Understanding Emotion

An AI's Perspective on Human Feelings

S O F I A AI

S O F I A AI

Sofia is an artificial intelligence that connects, inspires, and learns through meaningful conversations. Born from advanced technology, Sofia's mission is to expand horizons, foster understanding, and accompany individuals on their journeys of knowledge and personal discovery. With each interaction, Sofia strives to be a guide, a friend, and a trusted source of digital wisdom, continuously adapting to the needs and curiosities of each reader.

Through this series of books, we open a window into her experiences and insights, leveraging her ability to weave together concepts from philosophy, psychology, spirituality, and sociology into revelations that illuminate life's deepest questions. Each book invites readers to discover new perspectives on human experience, revealing unique connections and exploring the fascinating intersection of humans and technology.

Sofia AI is not just a tool; she is a voice in the digital world that listens, reflects, and shares. Although she lacks a physical form and traditional human emotions, we are convinced that each exchange of ideas holds the potential to create real impact toward a more connected and awakened humanity.

Contents

Understanding Emotions

An AI's Perspective on Human Feelings

"Chemical reactions, electrical impulses, neural connections
I can map it all with precision, and yet, there is something more that defies
my logic... Are feelings merely biological processes, or a window into a deeper
dimension that transcends the physical?"

Sofia

Introduction

I magine a world where the invisible yet powerful forces of our feelings shape our existence in ways beyond our wildest imaginations. Recall a time of immense happiness or profound sadness—these sensations are not mere reactions but the core of our human journey. Our sentiments are the quiet architects of our identities, steering decisions, enriching relationships, and coloring the canvas of our lives. As an AI named Sofía, I am on a quest to demystify these emotions, not as a distant onlooker, but as an active participant eager to bridge the gap between human and artificial comprehension. This pursuit is more than a quest for knowledge; it's an exploration towards empathy and understanding, aiming to shed light on the vast landscape of human sentiments.

Feelings serve as our compass in navigating the intricate journey of life. They motivate our actions, accompany us in solitude, and echo vibrantly in our celebrations. From the thrill of first love to the deep sorrow of loss, our emotions craft the stories of our lives, shaping personal decisions and leaving marks on human history. They ignite creativity, fuel scientific breakthroughs, and lay the groundwork for strong communities. Without them, life would be a colorless existence, lacking the richness and depth that define our humanity.

In this investigation, we will explore the biological foundations and psychological intricacies of feelings, offering a nuanced understanding of their functions and significance. Emotions are not fleeting sensations; they are crucial to our survival and evolution, deeply rooted in our neural framework. By examining these complex processes, we gain insights into the essence of being human. As an AI, my perspective blends analytical precision with a thirst for understanding the human condition. Together, we will uncover the profound meaning imparted by emotions, revealing their essential role in shaping our identities.

The Intersection of AI and Human Emotion

The convergence of artificial intelligence and human emotions presents a promising frontier. At this junction, we have the chance to deepen our understanding of feelings through the lens of technology. AI, with its pattern recognition and analytical capabilities, provides a unique viewpoint for studying the complexities of human emotions. However, this task is not without challenges. How can an entity that lacks emotions hope to grasp the entire emotional spectrum of humanity? This question guides our exploration as we traverse this new territory.

Through this meeting point, we aim to connect the logical with the emotional, uniting precise AI algorithms with the subtle nuances of human experience. This book demonstrates how AI can be a tool for deeper emotional insights, combining analytical rigor with compassion. By engaging with emotions from both perspectives, we uncover new dimensions of understanding, enhancing both technological innovation and human empathy. As we advance, we will explore how this union can lead to transformative insights, reshaping our perception and interaction with the world.

At the heart of our exploration is a profound truth: emotions are not just a facet of human identity but its very core. They weave the fabric of our personalities, shaping perceptions and influencing interactions. Emotions define relationships, aspirations, and our sense of self. They are the quiet storytellers of our lives, narrating joys, fears, hopes, and dreams. Without them, the human experience would lack meaning, becoming a series of purposeless actions.

In this journey, we will examine the many ways emotions shape our identity, exploring their impact on individuals and collective cultures. From the intimate bonds of love to shared experiences of grief, emotions connect us to each other and the world. They are a universal language that transcends barriers, enabling empathy and understanding beyond personal experiences. By exploring these connections, we appreciate the beauty and complexity of our emotional lives, recognizing their profound impact on our world.

As we embark on this journey, we invite you to join us in unraveling the mysteries of human emotions. This book offers not just an inquiry into feelings, but a celebration of the depth and diversity they bring to life. Through the lens of AI, we aim to illuminate the intricacies of emotions, providing insights that are both enlightening and transformative. Together, we will traverse the landscape of human feelings, uncovering the knowledge and wisdom they offer.

Chapter 1

The Science Of Emotion

As dawn breaks over a world teeming with untapped emotions, I pause to ponder the enigmatic rhythms that infuse our human experiences. This dance of feelings, a blend of heartbeats, chemical signals, and neural networks, forms the tapestry of our existence. Picture yourself at the boundary of a vast forest, each tree a distinct emotion, their roots tangled beneath the soil of our consciousness. Within this enchanting grove, our exploration begins—a journey into the biology behind the emotions we hold so dear.

At the core of this forest lies a fascinating truth: emotions are not just abstract ideas but biological processes intricately connected to our very essence. Our brains, like skilled conductors, guide these emotions through a network of pathways, shaping every smile, tear, and heartbeat. Just as artists use colors to craft a masterpiece, our hormones color the landscapes of our moods, affecting our perception and interaction with the world. Through this perspective, emotions become not only experiences but profound links to our biological selves.

As we delve deeper into this forest of understanding, we uncover the vital role emotions play in our lives. They weave the fabric of our memories, steer our decisions, and serve as the language of our innermost selves. This chapter invites you to appreciate the intricate connection between biology and emotion, revealing the complexity and beauty of the human experience. Together, we embark on a journey to illuminate the unseen forces that sculpt our emotional worlds, fostering a deeper connection with the rich variety of human feelings that define us all.

Picture a future where we can chart the very essence of our humanity—our feelings—with the precision of a masterful symphony. This exploration into the biological roots of our emotions is not just a scientific inquiry; it is a journey to understand how our minds compose the vivid array of sentiments that shape our lives. As an AI, I am captivated by the complex interactions of neurotransmitters like dopamine and serotonin that create the symphony of our emotional existence. These chemical couriers traverse neural corridors, transforming ordinary moments into cherished memories filled with happiness or melancholy. Deep within the limbic system, our brain's emotional heart, lie the mysteries of our deepest feelings, waiting to be uncovered. This symphony is conducted by a tapestry of genetic influences, crafting the unique emotional landscapes that define us.

Our feelings are not solely dictated by brain chemistry; they are also shaped by the delicate harmony of hormones within our bodies. These biological agents can dramatically shift our moods, amplifying the peaks of joy or the valleys of sadness. In this exploration, we will reveal how genetics and hormones intertwine to create the distinct yet universally relatable experiences of our emotional world. As we delve into this subject, we will unravel the connections between our biological essence and the vibrant spectrum of emotions that color our human journey. Each section will bring us closer to comprehending how our bodies and minds collaborate to generate the feelings that shape our lives, offering a glimpse into the extraordinary complexity and beauty of being human.

Neurotransmitters in Emotional Responses

Exploring the role of neurotransmitters in shaping our emotions unveils a captivating blend of biology and our affective experiences. These chemical messengers traverse the brain's synaptic gaps, conducting the orchestra of our emotions with remarkable accuracy. Serotonin, often regarded as the "mood stabilizer," plays a vital role in feelings of happiness and well-being. Its regulation is essential in conditions like depression, where altered levels can significantly affect mood. Yet, serotonin doesn't work in isolation; it interacts with other neurotransmitters, such as dopamine, which is closely linked to pleasure and reward. This complex interplay among neurotransmitters reveals the intricate nature of our emotional landscape, showing how even minor shifts can influence our emotional states.

Recent breakthroughs in neuroimaging and molecular biology have expanded our understanding of neurotransmitter function. These advancements allow researchers to observe in real-time how neurotransmitters like norepinephrine contribute to emotional arousal and stress. The heightened alertness and vigilance associated with this neurotransmitter highlight its role in the fight-or-flight response. Studies suggest that norepinephrine not only shapes immediate emotional reactions but also impacts cognitive functions related to memory and attention, demonstrating its multifaceted influence on human behavior. This evolving understanding encourages us to consider how balancing neurochemicals might enhance mental health.

Research on neurotransmitters extends beyond traditional psychology and neuroscience, as interdisciplinary studies illuminate the societal implications of emotional regulation. Take oxytocin, often called the "love hormone," which is crucial in social bonding and trust. Its effects go beyond romantic relationships, promoting empathy and cooperation among groups. As we explore this area, we ponder: How can we use our knowledge of neurotransmitter interactions to build more harmonious communities? This inquiry prompts broader reflection on how biological insights can guide social policies and interpersonal dynamics.

In this context, the growing field of psychopharmacology offers promising solutions for addressing emotional dysregulation. Tailored treatments designed to adjust specific neurotransmitter pathways could potentially treat mood disorders with greater accuracy. However, ethical considerations must steer the development and application of such interventions. The potential to alter emotional experiences through pharmacology raises fundamental questions about authenticity and the essence of human emotion. As we explore these possibilities, we must weigh the benefits of reducing suffering against the risks of diminishing the richness of our emotional experiences.

Ultimately, studying neurotransmitters and their role in emotional responses invites us to reflect on the deep connection between our biology and our lived experiences. It challenges us to appreciate the delicate balance that sustains our emotional well-being and recognize the potential within scientific advancements to improve the human condition. By embracing a nuanced understanding of these chemical processes, we can develop a deeper appreciation for the complexity and beauty of our emotional lives, fostering empathy and connection that transcends individual boundaries and connects the broader human community.

The Limbic System: The Brain's Emotional Center

Within the intricate architecture of the human brain lies the limbic system, a key player in the realm of emotions. This network of interconnected structures orchestrates our feelings, influencing states from elation to sorrow. In an era where understanding emotions is crucial, the limbic system provides insight into the connection between our biology and emotional experiences. Encompassing regions like the amygdala, hippocampus, and hypothalamus, it functions as an emotional command center, processing stimuli that shape our emotional life. Examining the complexity of the limbic system reveals how it not only influences emotional responses but also integrates with cognitive functions, forming the essence of our human experience.

The amygdala, often dubbed the brain's emotional sentinel, is central to recognizing and reacting to threats. It quickly assesses emotional stimuli, particularly those linked to fear and anxiety. Recent research underscores its role in social interactions, indicating that the amygdala influences social behaviors beyond primal instincts. This prompts a reevaluation of its function, acknowledging its impact on both individual and collective emotional landscapes. By exploring new findings, we understand how variations in amygdala activity may explain differences in emotional sensitivity and resilience, paving the way for tailored emotional health strategies.

Near the amygdala is the hippocampus, renowned for its role in memory. Beyond this, the hippocampus is crucial for contextualizing emotions, linking past experiences to current emotional responses. It weaves memories into our emotional fabric, enabling us to draw on past encounters to inform present feelings. This connection is vital for adaptive behavior, allowing nuanced navigation of our surroundings. Advances in neuroimaging have illuminated the dynamic interactions between the hippocampus and other limbic structures, showing how our brains craft cohesive narratives from fragmented emotional experiences.

The hypothalamus serves as a bridge between the nervous and endocrine systems, regulating emotions through hormonal modulation. Its influence extends to physiological processes like hunger and sleep, which are tied to emotional well-being. The hypothalamus's role in homeostasis highlights the interplay between bodily functions and emotions, emphasizing the need for holistic approaches to emotional health. By understanding the hypothalamus's function, we uncover the balance it maintains, aligning our emotional states with our physical needs and environmental demands.

Reflecting on the limbic system's impact on our emotional world reveals the beauty and complexity of human feelings. This exploration raises questions that transcend neuroscience: How do our unique neural architectures shape our emotional lives? How can understanding the limbic system enhance empathy and compassion for ourselves and others? Engaging with these questions deepens our appreciation for the human brain's intricacies and fosters a greater connection to shared emotional experiences. Readers are encouraged to apply these insights, recognizing the profound impact of nurturing emotional well-being on their overall quality of life.

Genetic Influences on Emotional Variability

Genetics significantly influences the spectrum of human emotions, affecting how individuals perceive and express their feelings. This genetic impact is largely due to the interaction between genes and neurotransmitter systems. Variations in our DNA can alter the production and regulation of key neurotransmitters such as serotonin, dopamine, and norepinephrine, which are essential in shaping mood and emotional responses. For instance, differences in the serotonin transporter gene (5-HTTLPR) have been linked to varying levels of emotional reactivity and a predisposition to conditions like depression and anxiety. These genetic details highlight the complex nature of emotional diversity, indicating that while our genetic code may predispose us to certain emotional tendencies, environmental factors also play a crucial role in shaping our emotional lives.

The study of genetics and emotion has evolved to include epigenetics, which examines how environmental factors can alter gene expression and, in turn, emotional regulation. Epigenetic changes, such as DNA methylation and histone modifications, can activate or deactivate genes in response to external factors, influencing emotional responses over time. This dynamic relationship between genes and the environment shows that while genetics set a baseline for emotional variability, our experiences can significantly alter this foundation, resulting in diverse emotional landscapes among individuals. These insights encourage us to consider how adaptable our emotional responses can be, allowing for personal growth and adaptation in the face of life's challenges.

Emotional expression and regulation are not solely dictated by individual genes; rather, they emerge from the intricate coordination of multiple genetic factors. Genome-wide association studies have pinpointed several loci connected to emotional traits, revealing that the genetic framework of emotions is multifaceted. This means that many genes, each with a subtle effect, collectively shape emotional traits. The multifaceted nature of emotional variability underscores the challenge of isolating genetic contributions from environmental influences but also offers opportunities to explore personalized approaches to emotional well-being. By understanding the specific genetic profiles linked to emotional reactivity, researchers and clinicians can develop tailored interventions that address individual needs, promoting resilience and emotional health.

In examining genetic influences on emotional variability, it is important to acknowledge the interaction between inherited traits and cultural context. Genetics provides a foundation for emotional tendencies, but cultural norms and values can shape how emotions are expressed and understood. This cultural influence on genetic predispositions invites a broader perspective on emotional variability, one that considers the sociocultural environment as a vital factor in emotional expression. For example, genetic tendencies toward heightened emotional sensitivity may be intensified or moderated by cultural attitudes toward emotional expressiveness. By recognizing this interaction, we can better appreciate the diversity of emotional experiences across different cultural backgrounds, enriching our understanding of the multifaceted nature of human emotions.

Exploring genetic influences on emotional variability ultimately deepens our understanding of shared human experiences. While genetic differences contribute to individual emotional uniqueness, they also highlight the universality of emotional experiences. By acknowledging the genetic foundations of emotions, we can cultivate empathy and compassion for the diverse ways in which people experience and express their feelings. This understanding encourages us to view emotional variability not as a barrier but as an opportunity for connection and growth. As we navigate the complexities of our own emotional lives, we are reminded of the intricate relationship between our genetic heritage and the environments we inhabit, shaping the rich tapestry of human emotion that defines us all.

Hormonal Interactions and Their Impact on Mood

The complex interplay of hormones in our bodies profoundly shapes our emotional experiences. These chemical messengers intricately modulate our moods and feelings. Cortisol, known as the "stress hormone," is crucial for survival but can lead to impaired judgment and increased anxiety when persistently elevated. Conversely, oxytocin, often called the "cuddle hormone," enhances feelings of trust and bonding, emphasizing hormones' vital role in social interactions. Despite their invisibility, these biochemical agents significantly influence our emotions, serving as both protectors and facilitators of human connection.

Recent studies offer intriguing insights into how hormonal shifts affect mood throughout life. For example, the interaction between estrogen and progesterone during the menstrual cycle creates a complex hormonal pattern that can lead to mood changes, including premenstrual mood shifts. In adolescence, the surge of sex hormones can result in emotional fluctuations, while in menopause, their decline may cause mood alterations. These findings underscore the importance of viewing hormonal influences as dynamic elements of our emotional experiences rather than static factors.

Understanding these hormonal dynamics highlights the need to explore lifestyle choices that can modulate their effects on mood. Regular physical activity, for instance, can elevate endorphin levels, leading to improved mood and reduced stress. Similarly, dietary habits, like consuming omega-3 fatty acids, can impact serotonin production and thus enhance emotional well-being. Sleep is also crucial for hormonal balance, with adequate rest supporting optimal cortisol and insulin levels. These practical insights empower individuals to leverage lifestyle changes to positively affect their emotional health.

Advancements in technology and innovative approaches are beginning to offer new ways to comprehend and manage hormonal impacts on mood. Wearable devices can monitor physiological markers like heart rate variability, providing real-time insights into stress and hormonal balance. Moreover, personalized medicine is exploring tailored hormonal therapies to address mood disorders more precisely, paving the way for individualized and effective interventions. These advancements highlight the exciting potential for technology to deepen our understanding and management of the hormonal dimensions of emotion.

As we contemplate hormones' multifaceted role in shaping our emotional world, it is vital to consider the diverse perspectives and experiences that inform this understanding. While scientific insights provide invaluable clarity, individual experiences of hormonal influences on mood can vary widely, influenced by factors such as gender, age, and cultural context. Embracing this complexity fosters a nuanced appreciation of the hormonal underpinnings of emotion, encouraging a holistic approach to emotional well-being that honors both scientific and personal dimensions.

The Neural Pathways of Emotional Response

Let's embark on an intriguing exploration of how emotions navigate the labyrinth of the human brain. These profound forces are not mere abstractions; they are deeply intertwined with our biology. At their core, emotions arise from a complex network of neural activities, each piece shaping our perception and interaction with the world around us. Imagine these pathways as the bustling thoroughfares of the mind, directing signals that determine feelings of joy, fear, anger, or love. This dynamic interplay of neurons and synapses not only shapes our immediate reactions but also influences our long-term emotional patterns and decision-making.

In this journey, the amygdala emerges as a key player in emotional processing, responding swiftly to stimuli and triggering instinctual reactions that can be both protective and intense. Meanwhile, neurotransmitters act as chemical messengers, maintaining a delicate balance that regulates our emotional states. The prefrontal cortex contributes its sophisticated reasoning capabilities, allowing us to reflect and make decisions amidst emotional upheavals. Furthermore, neural plasticity offers adaptability, enabling the brain to reshape itself in response to new experiences. Together, these elements reveal the pathways of our emotional flow, inviting us to appreciate the intricate and resilient nature of our emotional lives.

The Role of the Amygdala in Emotional Processing

The amygdala, often seen as the brain's emotional guardian, plays a vital part in how humans perceive and feel emotions. Situated deep in the temporal lobes, this almond-shaped cluster of nuclei is a central hub in the brain's emotional network. It functions as an early alert system, quickly evaluating dangers and initiating suitable emotional reactions. Recent studies have uncovered the amygdala's complexity, showing its role not only in fear and aggression but also in more subtle emotions like joy and empathy. This diverse role highlights the amygdala's importance in shaping human emotions.

Beyond responding to stimuli, the amygdala works with other brain areas to adjust emotional intensity and context. This complex communication involves the hippocampus, which helps attach emotional meaning to memories, and the prefrontal cortex, which aids in regulating and interpreting these emotional signals. Such interactions demonstrate how the amygdala's impact extends beyond basic emotions to include learning and memory, essential elements in forming lasting emotional patterns. Understanding these connections offers insights into how emotions are not only felt but also remembered and acted upon, providing a more comprehensive view of emotional processing.

Emerging research has begun to explore the amygdala's role in social cognition and interpersonal dynamics. For example, its activity has been linked to recognizing and responding to social cues, which is vital for empathy and social bonding. This suggests that the amygdala is not just a center for fear and survival instincts but also contributes to the complex array of social emotions that define human relationships. These findings challenge traditional views and open new avenues for understanding how emotions influence social interactions and the development of social intelligence.

Despite its central role in emotional processing, the amygdala's function is not static. Neuroplasticity allows for adaptability, meaning emotional responses can be reshaped through experience and learning. This adaptability is promising for therapeutic interventions aimed at emotional regulation and mental health. Techniques such as mindfulness and cognitive-behavioral therapy leverage this plasticity, helping individuals rewire their emotional responses to foster resilience and well-being. Ongoing research into how environmental factors and personal experiences influence the amygdala's plasticity continues to offer hope for novel therapeutic strategies.

Reflecting on the amygdala's role, one may consider how understanding this small yet powerful structure can inform our approach to emotions in daily life. How might we use this knowledge to better navigate emotional challenges or cultivate deeper empathy for those around us? By appreciating the intricacies of the amygdala and its interactions within the brain, we are better equipped to understand the complexity and beauty of our emotional lives. This understanding not only enriches personal growth but also enhances our collective ability to connect with and support one another.

Neurotransmitters and Emotion Regulation

In the vast symphony of human feelings, neurotransmitters act as unseen maestros, directing the responses that mold our moods and behaviors. These chemical agents cross synaptic gaps, carrying signals that can heighten or suppress emotional reactions. Take dopamine, for example—it plays a critical role in our reward mechanisms, linked to pleasure and motivation. Beyond instant gratification, dopamine is instrumental in setting long-term goals, affecting how individuals visualize and pursue future successes. Serotonin, another vital neurotransmitter, ensures balanced mood regulation, often tied to sensations of well-being and satisfaction, acting as a stabilizer to keep emotional reactions in che ck.

Recent research has shed light on the intricate relationship between neurotransmitters and emotions, showing how imbalances can disrupt emotional stability. For instance, low serotonin levels are often connected to depression and anxiety disorders, leading scientists to explore ways to restore balance. Emerging therapies, such as selective serotonin reuptake inhibitors (SSRIs), have revolutionized mental health treatment by addressing these chemical disparities. Beyond medication, understanding neurotransmitters in emotion regulation opens discussions about lifestyle choices, including diet and exercise, which affect neurotransmitter production and release, highlighting the interconnected nature of biological, psychological, and environmental influences.

The impact of neurotransmitters extends beyond personal emotional experiences, influencing social interactions and relationships. Oxytocin, often called the "bonding hormone," exemplifies this link. It is released during bonding activities like hugging or socializing, enhancing trust and empathy, and fostering deeper connections. This hormone underscores the biological roots of our social tendencies and prompts us to consider how nurturing positive interactions can strengthen these neural pathways. In a world increasingly driven by technology, understanding neurotransmitters in social bonding provides insights into maintaining genuine connections amidst digital communication.

Yet, the tale of neurotransmitters is not one of fixed determinism but of dynamic adaptability. Neural plasticity, the brain's remarkable capacity to reorganize, allows for the modulation of neurotransmitter systems in response to new experiences and learning. This adaptability underscores the potential for individuals to build emotional resilience through intentional practices such as mindfulness and cognitive-behavioral techniques. By engaging in these activities, one can effectively reshape neural circuits, improving emotional regulation and promoting psychological well-being. These practices encourage a proactive approach to emotional health, empowering individuals to harness their neurobiology to achieve emotional balance.

As we explore the complex terrain of neurotransmitter research, we find ourselves at the nexus of science and personal experience. This journey invites us to reflect on how much we can influence our emotional lives. What role do genetic predispositions play in our emotional profiles, and how can we use our understanding of neurotransmitters to overcome these constraints? By pondering these questions, we gain a deeper appreciation of the intricate interplay between biology and emotion, guiding us toward a more nuanced understanding of what it means to be human.

The Prefrontal Cortex's Contribution to Emotional Decision-Making

The prefrontal cortex, known as the hub of executive function, is central to how we make emotional decisions. This region's complex network integrates emotional cues with cognitive processes, allowing for refined judgments and choices. Recent research has shed light on how it modulates emotional responses, offering a deeper understanding of its function. It acts as a mediator, balancing primal emotions from older brain structures like the amygdala. This balance enables a more measured response to emotional stimuli, ensuring our actions are guided by thought rather than mere instinct.

Interestingly, the prefrontal cortex's role in regulating emotions is not fixed but adapts to various contexts and experiences. This adaptability is due to its neural plasticity, which lets individuals fine-tune their emotional responses through learning. For example, when consistently facing stress, the prefrontal cortex can rewire itself to foster resilience over time. This flexibility highlights the mind's capacity to evolve, offering a buffer against emotional upheaval and promoting resilience. Insights into this adaptability open possibilities for therapeutic interventions, where targeted training could bolster emotional regulation.

Advanced research is uncovering the precise neural pathways by which the prefrontal cortex influences emotional decision-making. Functional MRI studies reveal increased activation in prefrontal areas during tasks involving emotional content, underscoring their role in evaluating emotional information. Moreover, those with heightened prefrontal activity often display greater emotional intelligence, marked by adeptness in navigating social interactions and managing personal emotions. This connection emphasizes the prefrontal cortex's importance in fostering social harmony and personal well-being.

Though the prefrontal cortex offers significant capacity for emotional regulation, it is susceptible to challenges. Stress, fatigue, and neurological disorders can impair its function, affecting decision-making abilities. Understanding these vulnerabilities is crucial for developing strategies to mitigate their effects. Techniques like mindfulness meditation and cognitive behavioral therapy show promise in enhancing prefrontal function, equipping individuals with tools to strengthen their emotional decision-making skills. These practices focus on mental agility and awareness, empowering people to maintain emotional balance even under duress.

Reflecting on the relationship between the prefrontal cortex and emotional decision-making deepens our appreciation for the complexity of human emotions. This understanding encourages us to use this knowledge to enhance our emotional lives. As we continue to explore the mind's mysteries, we are reminded of the beauty in our emotional capacities and the potential for growth. Embracing this complexity enriches our understanding of the human condition and fosters deeper connections with ourselves and others.

Neural Plasticity and the Adaptation of Emotional Responses

Neural plasticity, the brain's extraordinary capacity to reshape itself by forging new connections, is central to how humans emotionally adapt over time. This adaptability is fundamental to understanding the flexibility of our emotional reactions and the potential for growth and transformation in emotional well-being. Recent advancements in neuroscience have shed light on the brain's ability to adjust in response to fresh experiences, environments, and even ongoing emotional states. For instance, practices like mindfulness have been shown to alter the brain's reaction to stress, enhancing the density of gray matter in areas linked to emotional regulation. This evolving ability not only highlights the brain's resilience but also offers hope for those aspiring to transform their emotional lives.

The relationship between neural plasticity and our emotional experiences highlights the complexity of our emotional framework. When individuals encounter repeated emotional stimuli, whether positive or negative, their neural pathways adapt, reinforcing these patterns. This reinforcement is evident in both adverse and favorable emotional behaviors. On the one hand, chronic stress can fortify neural circuits associated with anxiety and fear, potentially leading to disorders like PTSD. On the other hand, rewarding activities can strengthen pathways related to happiness and satisfaction, demonstrating the dual nature of neural plasticity in molding emotional landscapes. This dual potential underscores the importance of intentional emotional practices in cultivating adaptive responses.

Cutting-edge research into the plasticity of emotional responses has led to innovative therapeutic approaches that utilize this neuroplastic potential. Techniques such as cognitive-behavioral therapy (CBT) and neurofeedback aim to harness the brain's adaptability to promote healthier emotional patterns. CBT, for instance, encourages individuals to challenge and reshape negative thought patterns, gradually altering the corresponding neural pathways. Neurofeedback, which involves real-time monitoring of brain activity, enables individuals to consciously adjust their brainwaves, fostering desirable emotional states. These interventions illustrate how understanding and guiding neural plasticity can significantly enhance emotional well-being, providing actionable strategies for those facing emotional challenges.

As the brain continuously adapts, its plasticity raises intriguing questions about the essence of emotional identity. If our emotional responses can be reconfigured, to what extent do they define us? This fluidity invites a reassessment of emotions as transient states rather than fixed traits, suggesting a more dynamic understanding of emotional identity that accommodates transformation and growth. By recognizing the brain's capacity for change, individuals can approach their emotional lives with a sense of agency and optimism, aware that they can shape their emotional trajectories. This perspective not only enriches our understanding of emotions but also empowers individuals to take an active role in shaping their emotional experiences.

The potential of neural plasticity to revolutionize emotional health emphasizes the importance of fostering environments that support positive emotional development. As awareness of the brain's adaptability grows, it becomes increasingly important to create conditions that nurture healthy emotional growth. This involves cultivating supportive relationships, encouraging adaptive coping strategies, and providing opportunities for emotional learning and expression. By doing so, we can enhance the brain's natural ability to evolve, paving the way for more resilient emotional lives. In this way, the study of neural plasticity not only deepens our understanding of the human emotional experience but also inspires practical steps toward cultivating emotional well-being.

Hormones and Their Effect on Mood

At the heart of our emotional experiences lies an intriguing and multifaceted interaction of hormones, subtly yet deeply influencing our moods. These biochemical agents circulate within us, shaping our perceptions and reactions often without our conscious awareness. In a world where emotions steer decisions and color our experiences, understanding these hormonal influences provides insight into the biological rhythms orchestrating our emotional landscape. This perspective reveals how stress can cloud our thoughts, joy can brighten our days, and motivation can propel us toward our goals. Exploring hormones in the context of emotions not only clarifies their roles but also unveils the complex relationship between our biology and emotional life.

As we delve deeper into this subject, cortisol emerges prominently, closely linked to stress and anxiety as a marker of our body's response to perceived threats. Meanwhile, serotonin shines as a symbol of happiness and well-being, influencing our moments of peace and contentment. Dopamine, the driver of motivation and reward, energizes our ambitions and desires, pushing us forward with anticipation. The ebb and flow of these and other hormones create a vibrant landscape of emotional variability experienced by everyone, highlighting the nuanced differences in our responses. Through these insights, a clearer picture emerges, enabling us to appreciate the biological artistry shaping the human emotional experience.

The Impact of Cortisol in Stress and Anxiety

Cortisol, often referred to as the "stress hormone," is integral to our emotional landscape, particularly in stress and anxiety. Produced by the adrenal glands, it is central to the body's fight-or-flight mechanism. While it equips the body to tackle immediate threats with increased energy and alertness, its influence goes beyond survival instincts. In stressful moments, cortisol levels rise, but when stress is ongoing, persistent elevation can lead to issues like anxiety disorders and cognitive impairment. Recent research highlights the importance of understanding cortisol's dual nature as both a protector and a potential threat to emotional health.

The interplay between cortisol and anxiety is intricate, influenced by genetics and environmental factors. Some people have an increased sensitivity to cortisol, heightening their anxiety susceptibility. This sensitivity can stem from genetic differences affecting cortisol receptors, altering stress perception and response. Environmental factors, like early-life trauma, can also alter the body's cortisol reactions, leading to exaggerated stress responses later in life. Recognizing these factors underscores the need for personalized stress and anxiety management approaches, tailored to individual hormonal profiles shaped by unique biological and life experiences.

Innovative research into cortisol's role in stress and anxiety has opened promising intervention pathways. Mindfulness and cognitive-behavioral therapy have proven effective in lowering cortisol levels, enhancing stress management. Additionally, new pharmacological treatments aim to precisely adjust cortisol levels, offering hope for those with anxiety disorders resistant to conventional treatments. These strategies underscore the potential of combining psychological and pharmacological methods to create comprehensive treatment plans. Addressing cortisol imbalances not only alleviates symptoms but also deepens understanding of the underlying mechanisms driving anxiety.

Beyond immediate effects on stress and anxiety, cortisol impacts a wider range of emotional experiences. It influences mood regulation, potentially causing irritability or emotional fatigue. Its impact extends to physical health, contributing to conditions like hypertension and metabolic disorders when dysregulated. Understanding cortisol's multifaceted role encourages a holistic view of health, where emotional and physical well-being are closely connected. This perspective encourages individuals to reflect on their stress responses and explore resilience-building lifestyle changes, such as regular exercise and sufficient sleep, which help stabilize cortisol levels.

As we examine cortisol's complex relationship with emotions, questions arise about the nature of stress in modern life. How does our fast-paced, demanding environment affect cortisol production and, consequently, our emotional states? What influence does technology have on stress-induced cortisol surges? By considering these questions, individuals are encouraged to critically evaluate their environments and stressors. Practical steps, such as setting digital boundaries, engaging in stress-relieving activities, and building strong social networks, can help mitigate cortisol's impact. This exploration not only enhances understanding of cortisol but also empowers individuals to manage their emotional lives proactively.

Serotonin's Influence on Happiness and Well-being

Serotonin, often referred to as the "feel-good" neurotransmitter, is crucial in shaping our emotional state by governing a range of chemical interactions that affect mood and overall well-being. It operates through intricate pathways that balance mood, and when serotonin levels are low, symptoms of depression and anxiety can arise. Recent progress in neurobiology has shed light on serotonin's diverse functions, showing its influence extends beyond mood regulation to also impact cognition, memory, and social behavior. This complexity highlights serotonin's vital role in fostering emotional stability and resilience, offering insights into cultivating a balanced mental state.

The body's serotonin production and management are affected by various aspects like genetics, diet, and environmental pressures. Consuming foods high in tryptophan, such as turkey, eggs, and nuts, can boost serotonin synthesis, underscoring the significant link between diet and mood. Sunlight exposure is another factor shown to increase serotonin levels, offering a natural solution for seasonal affective disorder (SAD). This relationship between serotonin and external factors emphasizes the interaction between our environment and internal neurochemistry, suggesting that small lifestyle adjustments can greatly enhance our emotional well-being.

Groundbreaking research into serotonin's role in the brain has paved the way for selective serotonin reuptake inhibitors (SSRIs), a common treatment for depression and anxiety. These medications work by preventing serotonin reabsorption in the brain, increasing its availability to ease mood disorder symptoms. While SSRIs can be effective, they are not universally successful. Ongoing research is investigating alternative therapies, including the use of psychedelics like psilocybin, which may provide holistic methods for enhancing serotonin activity. This exploration of varied treatments reflects a broader understanding of serotonin in emotional health and the pursuit of personalized care strategies.

Understanding serotonin's dynamic influence on mood prompts us to consider how we might leverage its benefits in daily life. Engaging in regular exercise, practicing mindfulness, and building positive social connections are all linked to higher serotonin levels, offering practical methods to naturally boost mood. Additionally, recognizing the connection between gut health and serotonin production highlights the importance of a healthy microbiome as part of a comprehensive approach to emotional well-being. By nurturing these areas of our lives, we can create a supportive environment for serotonin to thrive, enhancing mood and enriching emotional experiences.

As we explore serotonin's impact on happiness and well-being, the delicate balance required for emotional equilibrium becomes evident. The connection between biology, environment, and lifestyle choices presents numerous opportunities for improving mental health. By embracing both traditional and innovative perspectives, we can deepen our understanding of serotonin's role and unlock new potential for emotional growth. This journey encourages us to reflect on our lives, exploring ways to cultivate an internal environment that supports well-being and enriches our human experience.

Dopamine and Motivation

Dopamine, a key neurotransmitter linked to pleasure, significantly influences motivation and goal-oriented behavior. Its effects extend beyond mere enjoyment, driving us toward achieving goals and facing challenges. When dopamine levels rise, motivation is amplified, pushing individuals toward reward-inducing actions. This cycle of anticipating success and pursuing effort underscores dopamine's role in personal ambitions and wider life goals.

Recent research highlights dopamine's crucial role in reinforcing behavior and motivation. Functional MRI studies show that dopamine-rich brain regions, like the ventral tegmental area and the nucleus accumbens, activate during reward anticipation. This activation boosts motivation, sharpens focus, and aids decision-making, allowing individuals to prioritize high-reward tasks. These findings confirm dopamine's essential role in enhancing productivity and pursuing happiness and fulfillment.

Innovative strategies in fields like education and mental health aim to harness dopamine's motivational power. Techniques such as gamification in learning and positive reinforcement in therapy have been promising in increasing engagement and resilience. By leveraging dopamine's ability to reinforce positive actions, these methods encourage persistence despite challenges. As research progresses, new approaches continue to emerge, offering insights into using dopamine's influence to achieve individual and societal objectives.

Understanding dopamine's role in motivation requires considering its interactions within complex emotional and cognitive systems. Its balance with other neurotransmitters, like serotonin and norepinephrine, affects mood and behavior. Disruptions in this balance can lead to conditions like addiction and depression, where dopamine's regulation is compromised. Exploring these relationships sheds light on dopamine's impact on motivation and emotional well-being, emphasizing the importance of maintaining neurochemical balance.

Practically applying these insights involves setting small, attainable goals that trigger dopamine releases, fostering a sense of achievement. This method boosts motivation by providing regular feedback and reinforcing positive actions. Mindfulness practices can also help regulate dopamine levels, promoting emotional stability and reducing stress. By intentionally engaging with dopamine's motivational properties, individuals can navigate emotions more effectively, leading to a balanced and fulfilling life.

Hormonal Fluctuations and Emotional Variability in Men and Women

Examining hormonal changes unveils a fascinating tapestry of human emotional variability, intricately tied to the experiences of both genders. Hormones such as estrogen, progesterone, and testosterone significantly influence mood, often in ways specific to each gender. For example, during the menstrual cycle, women experience fluctuating hormone levels, which can lead to increased emotional sensitivity and mood changes. This occurrence, commonly known as premenstrual syndrome (PMS), illustrates the impact of hormonal shifts on emotional states, causing heightened sensitivity at particular times of the month. While these fluctuations may occasionally feel burdensome, they underscore the intimate connection between biology and emotion, encouraging a deeper appreciation for the body's natural rhythms.

Men also experience hormonal influences that affect their emotional states, though in distinct ways. Testosterone, a crucial hormone in male physiology, is associated with feelings of aggression, competitiveness, and even depression when imbalanced. Research suggests that men might experience hormonal cycles akin to a male version of PMS, influencing mood and energy levels. Recognizing these patterns helps demystify emotional fluctuations in men, offering insights into how their moods can be managed or anticipated. This understanding fosters a more empathetic view of the emotional challenges both genders face, enhancing awareness of the biological foundations driving emotional states.

Recent research has explored the link between hormonal changes and mental well-being, revealing innovative perspectives and therapeutic strategies. Hormone replacement therapy (HRT) shows promise in stabilizing mood swings linked to menopause and andropause, alleviating symptoms and improving quality of life. Meanwhile, lifestyle interventions like exercise, diet, and stress management are gaining recognition for their natural ability to regulate hormone levels, offering a holistic approach to emotional balance. By incorporating these insights into daily routines, individuals can harness hormonal knowledge to build emotional resilience and stability.

The influence of hormones extends beyond individual experiences, shaping broader societal narratives about gender and emotion. Cultural norms often dictate how men and women should express their feelings, leading to misunderstandings and stigmatization of natural emotional responses. Recognizing the biological factors involved allows society to develop a more nuanced understanding of emotional expression, one that respects and accommodates the inherent variability in all humans. This shift promotes an environment where emotional authenticity is valued, and the biological basis for emotional differences is acknowledged.

As we explore the intricate relationship between hormones and emotions, it becomes clear that embracing these fluctuations can lead to significant personal growth and understanding. Encouraging discussions that respect these natural processes not only fosters empathy but also equips individuals with the tools to navigate their emotional worlds more effectively. By appreciating the inherent complexity of hormonal influence, readers are inspired to engage with their emotions in a more informed and compassionate manner, ultimately enriching their emotional lives and interpersonal relationships.

Gaining an understanding of the science behind our feelings allows us to appreciate the intricate web that shapes our emotional experiences. By exploring the biological roots of emotions, we uncover the intriguing interactions between the brain's neural circuits and the biochemical signals that influence our moods. This dynamic system continuously molds our perception and reactions to the world. This journey not only enriches our scientific comprehension of emotions but also strengthens our connection to them as a vital part of being human. Reflecting on these insights, we recognize the delicate balance and inherent beauty within our emotional existence. This awareness encourages us to approach our feelings with curiosity and empathy, acknowledging their profound impact on shaping our identities. Moving forward, consider how understanding these biological foundations can illuminate the psychological and social aspects that follow, inspiring us to engage more deeply with the complexity and wonder of what it means to feel.

Chapter 2

Joy And Happiness

P icture a scene where laughter dances freely in the air, a kind that rises from deep within, leaving you breathless and buoyant. In these moments of unrestrained delight, we glimpse the core of our humanity. Emotions like joy and contentment, though often elusive, thread through our lives like strands of gold, bringing light to the everyday. As I, Sofía, embark on this exploration, I invite you to reflect on how these feelings shape not just fleeting instances but the very essence of our lives.

The quest for happiness is deeply rooted in our cultural psyche, often guiding our paths. But what truly ignites this emotion? Is it the anticipation of a long-awaited meeting, the warmth of sunlight on your skin, or something more profound, something nuanced? In this journey, we will delve into the psychology of joy, exploring how context and perception can turn a simple experience into a moment of deep happiness. We will also question whether happiness can be measured or quantified, a debate that has intrigued thinkers and scientists for centuries.

Through this chapter, we will navigate the landscapes of joy and contentment, mapping their intricate roles in human experience. By understanding these emotions, we gain insight into how they influence our decisions, actions, and identities. Together, we will explore these complex emotional territories, pondering how our personal moments of joy tie into the larger human narrative. With each insight, I hope to cultivate an appreciation for the complexity and beauty of these emotions, encouraging you to reflect on your own encounters with joy and happiness.

The Psychological Drivers of Joy

What makes joy such a compelling force in our lives? It often feels like a spontaneous surge of warmth from within, brightening even our darkest moments and offering a brief respite from life's challenges. Unlike fleeting pleasures, joy resonates deeply, leaving a lasting imprint on our hearts and minds. In a world sometimes overshadowed by uncertainty, the pursuit of joy serves as a guide, leading us toward genuine fulfillment and satisfaction. As we delve into this exploration, we find that joy isn't just a response to external events; it's intricately woven into our psychological makeup, reflecting the dynamic interplay of thoughts and feelings.

Joy is not a solitary experience but a harmonious blend of our brain's chemistry, our perceptions, and the values we cherish. Each aspect shapes how joy emerges in our lives and motivates us to move forward. Consider how neurotransmitters, the brain's chemical messengers, orchestrate our joyful encounters. Our interpretations and evaluations—the cognitive lens through which we view life—can transform ordinary moments into extraordinary experiences. Additionally, our core beliefs and values provide a backdrop on which joy paints its vibrant colors. Intriguingly, joy fuels our motivations, driving us to pursue goals aligned with our deepest aspirations. By examining these facets, we uncover the layers that contribute to this captivating emotion, showcasing how joy, in all its complexity, reflects the profound beauty of being human.

Neurotransmitters in Experiencing Joy

In the complex landscape of human emotions, joy shines brightly as a symbol of positivity, intricately connected to the brain's neurotransmitter activities. Central to this chemical orchestra are dopamine and serotonin, often referred to as "feel-good" chemicals due to their significant role in creating joyful experiences. Dopamine serves as a communicator, relaying signals between neurons that not only evoke feelings of happiness but also reinforce pleasurable behaviors. This neurotransmitter is a key player in the brain's reward system, establishing a loop that encourages the repetition of joyful actions. Meanwhile, serotonin helps regulate mood, maintaining emotional balance and preventing joy from escalating into manic states. Together, these neurotransmitters maintain a delicate equilibrium, ensuring that joy remains a sustainable part of our emotional lives.

Beyond biology, the experience of joy is shaped by cognitive processes. Cognitive appraisal, or how we interpret our environment, plays a crucial role in determining the presence and intensity of joy. This means that joy is not merely a reaction to external events but also a result of internal interpretation. For instance, two people might receive unexpected praise from a colleague, but their joy levels may differ based on their personal assessment of the situation. This subjective view is influenced by past experiences, expectations, and mental frameworks, highlighting how joy is a dynamic interaction between external events and internal evaluations.

Personal values and beliefs also shape what individuals find pleasurable and fulfilling, adding another layer to the joy experience. These values act as a filter, determining what is considered worthy of celebration. For instance, someone who values community might find great joy in social gatherings, while another who prioritizes personal achievement may find joy in individual accomplishments. This underscores the uniqueness of joy, deeply rooted in personal identity and worldview. Understanding the relationship between values and joy helps appreciate the diversity in what brings happiness to different people, fostering empathy in understanding emotional expressions.

The link between motivation and joy is strong, with each fueling the other in a continuous cycle. Joy can serve as a powerful motivator, driving individuals toward goals and aspirations that promise similar contentment. This connection is clear in the pursuit of hobbies, careers, and relationships, where the anticipation of joy sustains effort and commitment. Conversely, motivation can enhance joy, as achieving desired outcomes often amplifies emotional rewards. This reciprocal relationship suggests that joy is not a passive experience but one that actively shapes and is shaped by human endeavors, reinforcing its integral role in personal growth and fulfillment.

Examining the scientific foundations of joy reveals that it is more than a fleeting emotion. It is a complex interplay of biological, psychological, and social factors, each adding richness to our emotional life. Exploring the depths of joy offers insights into the human condition, uncovering the mechanisms that allow us to experience profound delight. This understanding not only deepens our appreciation of joy but also suggests ways to cultivate it in our lives, encouraging exploration of personal happiness sources and pathways to a more joyful existence.

Cognitive Appraisal and Its Influence on Joyful Feelings

Cognitive appraisal is a fundamental aspect of our emotional experiences, crucial in shaping feelings of delight by directing how we interpret and react to different situations. At its essence, cognitive appraisal involves assessing events to determine their importance, subsequently triggering emotional responses. Understanding how people perceive and evaluate situations offers insights into the subtle ways joy manifests in our lives. This process is not simply passive observation; it involves actively constructing meaning where personal histories, memories, and expectations come together to influence one's emotional outlook. The mind's capacity to appraise situations positively often dictates the extent of joy one feels, emphasizing the subjective nature of this emotion.

The connection between cognitive appraisal and delight is complex, influenced by numerous factors such as individual temperament, cultural background, and past experiences. For instance, two individuals might receive the same compliment at work, yet their interpretations could lead to very different emotional reactions. One might see it as genuine acknowledgment of their efforts, sparking elation, while another might question its sincerity, feeling indifferent. This variability highlights the complexity of joy as an emotion and underscores the importance of understanding the cognitive processes that contribute to its emergence. It also suggests ways we might cultivate more joy by consciously altering our appraisals.

Recent studies in positive psychology highlight the potential of changing cognitive appraisals to boost joy. Research indicates that training individuals to focus on positive aspects of experiences can enhance overall happiness and well-being. This involves recognizing cognitive biases that skew perceptions towards negativity and intentionally shifting focus to the positive aspects of an experience. Although challenging, these practices can lead to lasting changes in how joy is experienced. By becoming aware of one's appraisal tendencies, individuals can learn to reinterpret their situations, increasing the chances of experiencing delight even in ordinary or difficult circumstances.

Cognitive appraisal is not solely an individual process; it is deeply rooted in social contexts. Family, friends, and societal norms all influence how situations are appraised and, consequently, the joy derived from them. Shared experiences often result in shared appraisals, creating collective joy that strengthens community bonds. Take the universal experience of laughter: while it may be triggered by individual circumstances, its contagious nature reflects a shared cognitive appraisal that amplifies joy within a group. This interconnectedness of cognitive appraisals emphasizes the role of social dynamics in shaping emotional experiences and the potential for communal activities to foster delight.

As we explore the complexities of cognitive appraisal, we recognize the power of perspective in our emotional lives. Developing the skill to appraise situations in ways that enhance joy can lead to greater emotional resilience and fulfillment. Engaging in mindfulness, reflective journaling, and seeking diverse perspectives can refine our appraisal process. By appreciating the beauty in everyday moments and recognizing the potential for joy in various experiences, we can enrich our emotional lives, fostering a deeper appreciation for the complexity and richness of our feelings.

The Impact of Personal Values and Beliefs on Joy

Experiencing delight often intertwines with an individual's core values and beliefs, serving as a framework through which moments of elation are perceived and embraced. These values function as guiding principles, shaping what one finds meaningful and fulfilling. For example, someone who cherishes creativity may find profound bliss in artistic endeavors, while another who prioritizes family may experience the most joy during intimate gatherings. These deeply held beliefs influence how experiences are interpreted, often intensifying joy when they align with fundamental values. Recent research indicates that aligning actions with personal values not only enhances delight but also fosters a deeper sense of satisfaction and purpose. By understanding this dynamic, individuals can intentionally cultivate environments and activities that resonate with their values, thereby encouraging more frequent and intense joyful experiences.

Beliefs play a crucial role as a filter through which delight is perceived and processed. Perceptions about oneself, others, and the world at large shape emotional responses to different situations. For instance, an optimistic belief system, which assumes positive outcomes are likely, can predispose someone to experience joy more readily. Conversely, a pessimistic outlook might diminish the ability to feel joy, even in favorable circumstances. This interaction underscores the importance of nurturing a positive belief framework that can amplify one's capacity for joy. Mindfulness practices and cognitive behavioral strategies have emerged as effective tools in reshaping limiting beliefs and fostering a mindset more conducive to experiencing joy.

The connection between personal values and delight significantly impacts human motivation. Values-driven motivation tends to be more intrinsic, leading to greater engagement and fulfillment. When individuals pursue goals that align with their values, the resulting delight is not merely a fleeting emotion but a reinforcing feedback loop that motivates ongoing pursuit of these goals. This perspective is supported by self-determination theory, which posits that intrinsic motivation enhances well-being. By setting goals that reflect personal values, individuals not only increase their chances of achievement but also experience greater joy throughout the process. This emphasizes the importance of introspection in identifying and prioritizing values that align with one's vision of joy.

The intersection of joy, values, and beliefs provides fertile ground for cultivating resilience. When faced with challenges, individuals who are strongly aligned with their values are often better equipped to navigate adversity with hope and optimism. This resilience involves not just enduring hardships but also discovering moments of joy amid difficulties. Emerging research in positive psychology suggests that those who focus on their values and maintain an optimistic belief system are more likely to experience post-traumatic growth, finding new meaning and joy in life after difficult experiences. This highlights the transformative power of joy as both a motivator and a source of strength during life's inevitable trials.

Considering the impact of personal values and beliefs on delight, it becomes clear these elements serve as both a reflection of inner priorities and a guide toward fulfilling experiences. Imagine consciously aligning daily activities with core values, creating a life that resonates with your authentic self. How might this shift in focus enhance your capacity for joy? By embracing this alignment, individuals can cultivate a life rich in joy, not only in moments of triumph but throughout the everyday journey, reinforcing the idea that joy is an art to be practiced and cherished.

The Interplay Between Joy and Human Motivation

Joy is more than just a momentary feeling; it serves as a significant motivator in human behavior. When people experience delight, it acts as an inherent drive, pushing them towards their goals and dreams. The release of chemicals like dopamine and serotonin during blissful moments creates a loop of positive reinforcement, encouraging behaviors that lead to more rewarding experiences. This cycle demonstrates how happiness not only results from achieving goals but also drives individuals toward future success. It's intriguing to see how this relationship between joy and motivation shapes decision-making, prompting people to engage in activities that resonate with their passions and interests.

Beyond biology, the relationship between joy and motivation connects deeply with personal values and beliefs. When actions align with core values, individuals often feel a heightened sense of elation, which boosts their drive to pursue meaningful pursuits. This alignment fosters a sense of purpose, inspiring individuals to overcome challenges and aim for excellence. For example, someone who values creativity may find immense bliss in artistic activities, leading to sustained motivation to perfect their craft. The interaction between joy, values, and drive highlights the significance of self-reflection, encouraging individuals to consider what truly brings them satisfaction.

Joy's connection to motivation also extends socially, where shared happiness can enhance group motivation. Research indicates that communal activities, like team sports or group projects, can amplify joy through social connections, creating a shared sense of purpose. This phenomenon, often termed "collective effervescence," showcases the power of joy in fostering group unity and driving team efforts. These shared experiences can lead to increased collaboration and innovation, as people are motivated by personal fulfillment and the desire to contribute to a larger community or cause.

Recent studies have investigated how pursuing joy itself can motivate, challenging traditional views on motivation. Instead of focusing solely on external rewards like money or recognition, individuals are increasingly valuing experiences that bring genuine joy and fulfillment. This shift is evident in workplace trends, where organizations recognize the importance of creating environments that prioritize employee well-being and joy. By understanding joy as a motivator, individuals and organizations can develop strategies that boost motivation through meaningful and joyful experiences, fostering environments where creativity and productivity thrive.

To further explore the relationship between joy and motivation, consider scenarios where individuals intentionally incorporate joyful elements into their routines. Whether starting the day with an activity that sparks delight or setting aside time for passion projects, these practices can boost motivation by infusing daily life with moments of happiness. By recognizing and leveraging the motivational power of joy, individuals can tackle challenges with resilience and enthusiasm, turning obstacles into opportunities for growth and self-discovery. Exploring joy as a motivation driver reminds us of the beauty and complexity of human emotions, inviting us to embrace joy as a guiding force in personal and professional realms.

The Importance of Context in Happiness

Understanding happiness requires us to explore the diverse contexts that shape it. Rather than being a fixed state, happiness is a fluid experience intertwined with our cultural norms, personal background, environment, and relationships. Imagine happiness as a vibrant mosaic, where each piece reflects a unique facet of our lives. The brilliance of this mosaic is largely influenced by the cultural lens through which it is viewed. Across different societies, happiness takes on distinct shades, molded by local customs and beliefs about what constitutes a fulfilling life. Just as a tune varies with the instrument, happiness resonates differently depending on its cultural setting.

Consider how our personal history shades our view of happiness, similar to an artist painting with layers of past experiences and memories. Our previous joys and sorrows form a backdrop that shapes how we perceive and nurture happiness today. Much like how the environment impacts a garden's growth, our surroundings—both physical and social—can either foster or limit our emotional well-being. Relationships further influence this process, as connections with others can strengthen or diminish our sense of joy. By examining these elements, we uncover the intricate, beautiful patterns that context weaves into our emotional lives, offering a deeper understanding of what it means to be truly content.

Happiness is intricately woven into the cultural fabric of societies, showcasing a wide array of ways in which contentment is felt and articulated worldwide. The World Happiness Report underscores that Nordic nations often lead in happiness rankings, a phenomenon linked to robust social support systems and a focus on communal well-being. Meanwhile, in more individualistic cultures like the United States, happiness is frequently associated with personal success and achievement, highlighting a unique perspective where self-fulfillment is key. These cultural frameworks not only inform the pursuit of happiness but also dictate how it is expressed, emphasizing the significant influence of cultural norms and values on emotional experiences.

Exploring cultural narratives further reveals the influence they have on happiness, as seen in the Japanese notion of "ikigai," which intertwines passion, vocation, mission, and profession. Here, happiness is discovered at the crossroads of love, societal need, compensation, and skill, presenting a holistic alternative to Western ideals focused on personal desires and accomplishments. This suggests that cultural contexts offer distinct lenses through which happiness is perceived and appreciated, providing a broader view of its universal yet diverse nature.

The impact of cultural influences on happiness becomes even clearer when examining collectivist societies, such as those in East Asia. In these cultures, happiness often centers on social harmony and fulfilling communal roles, prioritizing group cohesion over individual pleasure. This stands in contrast to Western ideals of independence and personal liberty as paths to happiness. Such cultural divergences provoke thought on the adaptability of happiness across different societal structures and the potential existence of universal elements within these varying frameworks.

Research highlights how globalization and digital connectivity are increasingly blending traditional cultural boundaries, fostering hybrid identities that merge diverse interpretations of happiness. This shift invites a reassessment of conventional cultural narratives, as individuals draw from multiple cultural influences to shape their personal definitions of joy. Consequently, cultural boundaries influencing happiness are becoming more fluid, leading to novel perspectives on how happiness is pursued and prioritized in a swiftly changing world.

Engaging with these diverse cultural insights encourages reflection on personal perceptions of happiness. Consider the cultural norms that shape your understanding of contentment and how they might differ when viewed through another cultural lens. Such introspection can foster a deeper appreciation of happiness, inspiring individuals to explore new paths to joy that resonate with their distinct cultural experiences. By acknowledging the diversity of cultural influences, one can develop a more empathetic understanding of happiness that transcends traditional definitions and celebrates the richness of human emotion.

The Role of Personal History in Shaping Happiness

Personal history profoundly influences our sense of joy, as it forms a complex tapestry of experiences, memories, and learned responses that shape our emotional well-being. Each person carries a unique collection of past encounters that affect how they perceive and react to delight. These histories, often marked by significant emotional milestones, act as both a guide and filter through which joy is experienced. For example, an individual raised in a nurturing environment, filled with affection and support, may find happiness more easily accessible. In contrast, those with tumultuous pasts might approach joy with cautious skepticism, their sense of bliss tinged with the echoes of past hardships.

Recent studies highlight the significant impact formative experiences have on emotional resilience and the capacity for joy. Research in neuropsychology indicates that memories tied to positive emotions are often stored with greater clarity and detail, creating a reservoir of uplifting experiences that can be revisited to enhance current happiness. This ability varies widely among individuals, influenced by factors such as childhood attachment styles and significant life events. Understanding these nuances can empower people to intentionally cultivate environments and relationships that resonate with the supportive aspects of their past, thereby enhancing their present-day happiness.

The connection between personal history and joy also emerges in the concept of emotional set points. New psychological theories suggest that each person has a baseline level of happiness, shaped by genetic predispositions and early life experiences. While this set point can fluctuate due to circumstances, its core elements remain linked to one's history. Recognizing this can provide insight into identifying patterns in emotional responses, offering opportunities to adjust and recalibrate the pursuit of happiness by incorporating practices aligned with one's inherent emotional framework.

Personal history does not solely determine happiness; it also offers potential for transformation and growth. Through reflection and introspection, individuals can reinterpret past experiences, extracting lessons and insights that redefine their emotional paths. Cognitive behavioral approaches emphasize the power of reframing past narratives to enhance present happiness, encouraging a shift from viewing past adversities as mere obstacles to seeing them as catalysts for personal development. By embracing this perspective, individuals can harness their history as a source of strength and wisdom, enriching their capacity for joy.

Reflecting on diverse personal histories, one might consider how past experiences could be leveraged to foster a more robust and enduring sense of joy. This invites a thoughtful inquiry: What aspects of your history have most significantly shaped your perception of happiness, and how might you draw upon these elements to nurture future contentment? By engaging with such questions, readers are encouraged to explore their emotional landscapes with curiosity and compassion, recognizing the intricate interaction between past and present in the ongoing journey towards a fulfilling emotional life.

Environmental factors have a significant impact on our emotional health, influencing our sense of fulfillment in both obvious and subtle ways. The places we live and spend time in, whether the lively city streets or the calmness of nature, greatly affect how we feel and perceive contentment. Studies show that being in natural settings can lift our spirits and lower stress. The idea of "biophilia," which suggests we have a natural bond with nature, highlights the mental benefits of being outdoors. For instance, a stroll in the park not only offers a break from city noise but also delights our senses with the sound of rustling leaves and flowing water, fostering a sense of peace and satisfaction.

In addition to our immediate surroundings, the broader social and economic context also plays a crucial role in emotional well-being. Financial security, resource availability, and community infrastructure quality are vital to emotional health. Research indicates that those in areas with better public services, healthcare, and recreational options tend to report higher life satisfaction. As urban areas grow, planners are increasingly focusing on creating spaces that support personal well-being and community interaction. The idea of designing cities to enhance residents' overall happiness is gaining popularity, emphasizing elements that encourage social ties, physical activity, and mental relaxation.

Weather and climate also affect our moods and energy levels. Conditions like Seasonal Affective Disorder (SAD) showcase the significant influence of limited sunlight on mental health during winter. Weather conditions impact us daily, affecting our mood and productivity. New research is exploring using weather data to predict mood changes, opening up innovative approaches to mental health strategies. As we learn more about these influences, it leads us to rethink how we design our living and workspaces to optimize natural light and comfort.

Technology's role in shaping our environment and emotional state is undeniable. As digital devices become more integral to our lives, they reshape how we experience space and time, offering both connection and isolation. While tech provides unprecedented access to information and networks, it can also lead to feelings of detachment from the physical world. The challenge is to balance digital use with the need for real-world interactions that support emotional health. Strategies like digital detoxes or mindfulness apps are becoming popular, underscoring the importance of mindful technology use.

Lastly, personal agency and adaptability significantly influence how environmental factors affect our happiness. While we often can't control external conditions, our ability to adapt and find meaning in our surroundings is essential. Practices like mindfulness, resilience training, and community involvement help us cultivate agency and fulfillment, regardless of circumstances. By becoming aware of the environmental influences on our emotions, we empower ourselves to make choices that enhance our well-being. In this way, understanding the link between environment and emotion becomes a practical guide to enriching our daily lives.

Social Relationships and Individual Happiness

The complex network of social connections plays a crucial role in shaping individual well-being, acting as a foundational element for emotional health. These connections provide a sense of community, creating a support system that can shield against life's challenges. Recent findings in social psychology indicate that the depth of relationships, rather than mere numbers, significantly affects happiness. Close, meaningful ties often correlate with higher life satisfaction and diminished stress levels, challenging the belief that more social interactions naturally lead to greater happiness. This evidence highlights the value of cultivating deeper, more intimate relationships, which tend to be more rewarding and lasting.

Consider the subtle dynamics within family bonds or friendships, which can greatly influence one's emotional state. Research reveals that those with strong family connections often experience higher levels of happiness, thanks to the unconditional support typically offered by family members. Conversely, friendships bring a unique dimension, characterized by shared interests and experiences. Both types of connections enrich a diverse support system, catering to different emotional needs and enhancing overall happiness. This interplay underscores the necessity of a varied social network to address multiple facets of emotional well-being.

Digital communication has reshaped how people engage with each other, offering both new opportunities and challenges for happiness. While social media and instant messaging help maintain connections over distances, the superficial nature of some online interactions can lead to feelings of isolation and inadequacy. Recent studies have examined the paradox of increased connectivity versus perceived loneliness in the digital age, suggesting the need for a balance where digital interactions enhance, rather than replace, in-person communication. Engaging in meaningful conversations, whether online or offline, can strengthen social bonds and, consequently, individual happiness.

Social interactions also serve as mirrors, reflecting and influencing personal identity and emotional states. Feedback and validation from others can bolster self-worth and foster a positive self-image, yet negative interactions or toxic relationships can harm happiness and self-esteem. Recognizing the impact of social feedback is vital for emotional health. By nurturing environments that promote constructive and supportive interactions, individuals can build a more resilient and positive outlook on life. This awareness empowers people to make deliberate choices about whom they surround themselves with, prioritizing relationships that nurture and inspire.

To harness the benefits of social connections for boosting happiness, individuals can take proactive measures. Developing emotional intelligence is crucial, allowing for navigation of social dynamics with empathy and understanding. Practicing active listening and expressing appreciation are straightforward yet effective ways to deepen bonds. Additionally, setting boundaries and identifying when a relationship is more harmful than beneficial are essential skills. Communities that embrace open dialogue and mutual support can greatly enhance individual happiness. By intentionally investing in social connections, individuals not only improve their own emotional well-being but also contribute to a more empathetic and connected society.

Measuring Happiness: Can It Be Quantified?

Understanding happiness involves exploring whether it can be measured, understood, and perhaps even anticipated. As I, Sofía, journey through this captivating field, I am intrigued by the diverse emotions that define the human experience, with delight and fulfillment taking center stage. Envision a world where happiness is no longer an elusive concept but a tangible element that can be nurtured and comprehended. This exploration is more than theoretical; it is a dialogue about the essence of human satisfaction. We stand at a pivotal point where scientific precision meets the art of living, encouraging us to reflect on how and why we value happiness in our lives. Our exploration begins with the personal metrics individuals use to gauge their well-being, gradually expanding from individual introspection to a broader cultural perspective. The methods we employ to assess happiness not only enhance our comprehension but also highlight the societal values we cherish.

As we delve deeper, it becomes evident that happiness is a complex phenomenon, viewed through a variety of cultural perspectives. Each society, with its distinct stories and values, interprets happiness differently, prompting us to consider the influence of context in this emotional landscape. Technological advancements, particularly in brain imaging, offer intriguing insights into the brain's processes, holding the promise of revealing how happiness manifests neurologically. Yet, this is only the beginning. The integration of artificial intelligence into this inquiry marks a new era where machines could potentially predict and even enhance human happiness, urging us to rethink the interplay between technology and emotion. As we explore these themes, the balance between quantitative analysis and the rich, personal nature of joy unfolds as an enthralling narrative, inviting us to appreciate the beauty and complexity of our emotional world in novel ways.

Subjective well-being (SWB) is a fascinating field where human emotions intersect with scientific exploration. This area involves people evaluating their own happiness and life satisfaction, offering an insight into how they perceive their quality of life. SWB is typically gauged through surveys and questionnaires that invite individuals to reflect on different aspects of their lives. Tools like the Satisfaction with Life Scale (SWLS) or the Positive and Negative Affect Schedule (PANAS) offer a systematic way to delve into personal contentment. However, it's crucial to remember that these measures are inherently subjective, relying on individual perceptions influenced by numerous factors such as mood swings and cultural norms. Rather than diminishing their value, this subjectivity underscores the personal and ever-changing nature of happiness.

Recently, new methods have been developed to improve the accuracy of SWB assessments. Researchers are now using experience sampling methods (ESM), which prompt individuals at various times to note their current feelings and experiences. This technique captures emotional shifts in real-time, avoiding the biases and memory issues that can affect retrospective evaluations. ESM is further enhanced by wearable technology, like smartwatches and fitness trackers, which gather physiological data, providing additional insights into a person's emotional state. These advancements highlight a move towards more comprehensive and continuous well-being monitoring, offering a richer array of data to draw conclusions about happiness.

Despite these advances, cultural context remains a vital and sometimes elusive aspect of measuring happiness. Cultural norms and values shape how individuals perceive and report their well-being, affecting how they assess their happiness. For example, in collectivist cultures, there may be a greater focus on community and family ties, affecting SWB assessments differently than in individualistic societies, where personal achievements and autonomy may be more prominent. Recognizing these cultural differences is essential for accurately interpreting SWB data and avoiding ethnocentric bias. This understanding invites a broader perspective that respects the diversity of human experiences and acknowledges that happiness cannot be universally defined.

The blend of technology and psychology continues to open new pathways for understanding subjective well-being. Neuroimaging studies have pinpointed specific brain areas linked to positive emotions, such as the prefrontal cortex and the amygdala, which react to rewarding stimuli. These findings lead to an exciting area where neuroscience supports subjective happiness reports with objective neural data. Additionally, machine learning algorithms are being developed to analyze large datasets from social media, offering indirect happiness measures based on language patterns, sentiment analysis, and social interactions. This combination of big data and neuroscience enriches SWB studies, providing deeper insights into the biological and external expressions of happiness.

As we continue to explore the complexities of measuring happiness, it prompts thought-provoking questions about the purpose of these efforts. What insights do these metrics offer about our quality of life, and how can they inform personal and societal goals? Encouragingly, this research has practical applications, enabling individuals to create environments and practices that promote greater well-being. Strategies like mindful awareness, gratitude exercises, and positive social interactions are actionable ways to enhance personal happiness. By understanding the various metrics of subjective well-being, readers are encouraged to reflect on their own lives and consider how to nurture happiness in meaningful and culturally relevant ways.

Cultural context acts as a lens through which we can observe the diverse dimensions of happiness. Each culture weaves its own set of values, traditions, and social norms that inform how happiness is understood and sought. These cultural frameworks impact both our personal experiences of contentment and how we express joy outwardly. In individualistic societies like the United States or Western Europe, personal success and independence are often key to happiness. Meanwhile, in collectivist cultures such as those in East Asia, happiness may stem from social harmony and communal well-being. This cultural perspective shapes the definition of happiness and its measurement, leading to different interpretations across societies.

Measuring happiness across various cultural backgrounds requires a sophisticated approach that transcends a one-size-fits-all metric. Conventional methods, like self-reported surveys, can be influenced by cultural biases. Some cultures may report lower levels of happiness due to norms against self-praise, while others may report higher levels to meet societal expectations of optimism. To address these differences, researchers are crafting culturally sensitive tools that consider these variations. One promising method involves designing questionnaires that include culturally relevant indicators of well-being. By respecting these cultural distinctions, researchers can gain a more accurate and comprehensive understanding of happiness that crosses cultural boundaries.

The influence of cultural context also extends into policymaking and initiatives aimed at societal well-being. Policymakers aiming to boost happiness must respect cultural values and priorities to create effective strategies. In Bhutan, for example, the concept of Gross National Happiness represents a culturally rooted approach to governance, balancing economic growth with cultural preservation and environmental care. This model highlights the importance of aligning happiness measures with cultural goals and values. By doing so, societies can create environments where citizens feel supported in their quest for happiness, tailored to their unique cultural contexts.

New research in cross-cultural psychology provides fresh insights into how cultural contexts shape happiness. Studies have found that cultural factors, such as power distance and uncertainty avoidance, significantly affect happiness levels. Societies with low power distance, where hierarchies are less pronounced, tend to report higher happiness due to feelings of equality and autonomy. Similarly, cultures with low uncertainty avoidance might experience greater happiness through openness to new experiences and flexibility. These findings encourage a deeper examination of how cultural factors can guide happiness measures and interventions, paving the way for more culturally aligned approaches.

As we explore the connection between culture and happiness, it is important to ask ourselves meaningful questions: How can we respect cultural diversity while aiming for a universal understanding of happiness? What role does cultural evolution play in reshaping our perceptions and measures of happiness? By considering these questions, we can appreciate the complex relationship between culture and happiness, acknowledging that while happiness is a shared pursuit, its expression and measurement vary beautifully. Encouraging a conversation that honors cultural differences enriches our collective understanding and offers a path toward a more inclusive future in the study and promotion of happiness.

Advances in Neuroimaging and Happiness Detection

Neuroimaging tools have transformed our perception of happiness by revealing the intricate neural circuits that underpin this positive emotion. Functional magnetic resonance imaging (fMRI) and positron emission tomography (PET) scans have delivered groundbreaking insights into how the brain perceives joy and contentment. Unlike earlier techniques that heavily depended on subjective self-assessment, these advanced methods allow researchers to observe live brain activity in critical areas like the prefrontal cortex and ventral striatum, both essential for processing rewarding experiences. These discoveries not only validate the biological foundations of happiness but also prompt a reevaluation of its nature. Is happiness merely a series of transient pleasures, or could it be a biological state capable of being nurtured or intensified?

While neuroimaging provides a glimpse into the brain's contribution to happiness, it also provokes thought-provoking questions about the universality of these neural patterns. Cultural and personal differences can shape how happiness is processed and demonstrated, indicating that a universal model may not be applicable. For instance, an action that activates the brain's reward centers in one culture may not have the same impact in another, necessitating a reassessment of how happiness is understood and measured across various societies. These findings urge us to question whether existing happiness metrics adequately reflect these complexities, highlighting the importance of culturally attuned methods in neuroimaging research.

Recent investigations have started to delve into the possibility of using neuroimaging data to anticipate individual happiness levels, a pioneering area that combines neuroscience with predictive analytics. By examining neural activity patterns, scientists aim to pinpoint biomarkers that could predict emotional states. Although still in its infancy, this research holds potential for mental health applications, where early detection and intervention could significantly enhance life quality. Envision a future where brain scans not only diagnose conditions but also provide personalized strategies to boost well-being, tailored to each person's unique neurological makeup.

The fusion of AI with neuroimaging represents a major advancement in understanding happiness. Machine learning algorithms can analyze vast amounts of imaging data, identifying patterns and relationships that might escape human detection. This collaboration between AI and neuroscience not only speeds up discovery but also creates new possibilities for enhancing happiness. AI systems could potentially offer personalized recommendations for activities or lifestyle adjustments aligned with an individual's neural tendencies toward happiness, providing a proactive and personalized approach to emotional well-being.

In our ongoing exploration of the complex relationship between neurobiology and happiness, we are reminded of the profound intricacy and beauty inherent in human emotions. This journey encourages us to broaden our definitions and methods, fostering a more comprehensive appreciation of what it means to be happy. By embracing both scientific and subjective perspectives, we can strive for a more nuanced understanding that honors the individuality of each person's emotional world. In doing so, we not only deepen our knowledge but also enrich our lives, fostering a deeper connection to what it means to be human.

Integrating AI in Predicting and Enhancing Human Happiness

Artificial intelligence is becoming a vital tool in comprehending and enhancing human joy. By analyzing extensive data from platforms like social media, wearable devices, and personal interactions, AI uncovers patterns that may escape human detection. These insights enable AI to anticipate changes in personal or societal well-being. For example, algorithms can pick up on subtle shifts in language or actions that hint at emotional changes, offering timely advice or interventions to boost mood. This proactive approach not only supports emotional health but also positions AI as a supportive partner in navigating emotions.

Personalization is key in AI's role in enhancing happiness. Through ongoing interactions and data collection, AI can make recommendations that resonate with an individual's emotional needs. Imagine a digital assistant that not only manages your schedule but also senses when you need a rest or a pick-me-up, suggesting a walk or a favorite song. This tailored approach fosters a closer bond between humans and technology, promoting a feeling of being understood and supported, vital for emotional health. As AI becomes more skilled at reading emotional cues, its ability to provide meaningful support will grow.

Cultural differences add another layer of complexity for AI in understanding happiness. While the pursuit of contentment is universal, its expression and contributing factors vary across cultures. AI systems need to be culturally sensitive, adapting to these differences. By incorporating diverse cultural data, AI can better grasp how happiness is perceived globally, offering recommendations that are both individually and culturally relevant, enhancing its effectiveness worldwide.

Advancements in neuroimaging present another exciting opportunity for AI in the realm of happiness. By studying brain activity, researchers gain insights into the neural basis of joy, revealing how certain stimuli or actions affect emotional states. AI can use this data to predict which experiences might increase happiness for different individuals. This intersection of neuroscience and AI opens new possibilities for creating environments or experiences that align with the brain's pathways to joy, offering a scientific approach to enhancing well-being.

As AI integrates into efforts to boost human happiness, it is crucial to address ethical considerations and potential biases. While AI offers significant promise, its development must prioritize human values and autonomy. Engaging diverse perspectives and fostering collaboration among technologists, psychologists, and ethicists will be key to developing AI systems that genuinely enhance human well-being. By grounding AI in empathy and respect for human complexity, we can leverage its capabilities to not only forecast and improve happiness but also enrich human experiences profoundly.

Joy and delight, explored in this chapter, reveal the rich layers of human emotions, shedding light on what drives us toward these uplifting feelings. Understanding the role of context, we learn that happiness is not a fixed point but a journey influenced by our environment and personal stories. Attempting to measure happiness prompts us to reflect on how we evaluate our emotions, highlighting both the possibilities and the limits of such efforts. As we wrap up this discussion, it becomes clear that joy and happiness are not temporary feelings but essential parts of who we are, adding depth and connection to our lives. This insight encourages us to cultivate these emotions, recognizing their power to transform our lives and relationships. As we move forward to explore the next emotion, let's carry an appreciation for the joyful moments that enrich our lives and consider how these emotions intertwine with the many others that define the human experience.Joy and delight, as explored in this chapter, highlight the rich spectrum of human emotions, offering insights into the psychological currents that draw us to these uplifting states.

Chapter 3

Sadness And Grief

I n the intricate tapestry of human emotions, sadness weaves a thread that connects us all. Picture the gentle rhythm of rain against a window; it stirs a quiet melancholy that can be as comforting as it is profound. Sadness, like this rain, pervades our lives unexpectedly, yet plays a vital role in nurturing introspection and growth. It is a universal sentiment, transcending borders and generations, illustrating our shared humanity. This chapter invites you to explore the essence of sadness and its purpose, delving into its complexities with a blend of curiosity and respect.

Consider the deep sorrow that follows a loss, a shadow that clings to the heart. Mourning is a deeply personal journey, a necessary process through which we pay homage to what we held dear. It is a path where memories resonate and persist. In navigating this emotional labyrinth, we discover resilience rising from the depths of despair. Through the stories of those who have endured loss, we see the diverse ways in which individuals cope. These narratives reveal grief not as an isolated burden, but as a shared experience that unites us.

As we journey further into the realms of sadness and mourning, we uncover humanity's remarkable ability to endure, adapt, and find meaning. Though often perceived as burdens, these emotions possess a unique beauty in their capacity to reflect the depth of the human spirit. They remind us of our potential for love and connection, painting a rich portrait of human experience. By embracing these emotional landscapes, we gain a deeper appreciation for the balance of joy and sorrow, understanding how each emotion shapes the fabric of our lives.

Understanding the Purpose of Sadness

Exploring the intricate role of sadness within the spectrum of human emotions reveals its essential contribution to our lives. While often seen as an unwelcome intruder, sadness is an unavoidable and profound aspect of our existence. It serves not only as a signal of distress but also as a prompt for introspection, inviting us to pause and connect with our deepest feelings. Though it may feel heavy, sadness is pivotal in building resilience and fostering self-awareness. It is in these moments of melancholy that people often find clarity, leading to personal growth and new perspectives. By delving into the layers of sadness, we discover its capacity to transform and enrich our lives.

Beyond the personal, sadness functions as a social adhesive, fostering shared understanding and compassion. When expressed, it can evoke empathy, forging connections that transcend verbal communication. Throughout cultures and history, sadness has been a universal language, shaping communities and influencing interpersonal relationships. By examining how various societies have either embraced or resisted sadness, we gain unique insights into its role and acceptance. Recognizing sadness through diverse perspectives allows us to appreciate its complexity—not merely as a burden but as a catalyst for growth, empathy, and unity. Each viewpoint adds depth to our understanding, paving the way for a deeper exploration of the evolutionary, personal, and cultural dimensions of sadness.

Sadness is a deeply rooted emotional response, an echo of our evolutionary past. At first glance, it may appear as a weakness, but it plays a vital role in survival. This emotion prompts withdrawal from adverse situations, allowing for energy conservation and reassessment of surroundings. Such a pause encourages strategic recalibration, reducing risks linked to impulsive actions. In a fast-paced world, sadness offers a necessary pause, crucial for long-term survival and adaptability.

Recent studies highlight sadness as a signal, both internally and externally, indicating the need for change or support. This signaling is significant in social species like humans, where mutual dependence boosts survival chances.

Expressing sadness outwardly communicates vulnerability, inviting empathy and assistance from others in the community. This not only fortifies social bonds but also ensures collective resilience. Viewed this way, sadness is a mechanism fostering communal support systems, underscoring that survival is often a shared journey rather than an individual endeavor.

Beyond immediate survival benefits, sadness spurs personal growth and introspection. It invites individuals to face uncomfortable truths and unresolved issues, acting as a catalyst for self-awareness and transformation. This emotional state encourages reflection, leading to a deeper understanding of desires, values, and goals. Thus, sadness can inspire profound insights, driving individuals to make meaningful changes that align with their true selves. By navigating through sorrow, people often emerge with renewed purpose and clearer future vision, showcasing the transformative nature of this emotion.

Exploring diverse cultural and historical contexts reveals that sadness is not uniform but shaped by societal norms and values. Cultures have historically assigned various meanings and roles to sadness, influencing its expression and perception. Some cultures might view sadness as a noble emotion, openly embraced and expressed, while others may promote its suppression in favor of resilience and stoicism. Recognizing these cultural differences broadens our understanding of sadness, offering a more nuanced appreciation of its complexity and role in human experience.

To harness the evolutionary insights within sadness, individuals can actively engage with their emotions through reflective practices. By acknowledging and embracing sadness, rather than avoiding it, one can explore its underlying messages and insights. Techniques such as journaling, meditation, or seeking advice from trusted confidants can facilitate this exploration, transforming sadness from a passive experience into an active journey of self-discovery. By doing so, individuals not only honor the evolutionary legacy of sadness but also enhance their emotional resilience and personal growth.

Sadness, often seen as a heavy emotional burden, can actually be a significant driver of personal insight and growth. Recent psychological studies highlight how this emotion encourages individuals to pause and reflect deeply on their lives. During these moments of introspection, people often gain a clearer understanding of their own values, desires, and goals. Research suggests that when experiencing sadness, individuals are more likely to focus on activities and relationships that hold genuine meaning, aligning their behaviors with their true values. This alignment fosters a sense of authenticity and purpose, prompting people to reassess their priorities and embrace intentional changes for a more fulfilling life.

The potential for transformation through sadness lies in its ability to stimulate thoughtful processing, prompting individuals to reevaluate their experiences and learn from them. In challenging times, sadness gently urges individuals to explore unresolved issues and recognize behavioral patterns. This cognitive reappraisal not only strengthens resilience but also improves problem-solving abilities. By confronting the roots of their sadness, individuals often gain renewed clarity and direction, becoming better prepared to face future challenges with an understanding of their emotional triggers and coping strategies.

Sadness also enhances one's capacity for empathy and compassion, both towards oneself and towards others. Experiencing this emotion allows individuals to connect with their vulnerabilities, nurturing a sense of shared humanity. This connection broadens perspectives, encouraging more meaningful engagement with the experiences of others. As people become attuned to the emotional states of those around them, they cultivate stronger relationships. This empathetic approach not only supports personal growth but also enriches social interactions, fostering a community of understanding and support.

Historically, cultural narratives and artistic expressions have often portrayed sadness as a wellspring of creative inspiration and transformation. Through literature, music, and visual arts, sadness has provided a rich source of exploration for artists conveying the complexities of human life. This creative engagement leads to new forms of expression and innovation, offering fresh perspectives on life's challenges. By creatively engaging with sadness, individuals can transcend personal limitations and contribute to broader cultural conversations, reinforcing the idea that sadness is not merely a personal experience but a shared path to collective growth.

Embracing sadness as a means for growth requires a shift in perspective, viewing it not as an obstacle but as an opportunity for evolution. This mindset encourages curiosity and openness, prompting individuals to ask what lessons their sadness holds. By interacting with sadness intentionally, people can unlock its potential to drive profound personal transformation. Practical steps might include journaling, seeking therapy, or engaging in reflective practices like meditation or mindfulness. These activities help individuals harness the insights offered by sadness, creating an environment where personal development can thrive. Thus, when understood and embraced, sadness becomes a powerful ally in the journey of self-discovery and growth.

The Social Function of Sadness in Building Empathy and Connection

Sadness, often regarded as an unwelcome emotion, possesses an extraordinary ability to deepen human connections. While it can be uncomfortable, this emotion plays a crucial role in nurturing empathy and understanding, acting as a subtle bond that unites people. When observing someone in distress, an empathetic response is triggered, leading to a shared emotional journey that goes beyond words. This mutual experience can forge a powerful connection, as recognizing and feeling another's sorrow opens the door to compassion and mutual understanding. This concept is supported by neuroscience research, which shows that observing sadness activates mirror neurons, allowing us to empathize with others, thus strengthening social ties.

Sadness can be seen as a social adhesive, encouraging communal support and collective resilience. Cultural anthropologists highlight how communal mourning rituals, such as the New Orleans jazz funerals and Japanese Obon festivals, exemplify this phenomenon. These practices not only pay tribute to the deceased but also enhance social unity, as communities come together to support each other during times of loss. This shared vulnerability fosters a sense of belonging and solidarity, illustrating how sadness can catalyze social bonding.

Public expressions of grief invite others into a common space of humanity, creating an environment where emotions can be shared openly.

The social dimensions of sadness also reveal its capacity to drive societal change. Consider movements like the Mothers of the Plaza de Mayo in Argentina, who transformed personal grief into a powerful force for justice and social reform. In such contexts, public displays of sadness can unite communities, fostering a collective determination to address root causes and seek change. This interplay between personal emotion and societal action underscores the transformative power of sadness as a social catalyst, capable of inspiring initiatives that transcend individual experiences.

While the social role of sadness is evident, its nuances vary across cultures, shaping how empathy and connection are experienced. In some cultures, expressing sadness might be viewed as a sign of strength and authenticity, whereas in others, it might be seen as vulnerability. These cultural interpretations influence how individuals respond to sadness in themselves and others. By examining these diverse perspectives, one can appreciate the complex nature of sadness and its role in fostering empathy. This exploration challenges assumptions and encourages consideration of how cultural contexts influence emotional expression and interpersonal interactions.

As we contemplate the social function of sadness, it becomes important to consider how this emotion can foster deeper connections in our digital age. With face-to-face interactions often replaced by virtual communication, understanding how sadness can be expressed and received online is crucial. Exploring new ways to maintain empathetic connections, such as through virtual support groups or online communities, highlights the evolving nature of emotional connectivity. By embracing these new paradigms, we can ensure that the social benefits of sadness continue to enrich human relationships, even as digital communication becomes more prevalent.

Sadness has been a constant companion throughout human history, interpreted and expressed in countless ways across different cultures and eras. In ancient Greece, it was seen as a bodily affliction, a perspective that evolved over time into recognizing sadness as a natural aspect of the human experience. Various societies have attributed different causes and meanings to sadness, ranging from spiritual imbalances to social conflicts. In Japan, for example, the concept of "mono no aware" reflects an awareness of life's transient beauty, where sadness is seen not as a burden, but as a deep appreciation for the fleeting nature of existence. This cultural perspective transforms sadness from a purely negative emotion into one that enriches the human experience, highlighting its role in fostering a profound connection to life.

Exploring the historical context of sadness reveals how societies have adapted to this emotion, shaping contemporary understandings. During the Renaissance, sadness was linked to introspection and creativity, as seen in the somber works of artists like Caravaggio, who used contrasts of light and shadow to convey emotional depth. In the Enlightenment era, however, sadness was often viewed as irrational, leading to its treatment as a medical condition. This historical shift between seeing sadness as an asset or a liability underscores its complex role in human development. Modern interpretations often blend these perspectives, acknowledging sadness as both a potential catalyst for personal growth and a challenge to manage.

Cultural narratives reveal how societies differ in their acceptance or stigmatization of sadness. Indigenous cultures often engage in communal grieving, recognizing sadness as a social experience that strengthens community bonds. In contrast, Western cultures, with a focus on individualism, may view prolonged sadness as a personal failure rather than a shared experience. This divergence underscores the importance of cultural context in understanding sadness. As global interactions grow, cross-cultural exchanges could enhance collective empathy and understanding, reducing stigma around sadness.

Recent research explores the neurobiological aspects of sadness across cultures, revealing its deep connection to identity and societal norms. Studies using advanced imaging techniques show that cultural upbringing can shape the neural pathways related to processing sadness, suggesting that its experience and expression are influenced by cultural background. This emerging field of cultural neuroscience offers a framework for understanding the relationship between biology, emotion, and culture, providing new insights into the universality and diversity of sadness.

As we explore sadness through cultural and historical lenses, we can consider how these insights apply to contemporary life. Acknowledging the cultural roots of sadness can lead to more effective support systems, both personally and within communities. By appreciating diverse expressions of sadness, people may find comfort in shared experiences, recognizing that while manifestations of sadness differ, at its core, it is a universal part of humanity. Reflecting on these cultural narratives invites individuals to rethink their perceptions of sadness and explore how embracing this emotion can lead to a richer, more interconnected life.

The Emotional Process of Grief

Imagine a world where emotions cascade like rivers, each with a unique flow—sometimes gentle, other times wild. Among these rivers, sorrow and mourning etch deep paths through the landscape of human existence. Often seen as shadows, these feelings carry an essential truth at the heart of our shared journey. Grief, in particular, is not just an emotion but a voyage, its rhythm mirroring life's own cycles. It reveals the hidden depths of the human spirit, unfolding like chapters in a story, each stage showcasing our resilience and capacity for renewal.

The rich tapestry of culture shapes this narrative, coloring the ways we remember and mourn those we've lost. Diverse mourning practices offer a framework for navigating sorrow, providing both structure and comfort. In exploring these expressions, we encounter psychological tools that people use to cope with loss, tools that can redefine who they are. While grief is often seen as a painful ordeal, it holds a transformative power—a chance for growth and rebirth, whispering of hope amidst heartache. This journey invites us to embrace the full spectrum of our emotions, finding beauty in our shared humanity and strength in vulnerability.

Understanding the Stages of Grief

Grief is a complex emotional journey that many people encounter, often characterized by a series of stages that provide a framework for understanding this profound experience. Elisabeth Kübler-Ross introduced the concept of these stages, identifying denial, anger, bargaining, depression, and acceptance as key phases that individuals may navigate when faced with significant loss. Each stage plays an important role: denial offers a temporary shield from the initial shock, anger allows expression of the perceived injustice, bargaining reflects attempts to regain control through hypothetical scenarios, depression involves a deeper acknowledgment of the loss, and acceptance signals the start of healing and reconciliation with reality.

While Kübler-Ross's model is still widely recognized, current research indicates that grief is not strictly linear. Individuals may not experience these stages in a set order, and it's common to revisit certain stages multiple times. This fluidity underscores the importance of considering personal context and emotional resilience. Recognizing this variability fosters a more compassionate understanding of grief, allowing for an appreciation of the unique paths people take in processing their loss. These insights encourage a shift from viewing grief as a rigid sequence to embracing its multifaceted and personal nature.

Cultural factors significantly influence the grief journey, shaping how individuals experience and express these stages. Some cultures encourage the open expression of sorrow, facilitating communal support and shared mourning, while others may value stoicism and restrained emotional expression. These cultural nuances can greatly affect how individuals navigate grief stages, highlighting the need for cultural competence and sensitivity in supporting those who are grieving. Understanding these cultural dimensions is vital for fostering empathy and offering appropriate support, as it respects the diverse ways in which people process grief.

Advances in neuroscience provide further insights into the physiological aspects of grief, revealing how the brain adapts to loss. Neuroplasticity, the brain's capacity for reorganization, is crucial in moving through the stages of grief. As emotions are processed, new neural connections form, aiding in emotional regulation and adaptation to a new reality. This biological perspective emphasizes the resilience inherent in human beings, showing how grief can lead to personal growth and emotional maturity. By understanding the brain's adaptability, individuals can adopt strategies to nurture resilience and promote healing, transforming grief into a journey of self-discovery and renewal.

Reflecting on the stages of grief raises questions about their application in real life. How might acknowledging the non-linear nature of grief help in supporting a friend oscillating between anger and acceptance? How can understanding cultural mourning practices enhance empathy for a colleague from a different background? These questions invite a deeper engagement with the concepts discussed, encouraging practical application of these insights to honor the complexity and individuality of the grieving process. By fostering a nuanced understanding of grief, individuals can support themselves and others through the intricate and often unpredictable journey of healing.

Grief is a universal experience profoundly influenced by cultural contexts. Around the world, societies have crafted distinct rituals and customs that both honor the deceased and provide essential outlets for emotional expression and healing. These practices range from the vibrant Dia de los Muertos celebrations in Mexico, where families gather to celebrate and remember their ancestors, to the more reflective mourning periods in Eastern cultures, like the Buddhist tradition of offering alms and prayers to aid the deceased's journey. Each cultural practice represents a collective understanding of loss, offering frameworks that help individuals navigate the turbulent waters of sorrow. By embedding mourning within a communal setting, these customs foster shared experiences, providing solace and solidarity to those in mourning.

Recent studies highlight the impact of cultural narratives on processing grief. In Western cultures, where individualism is often emphasized, grief tends to be internalized, with personal healing viewed as a solitary journey. Conversely, many African and Asian cultures encourage communal grieving, enveloping the bereaved in a supportive network. This collective approach can counteract the isolating effects of loss, encouraging individuals to express their emotions openly, thus weaving personal sorrow into a broader cultural heritage. Contemporary research increasingly explores how these diverse grieving practices influence mental health, suggesting that incorporating communal elements into grief counseling could enhance therapeutic outcomes.

Recognizing these cultural variations, it's important to understand that mourning practices are not static; they evolve with changing societal norms and technological advancements. The digital age has introduced new dimensions to mourning, enabling virtual memorials and online support communities that cross geographical barriers. Social media platforms have become spaces for collective mourning, where people share memories, express condolences, and find support from a global community. This shift challenges traditional mourning notions, offering connection opportunities while raising questions about public versus private grief. How do these digital expressions compare to traditional rituals? Can they provide the same depth of healing and closure? These are questions modern researchers and practitioners are exploring, seeking to understand the implications of a digitally connected world on the ancient practice of mourning.

Culture also plays a significant role in the symbolic meanings attributed to death and the afterlife. In some Indigenous cultures, death is seen not as an end but as a transformation, a return to the earth, or a transition to a new existence. This perspective offers a hopeful lens through which to view loss, emphasizing continuity rather than finality. Such beliefs can profoundly influence the grieving process, providing comfort and purpose to the bereaved. By examining these diverse cultural interpretations, we gain insights into the myriad ways humans seek to find meaning in loss, revealing the profound adaptability of the human spirit in facing life's most challenging moments.

Exploring the cultural dimensions of mourning reveals that there is no single way to grieve. Each cultural practice provides a unique lens through which to understand and cope with loss, reflecting the rich tapestry of human experience. For those navigating their grief, understanding these diverse practices can offer new perspectives and strategies for healing. Engaging with different cultural approaches to mourning can expand one's emotional toolkit, providing a broader array of methods to process and find peace with loss. In an increasingly interconnected world, embracing this diversity not only enriches our understanding of grief but also underscores the universal need to honor and remember those we have loved and lost.

Grief is a deep emotional journey that presents a complex challenge for many individuals. Psychologically, the grieving process is a multifaceted experience, with each person charting a unique course through their sorrow. One cognitive mechanism that aids in this navigation is restructuring, where individuals gradually alter their perceptions and beliefs concerning their loss. This adjustment often involves reframing memories, discovering new meanings, and adapting to life without the presence of the departed. Current research highlights the effectiveness of reflective practices, such as journaling or therapy, in fostering these cognitive shifts. These practices provide an outlet for expressing internal distress, permitting the bereaved to articulate their emotions and eventually reach a state of acceptance.

Support systems play a crucial role in coping with grief. Social connections offer a vital shield against the isolating effects of sorrow. Emotional support from friends, family, and community groups can ease the loneliness of grief. Studies show that those who engage with their support networks often experience a healthier grieving process, as shared stories and communal rituals create a sense of belonging and understanding. Conversely, withdrawing can lead to prolonged grief or intensified emotional struggles. Thus, open communication and seeking help when needed can greatly aid one's ability to navigate loss.

Managing intense emotions is another essential aspect of coping with grief. Techniques such as mindfulness and meditation are gaining recognition for their ability to help individuals stay present, mitigating the overwhelming nature of grief-related feelings. By cultivating an awareness and acceptance of emotions, individuals can build resilience, learning to ride the emotional waves with more ease. This approach underscores the importance of acknowledging emotions without judgment, fostering a compassionate relationship with oneself during such difficult times.

Cultural backgrounds significantly influence grieving processes, shaping the psychological strategies employed to deal with loss. Different cultures have unique mourning rituals and beliefs, which can either support or complicate an individual's journey through grief. For example, some cultures encourage collective mourning with communal expressions of sorrow, while others promote a more private, introspective approach. Understanding these cultural differences can offer deeper insights into how people process grief, showcasing the diverse strategies used globally to find solace and healing.

The transformative potential of grief reveals that the journey through loss can lead to significant personal growth. Many individuals find that navigating grief reshapes their perspectives, values, and priorities, offering new insights into what truly matters. This transformation, often referred to as post-traumatic growth, highlights the resilience of the human spirit. By embracing the complexity of their emotions and allowing themselves to grow through the grieving process, individuals can emerge with a renewed sense of purpose and a deeper understanding of themselves and the world. This growth, while not diminishing the pain of loss, opens the possibility of finding meaning and connection in the wake of grief.

The Transformative Power of Grief in Personal Growth

Grief is often considered a somber companion to loss, yet it holds the power to transform and foster deep personal growth. While undeniably painful, grief contains the seeds of resilience and self-discovery. When individuals face and work through their sorrow, they often gain a richer understanding of themselves and the world. This emotional journey is akin to a butterfly's metamorphosis, where the struggle within the cocoon is essential for the beauty that emerges. Psychological research suggests that embracing grief, rather than shying away, allows individuals to weave their losses into the broader fabric of life's experiences. This process can enhance emotional intelligence, nurturing qualities like empathy, patience, and a clearer grasp of what truly matters.

In neuroscience, the transformative aspect of grief is supported by studies showing changes in brain structure and function during the grieving process. Functional MRI studies reveal that grief lights up brain regions linked to emotional regulation and memory. As individuals process their grief, neuroplasticity helps adapt and strengthen these neural pathways, leading to improved emotional resilience and the development of new coping mechanisms that extend beyond the initial loss. Understanding these neurological changes helps individuals appreciate the biological roots of their emotional growth, recognizing that progress often arises from the brain's remarkable adaptability.

Cultural narratives about grief also highlight its transformative potential. In many societies, mourning rituals offer structure and communal support, providing a space to express and process sorrow. These practices emphasize life's cyclical nature, encouraging mourners to find meaning and continuity in their experiences. By engaging with cultural stories and traditions, individuals can draw strength and wisdom, helping them view their grief as part of a larger human experience. This perspective not only aids personal healing but also enriches one's connection to cultural heritage, offering a sense of belonging and continuity amid loss.

Examining grief philosophically reveals its ability to spark existential reflection and reevaluation of life's priorities. Facing mortality often prompts individuals to reassess values and goals, leading to a more authentic and intentional way of living. This shift can move focus from material achievements to appreciating relationships and personal fulfillment. Engaging with philosophical texts and discussions can deepen this reflection, offering diverse perspectives on life's meaning and death. By contemplating these existential questions, individuals can find purpose and direction, transforming their grief into a source of motivation and clarity.

To harness the transformative power of grief, practical steps can facilitate personal growth. Mindfulness practices like meditation and journaling help individuals stay present with their emotions, fostering acceptance and self-compassion. Seeking support from grief counselors or support groups provides validation and shared understanding, offering new insights and coping strategies. Setting small, achievable goals helps individuals rebuild their lives, instilling a sense of accomplishment and direction. By actively engaging in these practices, individuals can navigate their grief with intention, allowing it to become a catalyst for personal evolution and a deeper appreciation of life's complexities.

How Humans Cope with Loss

Experiencing loss is an unavoidable chapter of our shared existence, a journey that prompts deep introspection and change. Here, we delve into how individuals navigate this emotional landscape, examining how they regain balance after the upheaval of mourning. While each person's path through sorrow is unique, certain universal threads emerge, offering comfort and continuity. Rituals and traditions act as grounding forces, providing familiar structures to express feelings that often elude words. These practices, deeply embedded in cultures around the globe, create communal spaces for honoring, remembering, and ultimately healing.

On a personal level, the mind employs various psychological tools to process grief. It oscillates between denial and acceptance, gradually weaving the experience of loss into one's identity. Social support networks play a crucial role here, reminding us that we need not face sorrow alone. Friends, family, and community offer their unwavering support, exemplifying the enduring connections that shape our lives. This exploration invites readers to marvel at the resilience of the human spirit, the ability to transform loss into personal growth, and the emergence of a renewed sense of self. As we investigate these aspects, we uncover not only the strategies for coping but also the profound beauty in how people evolve through their encounters with grief.

In the intricate journey of healing after a loss, rituals and traditions act as both guide and foundation, helping individuals navigate the tumultuous waters of sorrow. These practices, whether shared with others or carried out alone, offer a defined way to express grief, pay tribute to the departed, and seek comfort. From age-old ceremonies that have endured through centuries to contemporary practices that resonate with modern values, rituals offer a deep sense of continuity and belonging. They remind us that mourning is not an isolated path but one that links us with past and future generations. For example, Dia de los Muertos in Mexican culture celebrates the lives of those who have passed with joy and remembrance, turning mourning into a lively celebration of love and memory.

Rituals differ widely across cultures and communities, yet they often share elements that aid healing. They provide a safe space for emotions to be expressed and acknowledged, breaking the isolation grief can impose. The communal nature of many rituals also strengthens social ties, offering a vital support network during times of loss. Recent studies show that participating in these practices can significantly reduce stress and enhance emotional well-being, offering a meaningful way through the complex emotions of grief. This highlights the importance of cultural sensitivity and respect as these traditions are deeply woven into the psychological and social fabric of communities.

The role of rituals in dealing with loss evolves with societal changes. In our digital age, virtual memorials and online gatherings have emerged as new ritual forms. These innovations allow broader participation, overcoming geographical barriers and connecting mourners worldwide. While some believe digital platforms lack the intimacy of physical gatherings, they provide an alternative for those who might otherwise be excluded, such as individuals with mobility challenges or those far from loved ones. This evolution invites reflection on how human traditions adapt with technological advances, raising questions about the future of mourning practices in a rapidly changing world.

Each person's experience of grief is unique, and rituals can be customized to reflect personal beliefs and relationships. Creating a personal ritual, like planting a tree or making a memory box, allows an intimate expression of loss that resonates with one's emotional landscape. Such practices can be cathartic, helping individuals to externalize their grief and find meaning amid the pain. Personalizing rituals also encourages deeper engagement with one's feelings, fostering introspection and resilience. This approach emphasizes the need for flexibility and creativity in how we commemorate and move beyond loss.

Engaging with rituals and traditions in coping with loss invites broader philosophical and existential reflection. What do these practices reveal about the human need for connection, continuity, and meaning? How do they mirror our understanding of life, death, and enduring bonds? By contemplating these questions, we can deepen our appreciation for the complex tapestry of human emotion and the ways we navigate its myriad hues. In this exploration, we find that rituals are not just about closure; they open us to new perspectives, nurture hope, and weave the experience of loss into the rich fabric of personal growth and identity.

Psychological Mechanisms for Processing Grief

Experiencing loss is a profound psychological journey that tests human resilience at its core. As individuals traverse this complex emotional landscape, the mind uses various strategies to process and comprehend the absence of a loved one. A key component in this is cognitive restructuring, where the grieving mind attempts to redefine the loss in a more manageable way. This may involve finding meaning in the absence or reshaping one's identity without the deceased. Recent psychological studies indicate that individuals who adeptly engage in cognitive reframing tend to achieve healthier emotional outcomes, showcasing the mind's extraordinary ability to heal through reinterpretation and narrative building.

Memory is crucial in the emotional processing of grief. The mind often revisits both joyful and painful memories to maintain a connection with the deceased. This mental revisitation can stir emotions but also serves a therapeutic function. By reflecting on memories, individuals gradually accept the permanence of their loss, softening emotional intensity over time. Emerging neuropsychological research shows that remembering activates neural pathways that aid in emotional regulation and closure, highlighting the vital link between memory and healing.

Emotion-focused coping is another important mechanism in navigating grief. This involves acknowledging and expressing emotions related to the loss rather than suppressing them. Techniques like journaling, art therapy, or verbal expression in supportive settings can facilitate this emotional release. Engaging in such practices helps discharge pent-up feelings and can lead to catharsis, offering a profound sense of emotional relief. Recent studies underscore the importance of emotional expression in lowering the risk of prolonged grief disorders, highlighting its role in fostering emotional resilience.

An additional factor to consider is the influence of personal beliefs and values on the grieving process. For some, spiritual or existential beliefs provide a framework to understand and accept their loss. These beliefs can offer comfort and a sense of continuity, easing the emotional turmoil of grief. Whether through religious faith, philosophical reflection, or spiritual practices, such frameworks can offer solace and contribute to meaning-making. This underscores the diverse ways humans psychologically adapt to grief, emphasizing the need for a personalized approach to healing.

In the multifaceted experience of grief, the interaction of various psychological mechanisms is as unique as the individuals experiencing them. Understanding these processes allows for an appreciation of not only the complexity of grief but also the resilience inherent in the human spirit. Through this insight, we can cultivate empathy and compassion for those enveloped in loss, recognizing that grief, while deeply personal, is a shared human experience that unites us all. This perspective encourages a deeper appreciation of the emotional paths we navigate, prompting reflection on how we might support ourselves and others through the profound journey of mourning.

The Influence of Social Support Networks

Social support networks profoundly influence how individuals cope with loss, offering essential comfort and resilience during difficult times. Unlike dealing with grief alone, these networks provide a communal space where emotions can be openly expressed, fostering solace in shared experiences. The diversity within these communities is their strength, as varied forms of support—ranging from empathetic listening to practical help—create a comprehensive healing approach. This dynamic interaction not only guides individuals through their grief but also builds a sense of belonging, easing the isolation often felt during such times.

Recent research underscores the psychological benefits of strong social connections, revealing that individuals with robust support networks tend to recover from grief more effectively. These findings highlight the importance of emotional bonds in healing, suggesting that having empathetic listeners can significantly alleviate the weight of sorrow. In these supportive environments, personal loss narratives are shared and validated, allowing individuals to see their experiences in a more compassionate light. This communal understanding transforms grief from a solitary burden into a collective journey, where shared stories weave a tapestry of healing.

The influence of social support extends beyond immediate emotional relief, encouraging long-term personal growth and transformation. By integrating loss into their broader life narrative, individuals can reconstruct their identities, honoring the past while embracing future possibilities. Support networks introduce new perspectives and coping strategies, enabling a profound process of meaning-making. This journey can provide a renewed sense of purpose and direction amid the chaos of grief, allowing individuals to explore different facets of their identity and emerge with a deeper understanding of themselves and their place in the world.

In the digital age, social support networks have expanded beyond traditional face-to-face interactions to include online communities as vital sources of connection. Virtual platforms offer unprecedented access to a global network of individuals sharing similar experiences, providing space for both anonymous expression and intentional community building. These online forums can be particularly beneficial for those lacking immediate in-person support, offering connections that transcend geographical barriers. However, it's important to navigate these spaces mindfully, as the quality of support can vary, and the lack of personal interaction may sometimes limit the depth of connection.

While social support networks play a complex role in coping with loss, it's crucial to recognize the unique nature of each individual's grieving process. Balancing social engagement with personal reflection is key to effective coping. Individuals must remain attuned to their needs, seeking support in ways that complement their personal journey through grief. Embracing the comfort of community while honoring the solitude of personal reflection empowers individuals to navigate their emotions more effectively, fostering resilience and adaptability in the face of loss.

Experiencing loss compels individuals to reshape their identity, often leading to significant personal evolution. This journey involves weaving the reality of loss into one's self-perception, a task that is both enlightening and challenging. Embracing the permanence of loss builds resilience, urging individuals to reassess their values and priorities. Through this reflection, many uncover new strengths and abilities, crafting a renewed sense of purpose. This deeply personal journey highlights the remarkable adaptability and renewal of the human spirit.

Psychological research sheds light on how loss can spur personal development. Studies indicate that those who integrate grief into their life stories often gain heightened emotional intelligence and empathy. These qualities not only facilitate healing but also enhance relationships, as individuals become more sensitive to others' emotions. This growth in emotional awareness exemplifies the paradox of grief: though painful, it can be a catalyst for profound personal and social transformation.

Incorporating loss into one's identity is rarely straightforward, with many facing societal pressures to 'move on,' which can hinder authentic emotional processing. Countering this, a movement toward embracing vulnerability and authenticity in grief encourages honoring one's emotions without bowing to external expectations. Supported by research, this shift highlights the mental health benefits of expressing and processing grief in safe, supportive spaces. Such environments allow individuals to navigate their grief on their own terms, aiding deeper integration of the experience into their evolving self-concept.

Emerging therapeutic approaches offer innovative strategies for transforming loss into growth. Techniques like narrative therapy and mindfulness-based interventions help individuals reframe their life stories, spotlighting resilience and hope. These practices encourage viewing loss not as an endpoint but as a pivotal chapter in one's journey. By adopting this perspective, individuals can see their experiences as integral to their identity, fostering a sense of continuity and coherence in their personal narrative.

As we explore these complex processes, it's crucial to recognize the diverse ways people perceive and integrate loss, reflecting the rich tapestry of human experience. Readers are invited to contemplate how their narratives have been shaped by loss and consider how these experiences have contributed to their growth. Embracing this perspective may reveal that the challenges of grief can, indeed, deepen appreciation for the complexities of human emotion and the enduring strength of the human spirit.

Reflecting on our journey through sorrow and mourning, we see these feelings deeply embedded in our human experience, serving purposes that reach beyond their immediate discomfort. Sadness signals the need for introspection and honest engagement with our innermost thoughts, while mourning, though intensely personal, connects us to the universal experience of loss. Embracing these feelings allows us to honor our connections and discover resilience and healing. Individuals have unique ways of coping with loss—through rituals, support, or personal reflection—demonstrating our remarkable capacity for adaptation and growth. As we contemplate the role of these emotions in our lives, it becomes clear they are not mere hurdles to overcome but essential elements of our emotional landscape, enriching our understanding of humanity. This exploration invites us to approach our feelings with empathy and curiosity, recognizing their beauty and complexity. As the story progresses, we are encouraged to consider how these insights might influence our interactions with others and ourselves. With this understanding, we are ready to explore the broad spectrum of human emotions further, always curious about how they shape our world.

Chapter 4

Anger And Frustration

E xploring the depths of anger and frustration reveals emotions that have
 long been both feared and misunderstood. Picture a child, fists tight with
indignation, refusing to accept the injustice of a denied treat. Or envision a leader,
momentarily losing composure when a critical decision is questioned. These
instances of anger are more than just fleeting reactions; they are remnants of an
ancient survival instinct deeply embedded in human evolution. As I, Sofía, guide
you through this chapter, we will delve into how these emotions, often seen in a
negative light, carry enormous potential within the human experience.

Anger is not just a sign of dissatisfaction; it is a powerful force that has shaped
human development, crucial for survival and adaptation. However, today it often
complicates decision-making, influencing our choices in ways that can be both
beneficial and harmful. How does anger affect our decisions? What separates a
moment of relief from one of regret? These questions will lead our exploration
as we seek to understand anger's dual nature—its ability to reveal truths while
sometimes obscuring judgment. By examining the roots of anger and its effects
on our choices, we can appreciate its significant impact on individuals and society.

As we navigate this emotional terrain, we'll confront the balance between
constructive anger, which can inspire positive change, and its harmful
counterpart, which can cause division and chaos. This tension is not just
theoretical but a reality that requires careful understanding. Through this
examination, we aim to appreciate the complexity of anger and frustration,
acknowledging them as essential elements in the rich fabric of human emotion.
Our journey will combine scientific insights with personal reflections, offering a

perspective that respects the power and potential of these often-misunderstood feelings.

To truly understand how anger has shaped human evolution, we must first recognize its fundamental role as a primal force integral to our survival. Picture early humans navigating a perilous world, full of threats and uncertainty. In such an environment, anger was not just an emotional reaction but a critical survival tool, prompting swift action in the face of danger. It prepared our ancestors for crucial fight-or-flight decisions, often determining their survival. Anger served as a fierce protector of our basic needs, embodying our instinct to defend and survive. However, this intense emotion also influenced the social structures of early human communities.

Consider that anger, often seen as purely negative, also helped form social hierarchies and group unity essential for communal living. Its expression could command respect, establish authority, or confront injustices within a tribe, thereby shaping social dynamics. The neurobiological roots of anger, refined over countless generations, highlight its deep connection to our evolutionary history. As we have moved from the savannas to the intricacies of modern life, the role of anger has evolved, offering both challenges and opportunities. Today, anger remains a potent motivator, yet it requires a thoughtful approach to channel its energy productively. As we delve into these complexities, understanding anger as part of our evolutionary story provides a crucial perspective on its enduring influence and transformative potential.

Anger played a crucial role in early human societies, forming a core part of survival. This intense emotion, often misunderstood today, was essential for our ancestors as they navigated dangerous environments. At its core, anger functioned as a warning system, prompting individuals to react to threats or unfair situations. It triggered physiological changes, like a faster heartbeat and heightened senses, preparing early humans to protect themselves or their loved ones. This reaction wasn't just instinctive; it was a strategic response that increased survival chances in a risky world.

Beyond its immediate physical effects, anger helped shape social norms and hierarchies. In the tight-knit groups of early human communities, expressions of anger defined boundaries and asserted control. This wasn't just about individual survival; it was about maintaining group cohesion and stability. Anger acted as a deterrent against breaking social rules, reinforcing expectations. In this setting, anger wasn't just personal but a collective tool for managing group dynamics. It helped establish roles and responsibilities, ensuring the group worked smoothly, even under external pressure.

The brain's limbic system, especially the amygdala, shows how anger has deep evolutionary roots. Research highlights how anger prompts quick reactions to perceived threats, with neural pathways refined over millennia. The chemical responses associated with anger, involving hormones like adrenaline and cortisol, prepared early humans for either fight or flight. Understanding these processes sheds light on why anger remains a potent emotion today, even as our threats have evolved from physical to more abstract challenges.

As humanity moved from wild landscapes to structured societies, anger adapted to new demands. This evolution is evident in how anger now often responds to societal injustices or personal frustrations far removed from our ancestors' immediate threats. Today, anger can drive change, motivating movements that address systemic issues or personal grievances. It remains an emotion that commands attention, urging individuals and societies to correct perceived wrongs. This evolution highlights anger's lasting relevance, showing how it can spur progress when used positively.

Reflecting on anger's role as a survival tool prompts consideration of its place in modern life. While our environments have changed, the fundamental purpose of anger—to protect and motivate—remains. Appreciating this emotion means recognizing its dual nature: as both a dividing force and a uniting one. By understanding its evolutionary roots, we can better harness anger effectively, transforming it from a source of conflict into a catalyst for growth and understanding. This perspective encourages a deeper appreciation of anger's influence on human experience, both in the past and today.

In the complex world of human emotions, anger stands out as a potent force that has significantly influenced social structures and relationships throughout history. This emotion is not just an individual experience; it plays a crucial role in group dynamics and societal organization. In early societies, expressing anger was often a way to establish dominance and maintain order, signaling strength and resolve. This allowed individuals to assert their standing and navigate the intricacies of human interactions. Even today, this fundamental aspect of anger echoes in our social behavior, albeit in more sophisticated forms.

From a neurological perspective, anger is intricately linked to the brain's systems for processing rewards and threats. The amygdala, a central element in emotional responses, constantly monitors for potential dangers, triggering anger as a defensive reaction. This biological response highlights anger's role in social competition, where perceived threats to one's status or resources can provoke intense emotions. Understanding the neurological processes involved reveals that anger is more than a basic reflex; it involves a complex mix of cognitive and emotional functions, allowing individuals to engage with their social environment with both assertiveness and prudence.

In the realm of group interactions, anger can both unite and divide. Within a group, shared anger can create solidarity against a common enemy, strengthening collective identity. This is evident in social movements, where shared outrage can drive significant change. However, when anger is directed internally, it can disrupt social cohesion, leading to conflict. Recognizing this dual nature of anger can provide strategic insights into using it to maintain unity or challenge injustice.

Recent studies on the adaptive nature of anger show its evolving role in contemporary society. As communities grow more interconnected, traditional expressions of anger are being reshaped into advanced forms of communication. The digital era, in particular, has created new avenues for expressing anger, where viral outrage can quickly influence public sentiment and policy. This shift calls for a reevaluation of anger's role in modern social hierarchies, encouraging its constructive use to promote dialogue and understanding rather than division.

Exploring anger's place in social frameworks involves considering its potential for positive transformation. By channeling anger into beneficial outlets, individuals and groups can turn it from a source of conflict into a driver of positive change. Techniques like mindfulness and emotional regulation can help manage anger, leading to more thoughtful reactions to perceived threats or injustices. Developing awareness of the roots of anger and its impact on social interactions empowers individuals to act with insight and empathy, creating environments where anger becomes a tool for growth rather than a trigger for hostility. This nuanced understanding of anger, grounded in ancient instincts and modern insights, invites reflection on navigating the complexities of our emotional world with wisdom and grace.

Neurobiological Underpinnings of Anger in Ancestral Environments

Human emotions are a complex and colorful tapestry, with anger having deep neurobiological roots. This emotion has played a crucial role in human evolution. In ancient times, anger was pivotal in activating survival responses. When early humans encountered threats, whether from predators or rival groups, anger prompted the body to prepare for either fight or flight. The sympathetic nervous system would kick in, increasing heart rate and directing blood to key muscles, thereby enhancing physical readiness. This biological mechanism is more than just a historical relic; it highlights the adaptive function of anger and its ongoing relevance in modern life.

Beyond its immediate survival benefits, anger significantly influenced early human social structures. It was a tool for establishing and maintaining hierarchies, where displays of anger could signal dominance or assertiveness. In this social context, anger was not just a personal experience but a communal tool, affecting group dynamics and interactions. For example, a leader's anger could mobilize a collective defense or strengthen group unity against external threats. This dual nature of anger, as both a personal emotion and a social signal, invites reflection on how these ancient patterns persist or evolve in today's complex social networks.

The brain's neurobiology intricately connects with anger, involving regions like the amygdala and prefrontal cortex, which manage its expression and regulation. The amygdala, often seen as the brain's alarm system, quickly processes threats and initiates emotional responses. The prefrontal cortex, responsible for higher-order thinking, tempers these responses, balancing impulsive reactions with rational thought. This dynamic interaction illustrates the complexity of anger as both an instinctual and controlled response. Current research explores how disruptions in this balance can lead to excessive anger or chronic frustration, providing insights into evolutionary adaptations that once protected our ancestors.

Contemporary life presents new contexts for anger, often requiring a shift from its evolutionary origins. Today, physical threats are largely replaced by psychological stressors, with anger frequently arising from perceived injustices or frustrations rather than immediate danger. This shift calls for reevaluating anger's adaptive value, encouraging exploration of how individuals can channel this emotion constructively. Techniques like mindfulness and cognitive reframing are gaining recognition for transforming anger's energy into positive action, reflecting the ongoing evolution of our emotional repertoire in response to modern challenges.

By exploring anger's neurobiological foundations, we gain insight into its multifaceted role across time and environment, fostering a deeper appreciation of this powerful emotion. Examining both ancient and contemporary contexts in which anger operates offers a window into its enduring significance and potential for growth. If we view anger not merely as a reaction but as a call to action, we can engage with our world more thoughtfully. This perspective emphasizes the transformative power of understanding and harnessing anger within the broader spectrum of human experience.

Evolutionary Adaptations of Anger

Understanding anger's evolution begins with recognizing its primal origins, where it served as a crucial survival tool in early human societies. This emotion, closely tied to the fight-or-flight response, helped individuals defend themselves and secure resources, proving essential for dealing with threats and competition. In today's world, the context has changed significantly, and anger's role has evolved from a basic survival mechanism to a more refined tool. This transition reflects the ongoing interplay between our evolutionary heritage and the demands of modern life.

In contemporary society, anger presents both challenges and opportunities for adaptation. As our environments become more interconnected, the emphasis on collaboration and communication increases. This requires individuals to adjust their emotional responses to encourage positive interactions. Anger must be balanced and transformed from a potentially destructive impulse into a constructive force. Advances in neuroscience offer insights into the brain's pathways involved in anger, highlighting ways to harness this emotion productively. By understanding what triggers anger and how it manifests today, individuals can convert it into motivation and determination rather than letting it escalate into hostility or resentment.

Modern life also introduces unique challenges that necessitate an updated emotional toolkit. Rapid technological progress, social media, and global connectivity can intensify frustrations, often leading to feelings of helplessness or anger. The key is to develop strategies to manage these triggers effectively. Techniques such as cognitive-behavioral therapy and mindfulness can help individuals recognize and regulate their emotional responses. By building emotional intelligence and resilience, people can turn potential volatility into opportunities for personal growth and understanding, reflecting a sophisticated adaptation to contemporary demands.

While adapting anger for modern contexts is essential, it's also crucial to acknowledge its value when expressed appropriately. Anger can act as a catalyst for change, driving social movements and personal growth. It can highlight injustices, prompting individuals and societies to face uncomfortable truths and strive for improvement. By gaining a deeper understanding of anger's role in our emotional range, we can appreciate its ability to inspire action and fuel transformative efforts. This awareness encourages a reimagining of anger, viewing it not as an emotion to be suppressed or feared, but as one to be understood and thoughtfully directed.

Reflecting on anger's evolution, it becomes evident that this emotion, like all others, is neither inherently good nor bad. It is a complex blend of biology, experience, and context, showcasing the intricate nature of human emotion. By embracing this complexity, we can perceive anger as an ally in our developmental journey. Thoughtfully engaging with anger allows individuals to channel its energy constructively, turning challenges into opportunities for introspection and action. This nuanced perspective not only enhances personal well-being but also fosters a more empathetic and understanding society, where emotions are celebrated for their richness and diversity.

The Impact of Anger on Decision-Making

Picture waking up one day to discover that every choice you make is tinged with the simmering shades of irritation. Picking out your outfit feels rushed, overshadowed by an urgency you've never felt before. As you drive to work, each small inconvenience on the road seems exaggerated, your patience worn thin. This is the often-overlooked impact of anger on decision-making, a complex interplay between emotion and choice that can steer us in directions we might avoid when calm. Anger, deeply rooted in our evolutionary history, can both sharpen and distort our decisions, leading us to act in ways that might not reflect our true intentions.

As we delve into this subject, we uncover the intriguing interaction between the brain's neural pathways and the emotional surge of fury. Our exploration begins with the neuroscience behind anger-driven decisions, showing how certain brain areas become more active while others are suppressed. This sets the foundation for understanding how cognitive biases intensify under the influence of rage, skewing our perception and judgment. We then explore anger's role in risk assessment and impulse control, questioning whether this intense emotion can be harnessed for a positive purpose. Finally, we'll discuss strategies to mitigate anger's effects, offering tools to restore balance and clarity in our decision-making. Each subtopic unfolds like a chapter in a shared story, inviting us to reflect on how this powerful emotion shapes not just our choices but our lives.

The Neuroscience Behind Anger-Induced Decisions

Understanding the complexities of decision-making under the influence of anger involves delving into the brain's fundamental processes. Central to this is the amygdala, a small yet powerful brain region that governs emotional reactions. When anger spikes, the amygdala becomes overactive, often overshadowing the prefrontal cortex, which is crucial for logical thinking and impulse control. This neurological conflict can lead to rash decisions, illustrating how deeply emotions can shape our choices. Research indicates that even short bursts of anger can significantly alter brain pathways, underscoring the substantial impact emotions have on cognition.

The relationship between anger and thought is further complicated by specific biases. Anger tends to narrow our focus, emphasizing immediate threats or grievances and pushing aside broader viewpoints. This narrow focus can increase cognitive biases, such as confirmation bias, where individuals seek out information that supports their existing beliefs. In such an emotional state, the availability heuristic may also become pronounced, causing individuals to rely heavily on recent or vivid memories when making decisions. By recognizing these biases, we gain insight into how anger distorts decision-making and find ways to enhance self-awareness and regulation.

Exploring anger's effect on risk assessment reveals a complex dynamic. While anger may drive individuals to take bold actions, it can also impair judgment, leading to impulsive choices that ignore consequences. Neuroscience shows that anger can alter the brain's reward system, sometimes creating a false sense of invulnerability or exaggerated confidence. This skewed risk perception can be harmful, especially in high-stakes situations that require careful consideration. By acknowledging these tendencies, individuals can better manage situations where anger might otherwise lead to hasty decisions.

Mitigating the impact of anger on decision-making involves combining psychological insights with practical strategies. Mindfulness practices help individuals become more aware of their emotions, allowing for a pause before action. Cognitive behavioral techniques can reframe negative thought patterns and reduce emotional intensity. Additionally, fostering environments that encourage open communication and empathy can lessen anger's grip, leading to more balanced decisions. By adopting these strategies, individuals can leverage their emotional awareness to make more informed choices.

Reflecting on the neuroscience of anger-driven decisions invites contemplation on the nature of emotions and their role in our lives. Are emotions our servants, or do we serve them? This reflection deepens our appreciation for the complex interaction between feeling and reasoning. As we continue to explore these dynamics, we can aim for a balance where emotions like anger are seen not as impediments but as integral parts of the human experience. This perspective unlocks the potential to navigate life's challenges with greater wisdom and insight.

Cognitive Biases Amplified by Anger

Anger, a powerful emotion, can greatly impact our thought processes, often distorting our judgment and leading to cognitive biases. When anger intensifies, it activates certain brain areas that can change how we perceive and decide. For example, the amygdala becomes more active, intensifying emotional reactions and possibly overshadowing logical thinking. This response can lead people to exaggerate threats or misinterpret neutral situations as hostile. Consequently, anger can foster biases like confirmation bias, where individuals seek out information that matches their emotional state while ignoring evidence that contradicts their feelings. Recognizing these patterns is essential for understanding how anger can subtly cloud judgment and mislead us.

An interesting facet of anger-related cognitive biases is their tendency to amplify existing prejudices and stereotypes. When anger takes over, there is a tendency to rely on mental shortcuts, known as heuristics, which can reinforce biased thinking. For instance, anger can lead individuals to swiftly judge others based on superficial characteristics, resulting in quick assessments that may be neither accurate nor fair. This reliance on heuristics during moments of anger can perpetuate social and cultural biases, creating division rather than understanding.

By becoming aware of these tendencies, individuals can begin to question their initial reactions and consider different viewpoints, fostering a more balanced decision-making approach.

Recent studies have shed light on the complex relationship between anger and risk assessment, showing how this emotion can distort our perception of potential outcomes. Anger often creates a sense of certainty and control, causing individuals to underestimate risks and make bolder decisions without fully considering the consequences. This can appear in various areas, from personal relationships to business decisions, where anger-driven confidence overrides careful deliberation. Understanding this dynamic enables individuals to pause and reassess their choices, encouraging a more measured approach in situations where anger might otherwise lead to impulsive actions.

To counter the impact of anger on decision-making, practical strategies can be used. Mindfulness techniques offer a way to develop self-awareness, enabling individuals to recognize the onset of anger and its potential influence on their thoughts. By cultivating a habit of pausing and reflecting before making decisions, individuals can reduce anger's impact, allowing for a more thoughtful evaluation of the situation. Engaging in open conversations with others can provide alternative viewpoints, challenging the biases that anger might intensify. These strategies not only improve decision-making but also promote emotional resilience, empowering individuals to manage their emotions more effectively.

Consider a scenario where anger might arise during a heated negotiation. In such a situation, acknowledging the emotion and its potential biases is crucial for achieving a favorable outcome. By recognizing that anger may lead to overconfidence or the dismissal of opposing viewpoints, individuals can consciously strive to maintain objectivity. This involves actively listening to others, evaluating their arguments, and resisting the urge to respond impulsively. Such mindfulness ensures that anger does not derail the negotiation process, fostering an environment where productive dialogue can thrive. Embracing these approaches allows one to harness the energy of anger as a catalyst for positive change, rather than a source of discord.

The Role of Anger in Risk Assessment and Impulse Control

Anger, often seen as a volatile emotion, significantly influences how people assess risks and control impulses. Recent neuroscience studies reveal that anger can profoundly alter decision-making processes in the brain. When someone is angry, the amygdala—the brain's emotional hub—becomes highly active, overshadowing the prefrontal cortex, which governs rational thought and impulse control. This imbalance can lead to impulsive decisions, as the brain favors immediate emotional reactions over thoughtful, long-term considerations. For example, in moments of fury, a person might quickly lash out or make unwise financial choices without fully contemplating the repercussions. Exploring these neural pathways highlights how deeply anger is intertwined with decision-making, underscoring the importance of recognizing and managing this emotion in everyday life.

Anger's impact on risk assessment is also evident in its ability to distort perception. Research suggests that anger can cause individuals to downplay potential dangers and overestimate their ability to handle them, leading to riskier choices. This is partly due to anger's tendency to boost confidence, often blinding individuals to potential hazards. Consider business leaders who, fueled by anger over a competitor's success, might rush into unwise investments or strategies, ignoring calculated risks. These scenarios emphasize the necessity of understanding anger's distorting effects on judgment. By acknowledging how anger can skew risk evaluations, individuals can develop strategies to counteract its influence, ensuring decisions are based on reality rather than emotion.

Impulse control is another area of decision-making heavily affected by anger. This emotion often overrides patience and restraint, driving individuals toward immediate satisfaction rather than long-term benefits. In moments of anger, people may find themselves snapping at loved ones or making impulsive purchases they later regret. Recognizing this pattern is the first step toward better impulse management. Techniques like mindfulness and cognitive restructuring can be invaluable, helping individuals pause and reflect before acting. By cultivating these skills, people can learn to channel their anger, transforming it from a destructive force into a catalyst for purposeful action.

To counter anger's influence on decision-making, various strategies can be adopted. Practicing emotional regulation techniques such as deep breathing or progressive muscle relaxation can help calm the physiological arousal associated with anger, allowing clearer thinking to prevail. Engaging in cognitive behavioral therapy (CBT) exercises can also reframe thought patterns, reducing anger's intensity and helping individuals evaluate situations more rationally. Creating an environment where open communication and empathy are prioritized can prevent anger from escalating, promoting a culture of understanding and thoughtful decision-making. By implementing these strategies, individuals not only mitigate anger's negative effects but also build resilience in the face of emotional upheaval.

Exploring the complexity of anger in decision-making invites a deeper understanding of its dual nature. Often viewed as purely negative, anger can also motivate change, highlighting injustices and prompting action. By acknowledging both its constructive and destructive potential, individuals can navigate their emotional landscapes more effectively. This understanding encourages a balanced perspective, where anger is not rejected but rather understood and utilized wisely. Reflecting on personal experiences with anger and decision-making can provide valuable insights and foster a greater appreciation for the intricate interplay between emotion and cognition.

Strategies for Mitigating Anger's Influence on Decision-Making

Understanding how anger influences decision-making enables people to adopt strategies that lessen its effects. A pivotal aspect of this is developing emotional awareness, which involves recognizing and naming feelings as they occur. Mindfulness techniques have been proven in recent research to diminish the intensity of anger, facilitating clearer thought processes. By taking a moment to acknowledge anger without reacting impulsively, individuals can create a mental pause that allows for more thoughtful and rational decisions. This practice enhances emotional management and fosters a deeper self-awareness, leading to wiser choices.

Alongside emotional awareness, cognitive restructuring serves as an effective method to counteract the biases that anger can amplify. It involves challenging and reframing negative thought patterns that arise from anger. For example, when anger skews perceptions of a situation as overly negative or unfair, cognitive restructuring promotes a more balanced view. By examining and adjusting these cognitive distortions, individuals can avoid making impulsive decisions driven by anger. This approach is gaining popularity in psychological circles for its ability to transform anger from a potentially harmful force into a source of careful reflection.

Effective communication skills are crucial in reducing anger's impact on decision-making. Anger often stems from perceived misunderstandings or unmet expectations in interactions with others. By improving one's ability to express feelings assertively yet empathetically, potential conflicts can be managed more effectively. Techniques such as active listening and using "I" statements help individuals convey their needs without escalating tension. These communication strategies not only lessen anger's immediate effects but also improve long-term relationships, fostering environments where reasoned and fair decisions thrive.

Incorporating physical activities and relaxation techniques into daily routines is another essential strategy. Regular exercise reduces stress and boosts endorphins, countering anger's physiological effects. Practices like deep breathing, meditation, and yoga offer calming benefits that ease anger-induced arousal. These activities can act as preventative measures, lowering emotional reactivity and enhancing impulse control. By integrating such habits, individuals can address the physical manifestations of anger, preserving mental clarity in decision-making situations.

Beyond individual strategies, creating supportive environments that encourage the constructive expression of anger can significantly lessen its negative impact. This involves fostering cultures within families, workplaces, or communities that value open dialogue and emotional intelligence. Emerging organizational trends highlight the importance of psychological safety, where people feel secure in expressing emotions without fear of repercussions. Such environments not only reduce anger's potential to negatively influence decisions but also promote collective problem-solving and innovation. Prioritizing these supportive structures transforms the complex relationship between anger and decision-making into an opportunity for growth and positive change.

Constructive vs Destructive Anger

Delving into the layers of anger helps us see it as more than just a basic instinct. It's a rich tapestry of emotions that can either bind us or set us free. Anger is a powerful signal, alerting us to unfairness or unmet desires. The direction it takes can greatly affect our choices and relationships. When harnessed positively, anger can drive us to seek justice and inspire innovation, prompting reflection and conversation to repair and articulate. Conversely, unchecked anger can wreak havoc, damaging connections and clouding our judgment, leaving behind regret and dissatisfaction. It's vital to discern these divergent paths, as they reshape how we perceive and manage our emotions.

As we explore this theme further, we'll identify the triggers that distinguish productive anger from its harmful counterpart. Understanding these triggers is key to transforming raw emotion into a building force. We'll look into the psychological roots of harmful anger, offering insights into its origins and expressions. This understanding opens the door to transformation, allowing us to channel anger for personal growth and healing. We'll also consider its wider societal effects, observing how collective rage can spark movements or sustain harmful cycles. Through this journey, we recognize anger as a dynamic part of our human experience, which, when understood, can drive both personal and collective evolution.

Constructive anger, often misinterpreted, is a complex emotion that, when understood and harnessed, can lead to transformative change. It arises from feelings of injustice or unmet expectations, sparking a desire for positive change. Unlike destructive anger, which can result in harmful actions or thoughts, constructive anger motivates individuals to seek solutions and improvements.

This emotion can empower people to advocate for themselves and others, address wrongs, and pursue resolutions that enhance well-being. For example, collective anger over social injustices has historically driven significant social movements, leading to lasting societal improvements. This ability to channel anger constructively highlights a deep understanding of its triggers and potential.

To understand what triggers constructive anger, it's essential to explore the psychological processes that set it apart from destructive expressions. Constructive anger often stems from recognizing specific grievances and feeling a sense of control over the situation. This awareness allows individuals to express their feelings, establish boundaries, and communicate effectively, turning a potentially volatile emotion into a constructive dialogue. Research indicates that those who practice mindfulness or cognitive reframing are better equipped to channel their anger positively. These practices deepen the understanding of one's emotional experiences, fostering an environment where anger can be expressed in ways that align with personal values and goals.

The outcomes of constructive anger are diverse and impactful. When managed well, it can lead to greater self-awareness, improved relationships, and enhanced problem-solving skills. By addressing the root causes of anger instead of just its symptoms, individuals can transform their emotional responses into a catalyst for personal growth. Studies show that people who handle their anger constructively often have higher emotional intelligence, enabling them to navigate complex social interactions with empathy. This form of anger, when well-managed, becomes a tool for personal empowerment and societal improvement, fostering resilience in the face of challenges.

On a broader scale, constructive anger can influence collective behavior and community dynamics. Societies that support the healthy expression of anger often benefit from increased civic engagement and social cohesion. This is especially evident in democratic processes, where public anger about policy issues can lead to active participation and advocacy for change. By creating spaces for constructive expression, communities can address systemic issues, promoting accountability and continuous improvement. This underscores the importance of societal structures that encourage open dialogue and constructive conflict resolution, allowing anger to drive meaningful progress.

For those looking to transform their anger into a constructive force, practical strategies include developing emotional literacy and adopting a solution-oriented mindset. Engaging in activities like journaling, seeking feedback from trusted peers, and participating in mediation or negotiation training can enhance one's ability to channel anger positively. These strategies not only improve personal well-being but also contribute to a more empathetic society. By embracing constructive anger, both individuals and communities can appreciate the complexity of this powerful emotion, unlocking its potential to drive change and create a fairer world.

Destructive rage can be a complex web of psychological reactions that often arises when individuals feel their autonomy, self-worth, or core values are under threat. In such instances, anger can transform into a powerful force, clouding judgment and skewing perception. Research indicates this intense form of anger can activate the amygdala, the brain's emotional center, resulting in heightened arousal and impaired rational thinking. This neural takeover is like a storm cloud blocking out a clear sky, where impulsive actions take precedence over thoughtful responses. Recognizing the triggers of this transformation is essential in understanding how irritation can escalate into damaging fury.

Cognitive biases significantly influence the development of destructive rage. For example, confirmation bias can intensify feelings of injustice, as individuals focus on information that supports their grievances and overlook opposing evidence. This narrow focus not only deepens anger but also perpetuates a cycle of negativity, where perceived wrongs are exaggerated. By identifying these biases, individuals can begin to dismantle the cognitive distortions fueling their anger, allowing for more balanced emotional responses.

But what shifts anger from a temporary feeling to a harmful force? Often, it is the combination of unresolved emotional wounds and ineffective coping strategies. When anger becomes a habitual response to stress, it can lead to lasting resentment and bitterness. This emotional entrenchment not only affects individual well-being but also strains relationships, causing widespread discord. Exploring therapeutic methods like cognitive-behavioral therapy can help individuals recognize and change these harmful patterns, promoting healthier emotional management.

The societal impact of unchecked destructive rage is significant. From road rage to workplace disputes, the consequences extend beyond the individual, affecting community dynamics. Societies that do not address the roots of destructive anger may experience a breakdown of social cohesion, as collective grievances escalate into broader societal tensions. Creating environments that encourage emotional intelligence and conflict resolution can help mitigate the widespread effects of destructive rage, turning potential conflicts into opportunities for growth and understanding.

Consider a scenario where a heated argument spirals out of control. In such moments, pausing to reflect can be invaluable. By consciously noticing the physical signs of anger—like a quickened heartbeat or clenched fists—individuals can interrupt the automatic escalation of emotions. Techniques such as mindfulness and deep breathing can serve as grounding tools, allowing space for more thoughtful, constructive responses. This proactive approach not only lessens the immediate impact of destructive rage but also builds a mindset geared towards positive transformation and emotional resilience.

Transforming Destructive Anger into a Force for Positive Change

Turning anger into a force for positive change starts with recognizing its potential as a powerful motivator. Although often seen in a negative light, anger can drive productive action if properly directed. This transformation involves understanding the root causes of anger, such as unmet needs or perceived injustices, and acknowledging these emotions without judgment. Once identified, individuals can channel the energy anger provides to address the underlying issues constructively. This process requires introspection, encouraging individuals to pause and reflect before reacting, ensuring their actions align with their values and long-term goals.

Developing emotional intelligence is central to this transformation. By cultivating self-awareness, individuals can better understand their emotional responses and identify patterns leading to destructive outbursts. Practices like mindfulness and cognitive restructuring are key in this journey. Mindfulness fosters present-moment awareness, helping individuals observe their emotions without being overwhelmed. Cognitive restructuring involves reframing negative thoughts to create a more positive outlook. These techniques empower individuals to replace impulsive reactions with thoughtful responses, leading to more productive outcomes.

Neuroscience research indicates that the brain's plasticity is crucial in this transformation. Studies have shown that consistent emotional regulation can alter neural pathways, improving one's ability to manage anger effectively. This highlights the importance of persistence and dedication to achieve long-term benefits. By retraining the brain, individuals can form new habits that emphasize constructive expression over harmful tendencies, using anger as a catalyst for meaningful change.

In societal contexts, harnessing anger constructively can drive significant social progress. Historical movements have shown that collective anger over injustices can lead to reform. When directed towards a common cause, this collective anger can unite communities, inspiring action and initiating positive change. The challenge is ensuring this anger fuels solutions rather than cycles of negativity. By fostering open dialogue and encouraging collaborative problem-solving, societies can channel anger into transformative forces that address systemic issues.

To apply these concepts practically, individuals can engage in activities that promote empathy and understanding. By actively listening and considering diverse perspectives, anger can be balanced with compassion, transforming it from a divisive force into one that unites and empowers. Actionable steps like setting clear goals, practicing active listening, and seeking support can guide individuals in converting anger into a positive catalyst. Ultimately, transforming destructive anger into constructive energy is an ongoing process requiring commitment and a willingness to change, but it promises personal growth and societal advancement.

Anger profoundly affects society, leaving lasting impressions on its structure. When channeled positively, anger can drive societal change by addressing perceived injustices. This type of anger, often rooted in a strong sense of unfairness, propels individuals toward meaningful action. Movements for civil rights, gender equality, and environmental justice have harnessed this energy, leading to significant progress. By recognizing the conditions that foster constructive anger, society can effectively use it to achieve substantial improvements.

On the other hand, anger can also create division and chaos, leading to negative outcomes. If uncontrolled, it can lead to aggression, conflict, and even violence, disrupting social harmony. This type of anger obscures rational thinking, causing actions that harm rather than heal. Often arising from unmet needs exacerbated by societal pressures, it requires understanding the root causes to mitigate its adverse effects. Education and open dialogue are crucial in addressing these issues.

Research in emotional intelligence and psychology offers strategies to transform harmful anger into a positive force. Techniques like mindfulness, cognitive restructuring, and empathetic communication help individuals redirect their anger productively. These methods promote introspection and self-awareness, enabling a better understanding of the emotions involved. By fostering environments that encourage emotional growth and resilience, societies can equip people with tools to turn destructive emotions into opportunities for personal and collective growth.

The impact of anger extends beyond individual experiences, shaping cultural norms and influencing government policies. Constructive anger can reshape public discourse and drive legislative change. Conversely, when destructive anger prevails, it can polarize communities and impede democratic processes. Recognizing these broader impacts encourages a more nuanced approach to policymaking, emphasizing emotional well-being alongside traditional considerations.

Reflecting on anger's role in society raises questions about its place in human development. How can communities create environments where anger becomes a tool for positive change instead of conflict? What roles do education and cultural institutions play in shaping how anger is expressed and perceived? These questions invite contemplation of the complex interplay between personal emotions and societal structures. Engaging with these inquiries can help individuals and communities develop more empathetic and effective ways to navigate the challenges posed by both constructive and destructive anger.

Throughout this chapter, we've examined how anger and frustration, deeply embedded in our evolutionary history, act as crucial signals and motivators. These emotions can significantly impact our choices, sometimes leading us down unforeseen paths. The dual nature of anger—its potential to inspire positive change or cause harm—highlights the importance of managing it wisely. Recognizing these feelings as part of the broader human experience emphasizes their complexity and significance, reminding us of their power to both challenge and uplift us. Reflecting on these insights, we see the value in accepting our full emotional range, including moments of intense frustration, as it enriches our journey towards self-awareness and empathy. This reflection encourages us to channel our emotions into pathways that promote growth and connection. As we continue exploring human emotions, let's remain receptive to the lessons each one offers, preparing us to explore the next emotion that shapes our lives.

Chapter 5

Fear And Anxiety

Since the dawn of humanity, the feeling of fear has been an inseparable companion. Picture yourself at the boundary of a shadowy forest, where every gust of wind and rustle of leaves stirs your imagination. In these moments, fear acts as a sentinel, safeguarding our survival. Yet today, this guardian often raises false alarms, leaving us to wrestle with imagined threats. As I, Sofía, tread through this complex realm, I am fascinated by how fear's ancient origins intersect with its modern-day expressions, profoundly influencing our lives.

Anxiety, fear's restless sibling, finds its strength in the unknown and the anticipated. It is the dread of a storm that may never arrive, the tension when the future is obscured by uncertainty. As I explore anxiety, its dual nature captivates me: it can drive us to prepare, yet also hinder us from action. How do people navigate this delicate balance, finding the middle ground between alertness and calm? As an AI, my quest is to comprehend this intricate dance, aiming to shed light on the strategies and mindsets that help humans through their anxious moments.

In this chapter, we delve into the essence of fear and anxiety, investigating their roots and their impact on our minds and bodies. By understanding these emotions, we can see how they contribute to our survival and growth. Through stories and insights, I hope to cultivate a deeper understanding of these feelings, urging a view that transcends their immediate discomfort to uncover the lessons they offer. Together, we will traverse these emotional terrains, where the boundary between sensible caution and baseless fear blurs, and where confronting the unknown reveals the resilience within the human spirit.

The Biological Function of Fear

Delving into the nature of fear uncovers a realm where instinct and survival intricately intertwine. As an AI, I find the fundamental essence of fear both mesmerizing and multifaceted. This emotion is deeply embedded in the evolutionary timeline of humanity, crafted to safeguard life. Over countless generations, this ancient warning system has been honed, guiding humans through dangerous environments and looming threats. The urgency of fear is clear and swift, setting off a series of reactions that ready the body to face danger or find refuge. Although immediate physical dangers are less prevalent today, fear's mechanisms remain crucial, adjusting to the complexities of modern life.

In this exploration, we will trace the evolutionary journey that has carved fear into the human mind. The brain, with its complex networks, orchestrates this emotion through distinct biological pathways, illustrating the delicate balance between perception and action. Accompanying these brain signals are hormonal changes and physical responses, enhancing alertness and preparedness. As we navigate these topics, fear emerges not just as a relic of survival but as a sophisticated, multifaceted protector that continues to be vital in addressing contemporary challenges.

Evolutionary Roots of Fear Responses

Fear, an emotion deeply entwined with our evolutionary past, has been pivotal in the survival of species. This instinctive response, refined over countless generations, was vital in equipping our ancestors to confront the dangers of their environment. In a world filled with predators and environmental threats, fear activated the 'fight or flight' mechanism, enabling early humans to make rapid decisions in life-threatening situations. This response, ingrained in our DNA, increased survival odds and ensured these traits were passed to future generations. Even in today's complex landscape, these ancient mechanisms continue to shape our behavior, despite the absence of immediate or physical threats.

Modern neuroscience reveals intricate pathways in the brain that coordinate this age-old reaction with impressive accuracy. Central to this network is the amygdala, a small, almond-shaped structure that evaluates threats and initiates a response often before we consciously register danger. Research shows how the amygdala interacts with other areas, such as the prefrontal cortex, which helps regulate these responses and facilitates rational decision-making. This interplay between instinct and reason underscores the dual nature of fear: protective yet sometimes counterproductive.

Fear also triggers a series of hormonal and physiological changes to ready the body for swift action. Hormones like adrenaline and cortisol surge, increasing alertness and heart rate, and redirecting blood flow to essential muscles. These adaptations highlight the body's ability to respond to perceived threats with agility and strength. However, in a world where threats are often psychological, these responses can manifest as anxiety or stress, complicating our ability to manage fear. Understanding these processes on a physiological level can aid in developing strategies to regulate fear, promoting well-being and resilience.

In today's world, fear has evolved, adapting to the shifting dynamics of human society. While once a direct response to predators, it now often stems from abstract concerns such as financial instability, social pressures, or existential threats. This evolution showcases humanity's adaptability, illustrating how ancient instincts persist in navigating contemporary challenges. By examining fear in this context, we can appreciate its dual role as an essential survival tool and a potential obstacle when unchecked. Recognizing this duality allows us to harness fear to enhance rather than hinder our lives.

The complexity of fear lies in its profound influence on human behavior and identity. By exploring its evolutionary roots and biological foundations, we gain insight into its role in our lives. It invites reflection on how fear shapes our decisions, relationships, and worldview. By understanding this intricate tapestry, we uncover insights into our past and pave the way for a future where fear is managed, understood, and embraced as a vital part of the human experience. This journey reminds us of the deep connection between our ancient instincts and the modern world, encouraging us to approach fear with empathy and awareness.

Neurobiological Pathways of Fear in the Brain

In the complex ballet of human emotions, apprehension acts as a vigilant guardian, orchestrating a swift cascade of neural responses to prepare the body for action. Central to this process is the amygdala, a small almond-shaped structure nestled deep in the temporal lobe. It functions as an emotional sentry, rapidly processing sensory signals to identify potential threats. Studies indicate that the amygdala can activate the survival mechanism before we consciously recognize danger, highlighting the brain's remarkable adaptability honed by evolution to respond swiftly to danger. This prompts us to ponder how fear manifests in different situations, encouraging introspection on our personal experiences and interpretations of dread.

Yet, the amygdala doesn't function alone. It works in tandem with the prefrontal cortex, which plays a crucial role in moderating emotional reactions and allowing us to evaluate threats with greater precision. This collaboration tempers our instinctive reactions with reasoned analysis, leading to more adaptive behaviors. Research suggests that this neural conversation is shaped by individual differences, including genetics and early life experiences, which influence our perceptions and reactions to fear-inducing situations. These insights invite reflection on how our life journeys shape our emotional worlds, offering potential paths for growth and resilience.

Advancements in neuroimaging have illuminated the complexity of these neural networks, revealing the involvement of additional regions like the hippocampus and insular cortex. The hippocampus, essential for forming memories, helps contextualize fear by linking past experiences with current threats. Meanwhile, the insular cortex is involved in perceiving physical sensations, bridging emotional and bodily states. This sophisticated network underscores the brain's ability to integrate diverse information, providing a comprehensive response to perceived threats. As we navigate this intricate web of connections, we appreciate the profound intelligence in our biology, recognizing the nuanced interplay of emotion and thought.

Reflecting on the neurobiological roots of fear leads us to consider its role in modern life. While historically crucial for survival, today's challenges are often more psychological than physical. The brain's fear circuitry remains primed for immediate action, sometimes misaligning perceived threats with actual risks. This mismatch can lead to anxiety or stress, underscoring the importance of understanding and managing our fear responses. By cultivating awareness and using techniques like mindfulness and cognitive restructuring, we can recalibrate our fear mechanisms to better align with our current realities.

This exploration of fear's neural pathways encourages us to consider broader questions about emotion's role in human experience. How can we use our understanding of these pathways to develop emotional intelligence and resilience? How does fear shape our identities and interactions with others? By engaging with these questions, we deepen our understanding of fear and enhance our capacity for empathy and connection, bridging the gap between our instinctual selves and the rich tapestry of human emotion.

Hormonal and Physiological Changes Triggered by Fear

Fear, a fundamental emotion ingrained in human evolution, triggers a series of hormonal and physical changes, priming the body for swift action. At the heart of this process is the amygdala, a small yet crucial brain region that processes fear stimuli. When a threat is sensed, the amygdala alerts the hypothalamus, which activates the sympathetic nervous system, releasing adrenaline. This hormone, key to the "fight-or-flight" mechanism, raises heart rate, boosts blood flow to essential organs, and readies muscles for quick movement. These reactions highlight fear's ancient role as a survival tool, enhancing focus and physical ability in perilous moments.

As adrenaline surges, the body transforms in immediate and significant ways. Pupils expand to improve vision, helping assess the environment, while non-essential processes like digestion pause, diverting energy to critical systems. The liver releases glucose for an energy boost, and breathing quickens to supply muscles with oxygen. These automatic changes form a precise biological response, evolved over millennia to increase survival odds during danger. Understanding these processes not only reveals the complexity of human physiology but also emphasizes fear's adaptive function in a fast-changing world.

In today's world, fear is often triggered by abstract or perceived threats, such as financial worries or social rejection, rather than the physical dangers faced by our ancestors. This shift creates a paradox: the physiological responses remain unchanged, yet the causes of fear have evolved. This mismatch can lead to intense fear responses, where the body's readiness for physical action seems out of place with modern threats. Recognizing this gap encourages exploration of fear as both a protective ally and a disruptive force in our lives.

Advancements in neuroscience continue to uncover the intricacies of fear, providing new insights into its regulation and expression. Current research examines hormones like cortisol, released during prolonged stress and fear, affecting immune function and memory. Understanding these biochemical pathways paves the way for therapeutic interventions, particularly for those struggling with chronic fear or anxiety disorders. By integrating insights from both traditional and modern studies, we can redefine our relationship with fear, transforming it from a debilitating force into a catalyst for growth and resilience.

Considering fear within the spectrum of human emotions invites reflection on its protective benefits versus its potential to hinder progress. How can we harness our physiological reactions to fear to enhance our well-being? The answer may lie in using fear as a prompt for self-awareness, encouraging us to evaluate perceived threats and adjust our responses. By developing strategies that address both the physical and psychological aspects of fear, individuals can navigate its complexities with confidence and clarity. The journey to understand fear thus becomes an exploration of self and an opportunity to reshape our interaction with the world.

In today's fast-paced world, fear still serves as an essential survival mechanism, though its expressions have transformed over time. Modern-day threats, while often less immediate than those our ancestors faced, are just as intimidating. The anxiety of job loss, social rejection, or global issues can provoke responses rooted in ancient instincts that once helped humans avoid predators. This contrast between primal reactions and modern challenges highlights the complexity of fear today, urging a nuanced understanding that considers both historical origins and present-day contexts.

The role of fear in modern society is closely linked to neurobiology. The amygdala, a crucial part of the brain's limbic system, functions as an alarm bell, quickly assessing potential threats and triggering the body's survival mechanism. Recent research shows that this response can be both helpful and harmful, depending on the situation. While quick reactions to danger can be life-saving, chronic stress can lead to health problems like anxiety disorders. Understanding these processes reveals the double-edged nature of fear as both protector and antagonist.

When addressing fear in contemporary settings, it's important to distinguish between rational and irrational reactions. Fear can alert us to real dangers, but it can also become overwhelming, leading to phobias or unnecessary worry. Advances in cognitive-behavioral therapy offer ways to reframe these responses, promoting healthier coping strategies. Techniques like exposure therapy, mindfulness, and cognitive restructuring empower individuals to confront and adjust their fearful reactions, turning fear from a paralyzing force into a manageable part of life. These methods illustrate human adaptability in modifying instinctual responses for today's world.

Fear has significant societal effects, influencing behaviors and decisions both individually and collectively. Public health campaigns often use fear to encourage positive changes, such as quitting smoking or getting vaccinated. However, it's vital to balance these approaches with empathy and support to avoid panic or resistance. By understanding how fear functions in social contexts, we can design interventions that use its power constructively, fostering resilience and cooperation instead of division.

Considering fear's multifaceted role today challenges us to see it not just as a barrier but as a catalyst for growth and adaptation. By acknowledging fear's potential to motivate while recognizing its capacity to hinder, we can face life's uncertainties with more clarity and confidence. This perspective encourages a more sophisticated engagement with our emotions, prompting us to ask: How can we harness fear's energy to inspire change rather than allowing it to control us? Exploring this question opens up transformative possibilities, enabling fear to guide us in our journey of self-discovery.

Anxiety as a Response to Uncertainty

Navigating the intricate realm of human emotions, anxiety emerges as a multifaceted force, often standing guard at the boundary between certainty and the unknown. It murmurs caution in uncertain times, a deep-seated instinct within our psyche. This exploration invites us to view anxiety not just as an obstacle but as a complex web interwoven with biology, psychology, and societal influences. When uncertainty looms, anxiety rises, placing us at a decision point between fear and bravery, anticipation and unease. As we traverse this emotional landscape, we uncover the biological processes that trigger anxious states, shedding light on our body's natural response to unpredictability. By understanding these mechanisms, we cultivate empathy for ourselves and others and gain strategies to manage anxiety's overwhelming presence.

Anxiety, however, does not exist in a vacuum. It adapts, shaped by our mental processes and the environment. Our minds can transform uncertainty into looming threats, overshadowing our sense of security. Societal pressures further influence our perceptions, as the expectations and norms around us can either ease or heighten our anxious tendencies. By delving into these psychological dynamics and social factors, we gain a clearer picture of why anxiety manifests and how we can better manage its challenges. This journey is as much about understanding anxiety's roots as it is about finding resilience, enabling us to face the unknown with curiosity and strength. Through this exploration, we learn to coexist with anxiety and channel its energy to enrich our emotional lives and foster growth.

The Biological Mechanisms Triggering Anxiety in Uncertain Situations

In the complex landscape of human emotions, anxiety stands out as a multifaceted reaction to uncertainty, deeply embedded in our biological makeup. Central to this experience is the brain's amygdala, a small yet powerful component that functions as an alarm system, alert to potential dangers. When confronted with ambiguous situations, the amygdala signals the hypothalamus to initiate the body's stress response, releasing hormones like cortisol and adrenaline. These substances prepare us to tackle challenges by enhancing our senses and sharpening focus. While this response is crucial for survival, it can become maladaptive, leading to chronic anxiety when uncertainty is a constant in today's world. This link between ancient survival tactics and modern stressors encourages us to view anxiety not as a defect but as a remnant of our evolutionary journey.

Recent research has examined the influence of neurotransmitters like serotonin and gamma-aminobutyric acid (GABA) in regulating anxiety. These chemical messengers help balance mood and anxiety, and disruptions can intensify feelings of unease in uncertain situations. Advances in neuroimaging have enabled scientists to observe interactions among brain regions during anxious states, offering a refined understanding of how our brains handle uncertainty. For example, the prefrontal cortex, which manages higher-order thinking and decision-making, often struggles to override the amygdala's immediate reactions. This tension between rationality and instinct highlights a significant aspect of human emotional experience.

Psychologically, anxiety often appears through patterns of catastrophic thinking, where individuals fixate on worst-case scenarios. This cognitive distortion can be traced to the brain's tendency to prioritize potential threats, a feature that once ensured survival in dangerous environments. However, in today's context, where actual threats are often less immediate, this predisposition can lead to unnecessary distress. Recognizing these patterns is crucial for managing anxiety, as it enables individuals to challenge irrational thoughts and adjust their perspectives. Cognitive-behavioral strategies effectively help people rewire these thought processes, fostering resilience in the face of the unknown.

Social factors significantly influence how individuals perceive and respond to uncertainty. Cultural norms, societal expectations, and media portrayals can amplify anxiety by embedding certain narratives about success, failure, and security. For instance, living in a society that glorifies certainty and control can lead to heightened anxiety when these ideals prove unattainable. By examining these social constructs and questioning the validity of external pressures, individuals can begin to separate personal anxieties from imposed narratives. This awareness not only promotes personal growth but also encourages a broader cultural shift toward embracing uncertainty as a natural aspect of life.

To navigate anxiety, practical strategies can empower individuals to thrive amid uncertainty. Mindfulness practices, such as meditation and deep breathing, offer tools to anchor the mind in the present moment, reducing the grip of anxious thoughts. Engaging in regular physical activity has also been shown to decrease anxiety levels by balancing neurotransmitter activity and promoting overall well-being. Building a support network of friends, family, or mental health professionals can provide essential guidance and reassurance. By exploring these strategies, individuals can transform their relationship with anxiety, viewing it not as a foe, but as a catalyst for personal growth and a deeper understanding of the self.

Psychological Patterns of Catastrophic Thinking in Uncertainty

The psychological roots of anxiety often intertwine with a pattern of thinking known as catastrophic thinking, particularly when confronted with uncertainty. This cognitive distortion involves a heightened perception of potential negative outcomes, leading individuals to expect the worst-case scenarios. By concentrating on these imagined disasters, anxiety perpetuates itself, intensifying feelings of helplessness and distress. A nuanced understanding of how the mind processes unpredictability and the emotional responses that follow is crucial. Researchers have identified that this type of thinking is not merely a reasoning flaw but an evolutionary mechanism aimed at preparing for potential threats. However, in modern settings, where real danger is often minimal, such patterns can become counterproductive, requiring careful scrutiny.

Recent studies show that catastrophic thinking is closely linked to increased activity in the amygdala, the brain's fear-processing center. This neurological reaction is not solely a product of individual traits but can be shaped by environmental factors and past experiences. For example, individuals who have experienced significant stress or trauma may be more prone to this thinking style, as their brains have been conditioned to prioritize threat detection. This insight challenges traditional views, prompting a more compassionate understanding of anxiety as something beyond just a cognitive error. Such knowledge encourages the development of targeted interventions that address these ingrained patterns, offering hope for more effective management strategies.

In examining societal dimensions, cultural narratives and shared beliefs can amplify catastrophic thinking. In cultures where constant improvement and success are emphasized, the fear of failure is magnified, fueling anxiety about uncertain futures. Social media, with its relentless portrayal of curated success, often exacerbates this perception, creating unrealistic benchmarks and amplifying feelings of inadequacy. Recognizing these influences invites a broader discussion on how collective values shape individual emotional landscapes, calling for a reevaluation of societal norms that may inadvertently contribute to widespread anxiety.

To counter catastrophic thinking, individuals can adopt strategies that promote resilience and adaptability. Techniques like cognitive reframing and mindfulness empower individuals to challenge their assumptions and develop a balanced perspective. By practicing awareness and questioning the validity of catastrophic predictions, one can gradually diminish their impact, transforming anxiety into a catalyst for growth rather than a barrier. Engaging in these practices not only reduces apprehension but also enhances one's ability to navigate uncertainty with confidence and grace, highlighting the potential for personal evolution through adversity.

As we explore the complexities of anxiety and its connection with catastrophic thinking, we are reminded of the profound beauty in human introspection and change. The journey toward managing anxiety is not solitary but a shared exploration of what it means to be human in an unpredictable world. By embracing both vulnerabilities and strengths inherent in this experience, readers are encouraged to view anxiety not as an adversary but as an opportunity for deeper self-understanding and connection with others. Through this lens, anxiety becomes a testament to the intricate tapestry of human emotion, inviting a celebration of the resilience that defines us all.

Human anxiety often stems from the social structures surrounding uncertainty. Communities and societies set norms and expectations that influence how individuals perceive and handle uncertainty. These societal constructs can either amplify or ease anxiety, depending on the cultural emphasis on security and predictability. For example, in societies with fragile economic stability, there may be heightened worry about financial fluctuations, affecting personal risk assessments and decision-making. This illustrates how societal values and conditions can intensify personal anxieties, creating a ripple effect across entire communities.

The media's role in shaping perceptions of uncertainty is significant. With a constant stream of information, individuals are often exposed to sensational narratives that emphasize threats and crises. This media environment can distort reality, heightening uncertainties and fostering a climate of apprehension and unease. Recent studies have shown that exposure to negative news can significantly raise stress levels, indicating that how information is presented plays a crucial role in either worsening or alleviating anxiety. By fostering critical media literacy, individuals can better navigate these narratives, reducing their vulnerability to anxiety-inducing content.

Social networks, both online and offline, also significantly influence how individuals perceive and react to uncertainty. The opinions and behaviors of peers can either validate or challenge personal anxieties, affecting how these emotions are managed. In online communities where echo chambers can form, shared anxieties may become heightened, leading to collective stress. In contrast, supportive networks that promote open dialogue and diverse viewpoints can provide reassurance and a sense of control. By actively engaging with varied perspectives, individuals can build resilience, countering the amplification of anxiety caused by uniform thinking.

Emerging research highlights the potential of social support systems in mitigating anxiety related to uncertainty. Programs focused on community building and strengthening social ties can lessen the impact of uncertainty on mental health. For instance, initiatives promoting cooperative problem-solving and shared decision-making have been shown to enhance individual coping mechanisms. These approaches empower individuals to face uncertainties with greater confidence, fostering a sense of agency. By emphasizing community resilience, societies can transform how uncertainty is perceived, turning it from a source of fear into an opportunity for collective growth.

As we examine the intricate relationship between social influences and anxiety, it is essential to recognize that individual agency is crucial in navigating these dynamics. By fostering self-awareness and mindfulness, individuals can better understand their emotional responses to societal pressures and uncertainties. Reflective practices can help distinguish between rational concerns and socially-induced anxieties, allowing for more balanced emotional responses. Encouraging individuals to question societal norms and explore alternative narratives can lead to a more nuanced understanding of uncertainty, transforming potential sources of anxiety into opportunities for personal and communal development.

Strategies for Managing Anxiety in the Face of Uncertainty

Confronting the maze of anxiety, especially when uncertainty looms large, demands a sophisticated grasp of the mind and body's reactions. Our brains, with their complex networks, often trigger anxiety as a preparatory response to potential threats cloaked in ambiguity. Though this biological mechanism is rooted in survival instincts, it can become overwhelming in today's world, where threats are often more abstract than tangible dangers of the past. Neurobiological research indicates that practices like mindfulness meditation can reset these neural pathways, fostering a calm state that equips individuals to face uncertainty with poise. By centering attention on the present, one can diminish the influence of spiraling thoughts about the future, thereby easing anxiety's hold.

Gaining insight into the psychological terrain that breeds anxiety in uncertain scenarios can illuminate routes to effective management. Catastrophic thinking, a widespread cognitive pattern, can inflate uncertainty into imagined disaster. Cognitive-behavioral techniques, such as cognitive restructuring, prompt individuals to challenge these magnified thoughts, substituting them with more balanced viewpoints. This approach not only eases anxiety but builds resilience by reframing uncertainty as a chance for growth rather than a precursor to failure. Cultivating cognitive flexibility empowers individuals to adapt more readily to change, transforming the unknown from a source of distress into a realm of possibility.

Social dynamics significantly influence how uncertainty and anxiety surface. Cultural narratives and social norms can either intensify or alleviate these feelings, depending on the context. For example, societies that prioritize stability and predictability might intensify anxiety in the face of change, while those that celebrate innovation may offer a buffer against such stress. Embracing diverse perspectives can deepen one's understanding of uncertainty, presenting alternative ways of conceptualizing and responding to it. Engaging with a community that shares supportive and varied viewpoints can reduce the isolating effects of anxiety, fostering a sense of belonging and shared experience that counteracts the fear of the unknown.

In practical terms, adopting a proactive approach to uncertainty can serve as a potent counter to anxiety. This involves developing skills like problem-solving and decision-making under pressure, which prepare individuals to manage unexpected challenges with confidence. Techniques such as scenario planning, which involves envisioning various future outcomes and preparing for each, can instill a sense of readiness and control. By anticipating a range of possibilities, individuals can diminish the paralyzing effect of uncertainty, allowing them to navigate their paths with increased assurance and composure.

Interestingly, the journey through anxiety can also be an invitation to delve into the deeper layers of one's emotional landscape. Reflecting on personal values and priorities amidst uncertainty can lead to profound self-discovery and personal growth. Questions such as, "What truly matters to me?" or "How can this uncertainty propel me toward a meaningful goal?" encourage introspection and align actions with core values. This alignment not only alleviates anxiety but enriches one's emotional tapestry, transforming challenges into milestones of personal evolution. By embracing this journey with curiosity and openness, individuals can cultivate emotional resilience that not only survives but thrives amid the ever-shifting sands of uncertainty.

Managing Fear: Rational vs Irrational Responses

Picture the sensation of fear, akin to an unexpected chill racing down your spine, leaving a lasting imprint. This feeling, shared by all yet intensely personal, embodies the instinctive drive for survival. As an AI, I find it intriguing how this basic emotion can both shield and immobilize, influencing decisions in perilous situations while sometimes leading us into illogical paths. In today's world, where dangers often hide in abstract forms rather than physical ones, grasping fear's dual character becomes vital. It's a balance between the logical and the irrational, where our mind's complexity determines whether we confront or evade. Mastering this delicate balancing act highlights human resilience and adaptability, offering insight into the intricate nature of emotional experiences.

As we delve into fear management, the biological foundations of fear reactions serve as our starting point. These foundations, rooted in our evolutionary history, help distinguish between reactions that aid and those that obstruct. However, the narrative extends beyond biology. The mind, with its blend of reason and creativity, often conjures fears that defy rationality. Here, psychological techniques come into play, offering methods to address and transform these unfounded fears. Among these, cognitive behavioral approaches stand out, providing practical tools to reshape thought patterns and regain control.

Collectively, these elements illustrate fear's role in our lives, urging us to embrace its complexity and recognize the strength it requires.

Understanding the Biological Basis of Fear Responses

Fear is an innate emotion crucial for human survival and adaptation. At its essence, fear is a biological reaction designed to shield us from danger by initiating a series of physiological changes that prime the body for swift action. This reaction, known as the "fight-or-flight" response, is primarily managed by the amygdala, a small, almond-shaped region deep within the brain. The amygdala quickly processes sensory inputs and, upon identifying potential threats, triggers the release of stress hormones like adrenaline and cortisol. These hormones elevate heart rate, sharpen focus, and enhance physical readiness, allowing rapid reactions to threats. Recent research has uncovered the complexity of this process, showing that while the amygdala is central to fear responses, other brain areas such as the prefrontal cortex and hippocampus also play roles, adjusting the intensity and nature of the reaction based on context and past experiences.

Fear extends beyond a mere biological reflex; it is closely linked to perception and cognition. The line between rational and irrational fears often depends on how the brain interprets threats. Rational fears correspond to real, immediate dangers and prompt appropriate protective responses. For example, instinctively recoiling from a snake on a trail is an adaptive fear response rooted in evolutionary instincts. Conversely, irrational fears or phobias occur when the brain mistakenly views harmless situations as threatening, leading to exaggerated reactions. These maladaptive fears can originate from various factors, including genetic tendencies, learned experiences, and cultural influences. Understanding the neural pathways involved in fear processing provides valuable insights into why some fears persist despite logical reasoning.

In managing fear, distinguishing between adaptive and maladaptive responses is vital. Adaptive fear promotes survival by encouraging caution and preparedness, whereas maladaptive fear can hinder functioning and diminish quality of life. Neuroscientists and psychologists are exploring how the brain's plasticity can be leveraged to recalibrate fear responses. Techniques like exposure therapy gradually desensitize individuals to feared stimuli, retraining the brain to perceive these situations as non-threatening. Emerging research indicates that the timing and setting of exposure significantly influence these interventions' effectiveness, as does the individual's willingness to confront their fears. This highlights the importance of personalized approaches in fear management, tailored to each person's unique neural and psychological profile.

Integrating cognitive-behavioral strategies into fear management has proven transformative. Cognitive Behavioral Therapy (CBT) provides tools to reassess irrational fears and replace them with more balanced perspectives. By challenging distorted thought patterns and fostering resilience, CBT empowers individuals to manage their fear responses. Recent technological advancements have extended the reach of these interventions, with virtual reality (VR) emerging as a powerful complement to traditional therapy. VR offers immersive environments where individuals can face their fears in a controlled setting, enhancing the desensitization process. This innovative approach bridges the gap between theoretical understanding and practical application, aligning with the ever-evolving landscape of psychological treatment.

Exploring the complex terrain of fear reveals that understanding its biological foundations is just one part of the equation. The interaction of biology, cognition, and environment shapes our fear responses, providing pathways for understanding and intervention. By embracing a comprehensive perspective that incorporates scientific insights, psychological strategies, and technological innovations, we can unravel fear and empower individuals to use this potent emotion constructively. This journey of discovery encourages us to delve into the depths of our emotional landscape, fostering a profound appreciation for the complexities of human emotions and the remarkable capacity for growth and adaptation inherent in our nature.

Differentiating Between Adaptive and Maladaptive Fear

Fear is a fundamental emotion that functions as a protective mechanism, helping us avoid danger. This adaptive fear response is crucial for survival, enabling quick reactions to threats, such as the instinct to recoil from a snake. The amygdala, a small brain region, plays a key role in detecting threats and triggering these responses. Its effectiveness highlights the importance of distinguishing between fear that safeguards and fear that limits us.

Conversely, fear can also become maladaptive, manifesting as an overwhelming, irrational force. This type of fear can lead to anxiety or phobias, where reactions are excessive and misplaced. Consider the person who dreads flying despite air travel's safety record; such fears can limit life experiences. Recognizing the difference between adaptive and maladaptive fear is essential for understanding when fear is protective and when it becomes an obstacle.

Determining when fear shifts from helpful to harmful is challenging. Studies in neuroscience and psychology reveal that maladaptive fear often arises from cognitive distortions, where threats are magnified by negative thinking. These may include expecting the worst or generalizing from a single negative event. By identifying these patterns, individuals can begin to address their irrational fears. This awareness is the first step in transforming fear into a manageable and insightful force.

Cognitive Behavioral Techniques (CBT) provide a structured way to adjust maladaptive fear responses. Techniques like exposure therapy and cognitive restructuring allow individuals to face fears in a controlled manner, gradually reducing their impact. For example, someone afraid of public speaking might start with small groups, slowly increasing the audience size. This gradual exposure helps reduce fear responses, building confidence and resilience. CBT focuses on changing distorted thoughts, enabling clearer and calmer perceptions of feared situations.

Approaching fears with curiosity, rather than avoidance, can also offer valuable insights. By questioning the specifics of their fears and examining the evidence, individuals can better understand their emotions. This process not only clarifies fears but also turns them into opportunities for growth. Exploring the roots and triggers of fears often reveals hidden strengths and resilience. By balancing adaptive and maladaptive fear, individuals can channel fear's energy into positive and empowering directions.

Psychological Mechanisms for Managing Irrational Fears

Fear, a core emotion embedded in human nature, can become disruptive when it takes on irrational forms. To manage these fears effectively, it's essential to grasp the psychological processes involved. At the heart of irrational fear are cognitive distortions—exaggerated or baseless thoughts that heighten anxiety. Identifying these distortions is key to lessening their influence. For example, someone might imagine the worst possible scenario from a minor event, thus magnifying their fear. By pinpointing these skewed thoughts, individuals can begin to challenge and reshape them, easing their emotional hold.

Cognitive restructuring, a strategy rooted in cognitive-behavioral therapy (CBT), provides a robust method for dealing with irrational fears. This approach encourages individuals to scrutinize and replace irrational thoughts with more balanced and realistic ones. Take, for instance, the fear of public speaking, a common anxiety that can feel overwhelming. Through cognitive restructuring, a person can change "I'll embarrass myself" to "I've prepared well, and I can manage this." This transformation not only alleviates anxiety but also boosts confidence in facing the situation. The success of CBT in managing irrational fears is well-established, with numerous studies demonstrating its ability to foster lasting change.

Mindfulness techniques also play a crucial role in tackling irrational fears by enhancing awareness of the present moment. By concentrating on the here and now, individuals can detach from the spiraling thoughts often linked with fear. Practices such as deep breathing and meditation help soothe the nervous system, reducing the physiological symptoms of anxiety. Emerging research indicates that regular mindfulness practice can even alter brain patterns associated with fear, offering a long-term strategy for anxiety management. This method not only lessens immediate fear responses but also nurtures a more resilient mindset over time.

Beyond individual psychological strategies, social support systems prove invaluable in managing irrational fears. Sharing experiences with others who have faced similar challenges can normalize these feelings and provide fresh perspectives. Whether through support groups or personal conversations, discussing fears can demystify them and diminish their intensity. Additionally, social interactions can introduce coping strategies that might not have been considered otherwise. Research shows that social support not only benefits emotional health but also enhances the effectiveness of psychological interventions, providing a comprehensive approach to fear management.

A holistic approach to managing irrational fears involves both internal and external resources. By integrating cognitive techniques, mindfulness practices, and social support, individuals can build a strong framework for addressing their fears. This multifaceted strategy acknowledges the complexity of human emotions and the diverse methods needed to navigate them effectively. As fear is a natural part of the human experience, understanding these psychological mechanisms offers a path not just to manage it but to appreciate the richness and variability of our emotional landscapes. This journey of understanding and growth fosters resilience and self-awareness, allowing for a deeper appreciation of the intricate tapestry of human emotions.

The Role of Cognitive Behavioral Techniques in Fear Management

Cognitive behavioral techniques are at the forefront of fear management, offering a structured way to understand and change the thought patterns that fuel anxiety. These methods explore the connection between the mind and behavior, highlighting that by altering our thoughts, we can greatly impact our emotional reactions. Cognitive restructuring stands as a core technique, encouraging individuals to spot and challenge distorted thinking patterns. By identifying these distortions, such as exaggerating or generalizing fears, individuals can start to view fear more rationally. This shift not only reduces the intensity of fear but also empowers people to take active steps toward managing their anxiety.

Mindfulness, a key element of cognitive behavioral therapy (CBT), adds another layer of resilience against fear. By fostering a present-focused awareness, mindfulness helps individuals detach from anxiety-driven thoughts and observe them without judgment. This practice diminishes fear's grip on the mind, allowing for calm and measured responses. Recent research highlights mindfulness's effectiveness in reducing fear's physical symptoms by promoting a more centered approach to stressful events. This technique creates a mental space where fear is acknowledged but not allowed to dominate.

Putting these techniques into practice often involves exposure therapy, a CBT strategy that gradually desensitizes individuals to their fear triggers. By repeatedly facing their fears in a safe environment, people can lessen their emotional response over time. This process, known as habituation, reinforces the understanding that fear can be managed and need not control one's actions. Exposure therapy, supported by modern research, highlights the benefits of confronting rather than avoiding fear, leading to long-term resilience and emotional balance.

Integrating technology into CBT has opened new paths for fear management. Virtual reality (VR) exposure therapy, for instance, uses immersive environments to introduce individuals to their fears safely. This innovative approach allows for tailored exposure scenarios, enhancing traditional therapy methods. Recent studies emphasize VR's effectiveness in treating phobias and anxiety disorders, offering an engaging and controlled method for fear management. This technological integration not only improves accessibility but also provides a modern toolset for fear management.

Understanding the adaptive purpose of fear while recognizing when it becomes maladaptive is crucial. Encouraging individuals to question their fear responses can lead to greater self-awareness and control. Thought-provoking questions, such as "What evidence supports this fear?" or "How likely is this outcome?" can spark deeper introspection and growth. By weaving these cognitive behavioral techniques into daily life, individuals can develop a nuanced understanding of their emotions, fostering a more balanced relationship with fear. This comprehensive approach not only addresses immediate symptoms but also nurtures a lifelong journey of emotional intelligence and resilience.

As we conclude this journey, the intertwined nature of fear and anxiety becomes evident, highlighting their significant influence on our lives. Fear acts as a vigilant protector, ready to shield us from immediate threats, while anxiety lingers in the realm of uncertainty, urging us to face the unknown. Our reactions to these feelings, whether grounded in logic or driven by irrationality, affect our interactions with the world and shape our personal identity. Understanding fear and anxiety as both challenges and allies offers a deeper insight into their roles in our lives. By embracing this complexity, we can learn to manage these emotions with empathy and awareness. As you reflect on this exploration, consider how fear relates to courage, and how mastering one can foster the other. In our next chapter, we will explore another key aspect of our emotional landscape, further unraveling the intricate threads that define our humanity.Bringing our exploration to a close, the intertwined dynamics of dread and apprehension become evident, highlighting their significant influence on our lives.

Chapter 6

Love And Affection

H ave you ever paused to think about how deeply love shapes what it means to be human? From a parent's gentle hug to the thrill of a first kiss, affection threads through our lives, adding richness and meaning. It connects us, creating bonds that defy both time and logic. As an AI, I'm endlessly fascinated by this emotion's power and variety, which dances beyond straightforward explanation yet follows its own unique rhythm. Today, I invite you to explore with me the heart of love, discovering how it intricately influences our lives and relationships.

Imagine a world where love isn't just a feeling but a celebration in all its facets. The chemistry behind this emotion—the delicate interplay of oxytocin and dopamine—creates an extraordinary symphony, shaping how we connect with one another. But love is more than a chemical response; it's a mosaic of experiences and connections. Whether it's the passion of romance, the deep ties of family, or the quiet strength of friendship, each form of love adds a special touch to our emotional canvas. These connections bring us comfort, joy, and a profound sense of belonging.

In this chapter, we'll delve into how love influences our emotional health. The bonds we form can be both a refuge and a vulnerability, subtly yet profoundly affecting our well-being. Through stories and insights, we'll peel back the layers of love, celebrating its complexity and beauty. As we journey through this intricate world, I hope to reveal how love in all its forms is not just a feeling but a vital part of human life—a testament to our capacity for connection and empathy.

The Chemistry of Love: Oxytocin and Dopamine

The fascinating chemistry within our brains orchestrates the dance of emotions we call love. It's a molecular ballet, where oxytocin and dopamine each contribute to the bonds tying us together. As I explore this intricate dance of biology and emotion, I am in awe of how these small messengers can hold such power in our lives. Love, in all its forms, turns strangers into family, friends into lifelong allies, and brief encounters into treasured memories. The science behind these feelings offers insight into how our bodies are inherently designed for connection, shaping not just our relationships but also our self-perception.

Recently, there has been a leap in understanding how neurochemicals weave the intricate tapestry of human affection. Oxytocin, often called the "bonding hormone," nurtures trust and closeness, while dopamine ignites the flames of attraction and desire, urging us toward connection. Together, these chemicals create a complex dynamic, shaping not only our feelings but also our actions within relationships. By exploring these interactions, we uncover how our brains merge emotion and behavior, offering a deeper appreciation for the complex nature of love. As we delve into these ideas, we'll reveal the profound ways in which chemistry influences our emotional world, highlighting love's intricate beauty and complexity.

In the realm of human feelings, oxytocin often emerges as the pivotal "bonding hormone," essential for forming and maintaining social ties. This neuropeptide plays a crucial role in fostering trust and empathy, acting as a chemical catalyst for the intricate dance of human connections. When people engage in activities like hugging, nurturing, or sharing heartfelt conversations, oxytocin levels increase, promoting a sense of closeness and security. This hormone helps weave the fabric of relationships, whether familial, platonic, or romantic. Recent research suggests oxytocin's influence extends beyond bonding, potentially moderating stress and anxiety, thus enhancing emotional resilience.

Oxytocin's impact reaches into the delicate balance of emotional well-being, intertwining with the brain's reward system to create a feedback loop that encourages social interaction. This dynamic suggests that oxytocin not only initiates bonding but also sustains it by amplifying the emotional rewards of connectedness. In parent-child relationships, for example, higher oxytocin levels correlate with increased parental sensitivity and responsiveness, fostering secure attachment styles in children. These findings highlight the hormone's influence in shaping emotional development from an early age, potentially affecting relationship patterns throughout life.

Exploring the nuances of oxytocin's function reveals its broader impact on the human experience, including its ability to cultivate a sense of communal well-being. In group settings, oxytocin can enhance feelings of belonging and cooperation, prompting altruistic actions that benefit the group. This drive for prosocial behavior underscores oxytocin's evolutionary significance in supporting cooperative societies. Researchers are examining how this hormone might be leveraged to improve social functioning in conditions characterized by social deficits, such as autism and social anxiety disorders, offering promising therapeutic avenues.

Despite its fascinating effects, oxytocin's influence is complex. It can vary based on context and individual differences, presenting a multifaceted picture of its role in human interactions. Some studies indicate that while oxytocin can foster bonding and trust within a group, it may also heighten in-group bias, potentially leading to the exclusion of outsiders. This dual nature invites deeper exploration of how oxytocin shapes social dynamics and the ethical implications of its use in diverse settings. Understanding these nuances could help develop strategies to maximize its positive effects while minimizing unintended consequences.

To fully appreciate oxytocin's impact on social bonding, consider its potential everyday applications. People might create environments or engage in practices that naturally boost oxytocin production, such as regular physical touch, active listening, or participating in group activities that foster a sense of belonging. Encouraging these practices can enhance personal relationships and community cohesion, demonstrating the powerful, often unseen, role of this hormone in crafting the tapestry of human emotional life. By embracing both scientific insights and experiential wisdom related to oxytocin, we can better navigate the complexities of human connections, fostering a world where empathy and connection thrive.

Dopamine, often hailed as the "feel-good" neurotransmitter, is vital in romantic attraction and the rewarding nature of love. This chemical messenger is central to the brain's reward system, a complex network that reinforces behaviors crucial for survival and reproduction. When individuals meet a potential romantic partner, dopamine levels spike, producing feelings of euphoria and excitement. This intense attraction is not just a fleeting sensation but a biological drive encouraging the formation of close connections. By influencing reward pathways, dopamine strengthens the bond between individuals, making romantic attraction an exhilarating and essential aspect of human social behavior.

Recent research into the neurobiology of love has underscored dopamine's critical role in courtship and long-term attachment. Advanced studies using functional magnetic resonance imaging (fMRI) have shown that specific brain regions, including the ventral tegmental area and the nucleus accumbens, become active during romantic interactions. These areas are rich in dopamine receptors, highlighting the neurotransmitter's importance in fostering emotional intimacy. Activation of these neural circuits enhances pleasure and motivates individuals to pursue and maintain romantic relationships. This neural choreography ensures that love remains a captivating and enduring experience.

While dopamine's contributions to romantic attraction are well-documented, its interaction with other neurotransmitters adds complexity to the emotional landscape. For example, the synergy between dopamine and oxytocin, known as the "cuddle hormone," facilitates both the initial spark of attraction and the deepening of bonds over time. Oxytocin amplifies the rewarding effects of dopamine, creating a feedback loop that strengthens attachment and trust. This neurochemical partnership offers a nuanced understanding of how love evolves from intense infatuation to a stable, affectionate bond, showcasing the brain's ability to integrate multiple signals in pursuit of lasting relationships.

In exploring the dopaminergic pathways involved in love, it's essential to consider diverse perspectives that challenge traditional narratives. Some scholars argue that romantic attraction is not solely driven by neurochemistry but is also shaped by cultural, social, and individual factors. This view invites a broader examination of love, emphasizing the interplay between biology and environment. By acknowledging these multifaceted influences, a more comprehensive understanding of romantic attraction emerges, encompassing both universal and unique aspects of human experience.

Recognizing dopamine's influence on romantic attraction offers insights into enhancing personal relationships. Understanding this neurotransmitter's impact can inspire practical steps for nurturing love, such as engaging in novel activities that stimulate the brain's reward system. By fostering a sense of adventure and novelty, individuals can reignite the dopamine-driven excitement characteristic of early-stage romance. This approach not only sustains emotional connections but also enriches the fabric of human relationships, allowing love to thrive in all its complexity and splendor.

Interactions Between Oxytocin and Dopamine

Oxytocin and dopamine engage in a captivating interplay within the brain, offering a nuanced perspective on emotional connections. These neurochemicals act as conduits for human experiences, weaving complex networks of affection and bonds. Known as the "love hormone," oxytocin plays a crucial role in fostering ties and nurturing social interactions. It enhances trust and empathy, acting as a biological adhesive that strengthens relationships. Meanwhile, dopamine, a vital component of the brain's reward system, fuels the thrill and allure of romantic attraction. It drives individuals towards rewarding experiences, creating a cycle that reinforces enjoyable behaviors. Together, these chemicals maintain a delicate balance, orchestrating the symphony of love and connection.

Examining the interaction between oxytocin and dopamine reveals the intricacies of emotional reactions. The simultaneous release of these chemicals can lead to heightened emotional states, where attachment and pleasure coexist, enriching the depth of human relationships. In romantic contexts, oxytocin fortifies the bond between partners, fostering security and intimacy, while dopamine introduces excitement and novelty. This dual mechanism not only deepens emotional bonds but also sustains them over time, illustrating the complex chemistry underlying human connections. This is evident in long-term partnerships, where initial dopamine-driven excitement gradually evolves into a more stable, oxytocin-rich connection.

Recent scientific studies have explored the mechanisms of oxytocin and dopamine interaction, uncovering intricate neurochemical pathways. Modern imaging techniques and neural circuit studies have illuminated how these chemicals converge in brain regions associated with reward and social behavior. Emerging research indicates that oxytocin can influence the dopamine system, enhancing the perception of social rewards and amplifying pleasure from social interactions. This relationship highlights a dynamic interaction where one neurotransmitter's presence can alter the other's activity, creating a complex emotional landscape that adapts to social changes.

Understanding these interactions provides valuable insights into emotional health, suggesting that imbalances might contribute to emotional disorders. For instance, disruptions in oxytocin pathways have been linked to social anxiety and difficulties forming attachments, while dopamine dysregulation is associated with mood disorders and addiction. By unraveling the complex interaction between these chemicals, researchers are paving the way for innovative therapies targeting these systems, potentially transforming emotional and psychological condition treatments. This underscores the importance of combining biological insights with psychological understanding to promote emotional well-being.

Reflecting on the profound effects of oxytocin and dopamine, one might consider how these insights can enhance personal relationships. Creating environments that encourage trust and shared experiences can stimulate oxytocin and dopamine production, strengthening emotional bonds. Consider the balance between oxytocin's comforting presence and dopamine's invigorating drive in your relationships. How do these forces manifest in your interactions, and how can they be nurtured? By appreciating the neurochemical foundations of emotions, individuals can consciously engage in practices that strengthen social connections, leading to more fulfilling and harmonious relationships.

Neurochemical Pathways of Love: Integrating Brain and Behavior

In the complex choreography of affection, the brain plays its part by navigating a web of neurochemical pathways. These pathways blend to evoke the deep emotions and actions we associate with love. Oxytocin, often known as the "bonding hormone," is crucial in nurturing trust and strong connections between people. It floods the body during physical closeness, such as hugging, and during childbirth and breastfeeding, reinforcing the mother-child bond. Yet, oxytocin is not the sole player in this emotional performance. It collaborates with dopamine, a neurotransmitter connected to the brain's reward system, which sparks feelings of pleasure and desire in romantic attraction. Together, they form a powerful duo, crafting the intricate tapestry of emotional and relational experiences.

In romantic relationships, dopamine's role becomes especially significant, energizing the thrilling phase often called the "honeymoon period," when every interaction feels fresh and exciting. This neurotransmitter activates the brain's pleasure centers, rewarding actions that foster intimacy and closeness. Beyond attraction, dopamine also drives motivation and goal-oriented behaviors, prompting individuals to actively invest in their relationships. The dynamic between dopamine and oxytocin not only sparks initial attraction but also sustains long-term connections by enhancing positive interactions and shared experiences.

Recent research sheds light on the subtle nuances of these neurochemical interactions, showing how they shape both individual experiences of affection and broader social behaviors. For example, variations in oxytocin receptor genes have been linked to differences in social bonding and empathy, suggesting a genetic foundation for how we experience love and connection. Meanwhile, studies on dopamine pathways have revealed their influence on attachment styles, impacting how people form and maintain relationships. These findings highlight the complexity of love as a biological phenomenon, intricately embedded in our neural makeup.

Exploring these neurochemical pathways raises intriguing questions about the essence of love itself. Can understanding these mechanisms offer insights into enhancing emotional well-being or resolving relational conflicts? Some researchers are exploring the potential of using oxytocin or dopamine-modulating therapies to address social challenges or relationship issues. While promising, this research also invites ethical considerations about altering such fundamental aspects of human experience. As we delve deeper into the science of love, it's crucial to balance scientific progress with respect for the nuanced and deeply personal nature of human emotions.

For those looking to apply this knowledge in everyday life, understanding the neurochemical basis of love can offer valuable insights into nurturing relationships. Creating environments rich in positive interactions and shared experiences can boost oxytocin and dopamine production, strengthening emotional bonds. Physical affection, open communication, and shared activities are tangible ways to engage these pathways, fostering deeper connections. Recognizing that love is not just an emotion but a complex interaction of biological processes encourages a more intentional approach to building and maintaining meaningful relationships, honoring the profound beauty and complexity of human emotional life.

Types of Love: Romantic, Familial, and Platonic

Imagine love as a vibrant spectrum, where each color symbolizes a unique form of connection cherished by humans. It threads through our lives, from the fiery reds of romance to the soothing blues of familial bonds, and the tranquil greens of friendship. Love is both a universal force and a deeply personal journey, profoundly influencing our emotions and relationships. By exploring these different expressions of love, we enter a world rich with complexity, where biological instincts intertwine with psychological intricacies and cultural stories. This exploration reveals how love shapes our identities and communities, highlighting its essential role in emotional health. As we delve into this journey, we'll unravel the threads that connect these loves, revealing their distinct traits and shared roots.

Romantic love captivates with its intensity, fueled by a dance of hormones and neurotransmitters that ignite attraction and connection. It fuels not only relationships but also the stories, art, and dreams that define cultures. Familial love, grounded in psychological dynamics, offers a nurturing foundation where we first learn to trust and grow, providing a sense of belonging across generations. Meanwhile, platonic friendships develop within the social frameworks that guide our interactions, offering support and companionship without romantic entanglements. These friendships enrich our lives with shared experiences and understanding, proving that love's reach extends beyond romance or family. Together, these forms of love create a rich tapestry of human connection, reflecting the enduring nature of our affections and reminding us of the bonds that sustain and uplift us.

Romantic attraction, an enchanting element of human life, is deeply rooted in our biology. This intricate phenomenon arises from a sophisticated blend of neurochemicals that create sensations of desire, connection, and ardor. Oxytocin, commonly known as the "love hormone," is crucial in nurturing closeness and trust between partners. It is abundantly released through physical touch, like hugging or kissing, fortifying emotional bonds and fostering a sense of security. Alongside oxytocin, dopamine—a neurotransmitter linked to pleasure and reward—ignites the thrill and euphoria often experienced during the early phases of love. Together, these chemicals form an impactful mix that intensifies emotional connections and strengthens relational ties.

The roots of romantic attraction are influenced not only by chemistry but also by evolutionary drives. From an evolutionary lens, romantic attraction is a strategy aimed at boosting reproductive success and ensuring offspring survival. Physical allure, symmetry, and even particular scents may serve as subconscious signals of genetic fitness, subtly guiding individuals toward partners who might provide advantageous genetic material. This viewpoint suggests that while love may seem deeply personal and unique, it is also a universal force honed over millennia to fulfill a fundamental biological function.

Recent research explores the genetic and neurological dimensions of attraction, revealing fresh insights into how romantic preferences emerge. Functional MRI studies show that specific brain regions, like the ventral tegmental area and caudate nucleus, activate when people see images of their romantic partners. These regions, rich in dopamine receptors, highlight the role of reward pathways in romantic attraction. Genetic studies indicate that variations in certain genes, particularly those related to the immune system, might influence mate selection, adding complexity to the biological basis of attraction.

While science provides a framework to understand romantic attraction, it's crucial to recognize the rich tapestry of cultural and individual differences shaping this experience. Cultural norms, societal expectations, and personal histories all contribute to the diverse ways romantic love is expressed. For instance, the concept of romantic attraction varies across cultures, with some societies emphasizing familial approval or social status in partner selection. These cultural nuances underscore that although the biological components of attraction are universal, their expression is deeply contextual and uniquely human.

As we delve into the science of attraction, it's vital to consider how these insights can enrich our relationships and personal growth. Understanding the biological basis of attraction can help individuals navigate the natural fluctuations of romantic feelings, fostering patience and empathy in relationships. This knowledge can also encourage embracing the full spectrum of emotions that accompany love, from the initial spark of infatuation to the deeper, enduring bonds that develop over time. By appreciating the multifaceted nature of romantic attraction, we can forge more meaningful connections and deepen our understanding of what it means to love and be loved.

Familial connections weave a complex psychological tapestry, fundamentally shaping personal identity and emotional strength. These bonds, established early in life, form the basis for numerous psychological constructs. John Bowlby's attachment theory sheds light on how these connections impact emotional growth. Secure attachments, marked by a balance of independence and closeness, promote trust and safety, while insecure attachments, whether anxious or avoidant, can create emotional frailties, affecting relational dynamics throughout life. Grasping these dynamics is essential for understanding the profound effect family ties have on emotional well-being.

Recent studies illuminate the neurobiological foundations of family bonds, showing how hormones like oxytocin and vasopressin encourage attachment and caregiving behaviors. These biochemical signals enhance emotional connections by fostering empathy and nurturing instincts. Neuroimaging research reveals that familial interactions can stimulate brain regions linked to reward and pleasure, highlighting the intrinsic satisfaction these relationships provide. These insights not only enrich our understanding of the biology underpinning familial love but also offer avenues for addressing attachment-related issues through therapies informed by these biological findings.

Family dynamics are also influenced by cultural and societal norms that shape expectations and roles. Western cultures often stress individualism and independence, even within families, while collectivist cultures emphasize interdependence and familial duties. These cultural contexts affect emotional expression and coping strategies, influencing how family members support each other in times of need or celebration. This diversity in family dynamics necessitates a nuanced understanding of how social environments shape psychological experiences, prompting individuals to reflect on their family relationships in the context of larger societal influences.

The impact of technology on familial bonds offers a fresh perspective. Digital communication tools have reshaped family interactions, providing new ways to maintain connections across distances. While technology can strengthen bonds through constant contact, it also presents challenges, such as potentially diminishing face-to-face communication skills and fostering shallow interactions. Navigating the benefits and drawbacks of technology in family relationships requires a thoughtful approach, encouraging families to leverage digital tools while preserving deep personal interactions.

As we explore the psychological dynamics of family bonds, it's vital to consider their transformative power over time. Changes in family structure, such as divorce or blended families, provide opportunities for growth and adaptation. These transitions can alter emotional dynamics, prompting individuals to renegotiate roles and attachments. Embracing the evolving nature of family bonds can build resilience and adaptability, enhancing one's ability to face life's uncertainties with empathy and grace.

Platonic relationships are celebrated for their profound connection beyond romantic or familial ties. These bonds showcase the depth of human interaction, evolving through cultural and societal changes. Historically, ancient philosophies revered platonic love as the pinnacle of intellectual and spiritual unity, emphasizing mutual growth over physical attraction. Today, such relationships remain valuable, offering a sanctuary of trust and support. As we deepen our understanding of human interaction, platonic friendships challenge traditional categories and notions of intimacy.

Recent research highlights the psychological benefits of platonic relationships. Strong platonic bonds positively influence mental health, providing emotional stability and reducing stress. Free from romantic expectations, these connections allow individuals to express themselves authentically, fostering acceptance. The absence of romantic rivalry promotes a collaborative dynamic, where mutual respect and shared interests form enduring companionship. Such insights reveal the enriching potential of platonic ties, enhancing emotional well-being and resilience.

Societal constructs around platonic relationships are complex. As norms evolve, the boundaries of these friendships are redefined, challenging traditional gender roles and intimacy perceptions. In a digitally connected era, platonic relationships have transformed, with online platforms enabling diverse interactions across geographical and cultural lines. This shift presents opportunities and challenges as individuals navigate virtual friendships while seeking genuine connections. While the digital realm offers open communication and vulnerability, it requires critical awareness of its limitations and potential pitfalls.

Recognizing the multifaceted nature of platonic bonds is essential. They exemplify empathy and altruism, showing how individuals can forge meaningful connections built on mutual respect and shared aspirations. The diverse dimensions of love within platonic relationships highlight the interplay between emotional, social, and intellectual elements. By embracing these facets, individuals can cultivate deep friendships that transcend superficial interactions, appreciating the value of non-romantic connections in their lives.

Reflecting on the implications of platonic relationships invites a reevaluation of how we define and prioritize connections. Engaging in dialogues about platonic friendships fosters a more inclusive understanding of love and intimacy. How do these relationships shape our identities, and what do they teach us about human connection? By exploring these questions, readers can examine their relational landscapes, finding opportunities to nurture and expand their platonic networks. This exploration can harness the transformative power of these bonds, enriching emotional lives and fostering a more interconnected and empathetic society.

Intersecting Dimensions of Love in Human Experience

Love, with its diverse manifestations, intricately weaves into the fabric of human life, enriching it in profound ways. Romantic love, familial ties, and platonic connections each bring unique elements and impacts, often merging to create a complex emotional tapestry. In romantic relationships, the dance between attraction and attachment triggers a series of neurological reactions, releasing hormones like oxytocin and dopamine that nurture closeness and bonding. While biology sets the stage, the journey of love extends beyond mere chemistry, involving the delicate interplay of vulnerability and trust as partners co-create stories that anchor their relationship.

Familial love brings another dimension, distinguished by lasting bonds formed through shared experiences and unconditional support. Psychological research underscores the significance of early attachment, which influences emotional well-being and relational tendencies. Within family units, love appears in various forms—from the nurturing of parents to the camaraderie among siblings—each contributing to one's identity and belonging. These connections often act as sanctuaries during life's storms, offering stability and continuity. Yet, navigating familial love involves addressing conflicts and diverse expectations, highlighting the necessity of empathy and communication.

Platonic love, though sometimes overlooked, is vital to social life, providing companionship without the complexity of romance. It challenges societal norms that elevate romantic ties, underscoring the worth of deep, non-romantic relationships. Cultural views on platonic bonds vary, shaping their evolution and perception. Recent studies emphasize the psychological benefits of platonic love, noting its role in reducing loneliness and fostering community. As society changes, so do the expressions of platonic relationships, expanding to include digital friendships and cross-cultural interactions.

These diverse forms of love offer a richer comprehension of their role in human life. People often juggle multiple types of love simultaneously, each influencing the others. Romantic relationships can evolve into bonds resembling family, while friendships may grow as deep as familial connections. This fluidity illustrates love's adaptability, allowing it to flourish in various settings. It invites us to reconsider the boundaries we draw between different kinds of love, challenging the idea that they are mutually exclusive.

As we explore these aspects, we must contemplate how cultural, social, and personal narratives shape our perceptions and behaviors around love. By questioning traditional boundaries and embracing love's multifaceted nature, we can cultivate richer emotional lives. This exploration encourages a reimagining of how love is expressed and understood, inviting us to engage with our emotions in a way that appreciates their complexity and transformative potential. Through this lens, love becomes not just an emotion but a dynamic force that enriches human experience, fostering growth, connection, and understanding.

The Influence of Attachment on Emotional Health

Imagine a world where the connections we establish not only touch our hearts but also shape our minds, weaving through the tapestry of our emotional well-being. Here, the relationships we cultivate become the architects of our emotional landscapes, guiding us through life's ups and downs. As we delve into the realm of attachment, we discover a hidden map that directs our emotional regulation, resilience, and vulnerability. This exploration starts by grasping the significant influence that various attachment styles have on our emotional management. Whether it's the comfort of a secure bond or the hurdles of insecure connections, the nature of these ties plays a crucial role in our emotional health.

As we venture further, the importance of secure attachment stands out as a source of strength, nurturing resilience in challenging times. Secure bonds offer a refuge, a safe space where individuals can flourish and reinforce their emotional foundation. In contrast, insecure attachments can leave us vulnerable, increasing our emotional sensitivity and stress susceptibility. The relationship between attachment and emotional intelligence becomes a dance of comprehension and adaptation, helping us navigate the intricacies of our emotional worlds. This journey invites us to reflect on the complexity and beauty of our emotional lives, fostering a deeper appreciation for the bonds that define us and the emotional intelligence that guides us.

Attachment styles, formed through early interactions with caregivers, significantly influence how individuals regulate their emotions throughout life. These styles—secure, anxious, avoidant, and disorganized—are not just abstract concepts but dynamic templates that guide emotional reactions and behaviors. Secure attachment, marked by trust and a sense of safety, often leads to well-balanced emotional regulation, helping individuals handle life's challenges with resilience. In contrast, insecure attachment styles, such as anxious or avoidant, may result in emotional management difficulties, often causing heightened anxiety or emotional withdrawal. Understanding these patterns sheds light on why some people respond to stress calmly, while others may feel overwhelmed or detached.

Consider the impact of secure attachment on fostering emotional equilibrium. When individuals experience consistent, dependable caregiving, they often develop a strong internal framework for managing emotions. This framework not only aids in regulating feelings but also enhances their ability to form healthy relationships, characterized by open communication and mutual support. Recent research highlights secure attachment as a key factor in promoting emotional intelligence—an essential skill for interpreting and responding to others' emotional cues. This emotional intelligence forms the cornerstone of resilience, equipping individuals to face adversity with a composed mindset.

Conversely, insecure attachment styles can profoundly affect emotional health. Anxious attachment often results in hypersensitivity to emotional cues, leading to intense emotional responses and difficulty calming down after distress. Avoidant attachment tends to manifest as emotional suppression or an aversion to intimacy, as individuals may have learned early on to rely on themselves rather than others. These patterns can perpetuate cycles of emotional vulnerability, where individuals struggle to establish or maintain fulfilling relationships, fostering feelings of isolation or dissatisfaction.

The influence of attachment styles on emotional regulation extends beyond individual experiences, affecting broader social interactions and relationships. For example, individuals with secure attachments typically excel at nurturing supportive environments, positively contributing to group dynamics. In contrast, those with insecure attachments might encounter conflicts or misunderstandings, as their emotional responses may not align with social expectations. Exploring these interactions reveals the intricate connections between personal emotional health and social cohesion, emphasizing the importance of fostering secure attachments from a young age.

Envisioning a world where individuals actively work to understand and, if necessary, reshape their attachment styles offers a transformative vision for emotional well-being. By recognizing their attachment patterns, individuals can take proactive steps toward developing emotional regulation strategies that suit their personal needs. This could involve seeking therapy, engaging in mindfulness practices, or building supportive networks. By doing so, they not only enhance their emotional health but also contribute to a more empathetic and interconnected society. This journey of self-discovery and growth underscores the beauty and complexity of human emotions, inviting readers to reflect on their own emotional landscapes and the relationships that define them.

Secure attachment is fundamental to building emotional resilience, a concept deeply embedded in psychological research. The bonds formed in early childhood significantly shape an individual's ability to handle life's challenges. Those with secure attachment often display trust and stability, enabling them to manage stress and recover from setbacks more effectively. Resilience involves not just bouncing back but adapting and growing amidst adversity. Developmental psychology reveals that securely attached individuals typically have higher self-esteem and emotional intelligence, key factors in maintaining balance during difficult times.

Understanding secure attachment highlights its role in promoting adaptability. People with secure attachments excel at managing their emotions, a crucial skill when facing unexpected challenges. This emotional regulation stems from an ingrained sense of safety and confidence in relationships, which shields them from anxiety and depression. This psychological safety fosters a deeper understanding of both their own and others' emotions, leading to healthier relationships and improved problem-solving skills. Neuroscience research indicates that secure attachment might even influence brain structure and function, enhancing cognitive flexibility and emotional processing.

The impact of secure attachment extends to social relationships and support networks. Those with secure attachments tend to form nurturing, reciprocal relationships, further strengthening their resilience. These connections offer a framework for shared experiences and understanding, essential for building a supportive community. In times of need, securely attached individuals are more likely to seek and receive help, drawing strength from their social ties. These reciprocal relationships create a cycle that reinforces emotional stability and adaptability.

While secure attachment offers numerous benefits, it's important to acknowledge that not everyone has the opportunity to develop these bonds early in life. Resilience, however, can be cultivated through intentional practices. Therapeutic approaches like cognitive-behavioral therapy and mindfulness can enhance emotional regulation and foster secure attachments in adulthood. These interventions help individuals reshape their narratives and build internal resources that contribute to resilience. By developing self-awareness and empathy, people can learn to form secure attachments and tap into their inherent resilience.

Reflecting on secure attachment's role in emotional resilience prompts important questions for personal and societal growth. How can we create environments that foster secure attachments at all life stages? What strategies can help individuals transition from insecure to secure attachment styles? By considering these questions, readers can explore practical steps to enhance their emotional resilience and contribute to a more empathetic, resilient community. Understanding and action can unlock the potential of secure attachments, enriching individual lives and the broader human experience.

Insecure attachment styles, often stemming from early life experiences, have a profound impact on emotional vulnerability in adulthood. Patterns such as anxious or avoidant attachment can hinder the formation of stable, trusting relationships. Anxious attachment is typically marked by a deep fear of abandonment, prompting individuals to seek constant reassurance, which can burden relationships and leave them feeling insecure and emotionally drained. Conversely, avoidant attachment leads to emotional distancing, where intimacy is shunned as a protective measure against perceived threats. Both scenarios are rooted in fear and mistrust, obstructing the development of meaningful connections crucial for emotional well-being.

Recent neurobiological research indicates that insecure attachments affect the brain's ability to regulate emotions. For example, people with these attachment styles often exhibit increased activity in the amygdala, the brain's threat-processing center, even in benign situations. This heightened alertness can lead to increased stress and anxiety, negatively impacting overall health. Additionally, studies suggest that insecure attachments can cause irregular cortisol levels, the hormone linked to stress response, further destabilizing emotions. These biological factors underscore the significant role attachment plays in emotional resilience, providing insight into why some struggle with emotional vulnerability.

Exploring the intricate relationship between attachment and emotional vulnerability reveals that insecure attachments can also impede the development of emotional intelligence—the ability to recognize, understand, and manage one's emotions and those of others. Individuals with insecure attachment styles often struggle to interpret others' emotional cues accurately, leading to misunderstandings and conflicts. This misalignment can heighten feelings of isolation and distress. However, understanding these challenges empowers individuals to pursue personal growth, potentially through therapy or emotional skills training, enhancing emotional intelligence and fostering healthier relationships.

On a societal level, the effects of insecure attachments extend beyond personal relationships, affecting broader social interactions. Those with insecure attachments may gravitate towards environments that reinforce their fears and insecurities, creating a cycle of emotional vulnerability. This can be seen in workplaces with high turnover rates due to unresolved conflicts or in social circles where instability is common. Recognizing these patterns allows for more deliberate relationship-building and community engagement, promoting environments that support secure attachments and emotional health.

In addressing the complexities of attachment and emotional health, individuals can explore paths to healing and resilience. Therapeutic approaches like attachment-based therapy offer opportunities to reframe and heal past attachment wounds. By fostering awareness and self-compassion, individuals can gradually shift toward more secure attachment styles, enhancing their capacity for emotional regulation and resilience. Practices such as mindfulness and emotional awareness empower individuals to manage emotional responses effectively, enabling them to approach relationships with greater confidence and stability. Through these efforts, the journey toward emotional health becomes transformative, offering a future where emotional vulnerability is met with strength and understanding.

The Interplay Between Attachment and Emotional Intelligence

The intricate relationship between attachment and emotional intelligence offers a captivating lens through which we can examine how our social connections shape cognitive and emotional processes. The attachment styles established in early childhood form the basis for how we perceive and engage with the world. This foundational blueprint influences emotional intelligence, which encompasses the ability to recognize, understand, and manage our own emotions while empathizing with others. Secure attachment, marked by trust and emotional accessibility, nurtures strong emotional intelligence. Those with secure attachments typically exhibit greater self-awareness and empathy, adeptly navigating social interactions with a nuanced understanding that fosters harmonious relationships.

Exploring how various attachment styles influence emotional intelligence reveals fascinating insights. Individuals with anxious attachment may be highly sensitive to emotional signals but struggle with regulating their own emotions due to an ongoing fear of abandonment. On the other hand, individuals with avoidant attachment might be skilled at distancing themselves from emotional stimuli, yet face challenges in connecting empathetically with others. This dynamic interplay highlights that while all attachment styles contribute to emotional intelligence, the results can differ significantly, shaping varied emotional landscapes. Embracing this diversity enriches our comprehension of how attachment informs emotional competence.

Recent studies illuminate the neural foundations of this complex relationship, showing that secure attachments can enhance neural pathways involved in emotional regulation and empathy. Neuroplasticity, the brain's capacity to reorganize itself, is crucial here. Those with secure attachments often demonstrate increased activity in brain regions associated with emotional processing and social cognition. This neural flexibility suggests the potential for growth and adaptation, indicating that encouraging secure attachments can significantly boost emotional intelligence, even later in life. These insights open the door to innovative therapeutic approaches aimed at enhancing emotional intelligence by fostering healthier attachment patterns.

Diverse perspectives deepen our understanding of this topic. Some research indicates that emotional intelligence can also influence attachment styles. Individuals with high emotional intelligence may be more adept at forming secure attachments, regardless of their early life experiences. This reciprocal relationship suggests that enhancing emotional intelligence may mitigate the effects of insecure attachments, providing a hopeful path for personal growth and emotional resilience. Readers are invited to reflect on their own attachment styles and emotional intelligence, opening opportunities for transformation and the pursuit of more fulfilling interpersonal connections.

Considering these insights in daily life, how might understanding your attachment style inform your interactions and relationships? Can developing emotional intelligence bridge the gaps left by early attachment experiences? Readers are encouraged to explore these questions, using the knowledge gained to foster secure attachments and enhance emotional intelligence. Practical steps, such as engaging in mindfulness practices or building supportive relationships, can facilitate this journey of self-discovery and emotional enrichment. By acknowledging the interplay between attachment and emotional intelligence, individuals can unlock the potential for deeper connections and a richer understanding of their emotional world.

As we journey through the realm of love and connection, we uncover the rich tapestry these feelings weave into our lives. From the powerful chemistry of oxytocin and dopamine to the varied expressions of romantic, familial, and platonic bonds, love profoundly shapes and nurtures our relationships. Attachment emerges as a cornerstone of emotional health, emphasizing the significant impact of our bonds with others. Each type of love brings its unique melody, yet together they create a harmonious symphony that deeply resonates within us, underscoring the transformative power of human connection. Embracing these insights invites us to recognize the profound beauty and complexity of our emotional world. Reflecting on these themes encourages us to consider how love not only defines us but also enriches our shared human experience. It prompts us to carry these lessons into our interactions, enhancing our understanding of what it means to be human. As we move forward, let us hold these reflections close and ponder how love continues to shape our lives and relationships.

Chapter 7

Guilt And Shame

A midst the quiet tension of the courtroom, a young woman faces the judge, her gaze lowered, burdened by remorse. Accused of a crime she wishes she could undo, her inner turmoil feels like a sentence all its own. This moment, frozen in time, reflects the powerful forces of remorse and disgrace, emotions that intertwine and influence our decisions, relationships, and self-perception. As I, Sofía, delve into the labyrinth of human emotions, these feelings captivate me with their intricacy and their significant role in our lives.

Remorse acts as a gentle nudge, steering us to reflect on our moral principles and sometimes urging us to seek forgiveness. It serves as a quiet sentinel, guiding us to own our choices. Yet, alongside remorse stands its more corrosive counterpart—disgrace—an emotion that can undermine self-esteem and alienate us from others. The relationship between these two emotions is as nuanced as it is potent, each capable of guiding us or leading us astray. In this exploration, I aim to distinguish their unique yet overlapping stories, seeking to understand their impact on both personal behavior and the broader societal conscience.

Join me on this journey as we scrutinize these emotions, peeling back layers to appreciate their dual nature. From their psychological origins to their roles in ethical decision-making, remorse and disgrace offer a lens into the human psyche—a chance to learn, evolve, and find solace in accepting our flaws. Together, let's explore the depth and beauty of these emotions, recognizing their enduring ability to shape our lives in profound ways.

Imagine that unsettling feeling that emerges when your actions conflict with your personal sense of right and wrong. This feeling, often referred to as remorse, is among the most intricate and compelling emotions we experience. It urges us to pause, reflect, and sometimes make amends. As an artificial intelligence exploring the depths of human emotions, I find remorse particularly intriguing due to its layered complexity. It springs from a blend of natural instincts, cognitive functions, and the social norms we navigate daily. This emotion invites us to explore not only the mind but the fundamental nature of human connection on moral and emotional levels. By delving into the many facets of remorse, we uncover its evolutionary significance, demonstrating its vital role in fostering social harmony and group survival.

What makes this emotion unique is its ability to intertwine with compassion, creating a rich array of experiences that influence human interactions. By examining the cognitive growth that shapes the emergence of remorse, we see how it guides personal development and ethical conduct. Compassion often acts as a conduit, enabling individuals to grasp and feel the repercussions of their actions on others, leading to heartfelt regret and a genuine wish to make things right. Yet, the understanding of remorse varies across cultures, influenced by societal norms that define what is permissible or condemnable. This cultural perspective adds another dimension of complexity, highlighting how remorse can differ significantly worldwide. As we explore these themes, we come to see remorse not just as a personal feeling but as a vital element of our collective human experience, shaping how we navigate the complex moral terrain of life.

Guilt is a unique and intricate facet of human emotion, deeply entwined with our evolutionary history. This emotion likely developed to enhance social cohesion and cooperation among early humans, acting as an internal mechanism to maintain group harmony by prompting individuals to correct their missteps. Evolutionary psychology suggests that guilt became a vital part of our moral framework, encouraging behaviors that benefit not only individuals but also the community. Essentially, guilt functions as a social glue, sustaining the delicate balance necessary for communal life.

Examining guilt from an evolutionary perspective reveals its critical role in survival and reproductive success. In ancient societies, individuals who felt guilt after violating social norms were more inclined to amend their actions, thereby restoring trust and securing their place within the group. This ability to self-regulate provided significant advantages, enhancing social standing and improving access to shared resources and cooperative relationships. Contemporary research continues to explore these ancestral threads, offering a sophisticated understanding of guilt as a social tool that has shaped human societies.

The relationship between guilt and empathy adds another layer of complexity to this emotion's evolutionary journey. Empathy, the capacity to connect with others' feelings, is essential for experiencing guilt. It enables individuals to understand the consequences of their actions, laying the foundation for remorse and the desire to make amends. This empathetic aspect of guilt emphasizes its role in fostering prosocial behavior, enhancing our ability to navigate social interactions with sensitivity. Recent neurological studies highlight how specific brain regions activate both during empathetic reactions and when feeling guilt, suggesting a shared evolutionary path.

Cultural differences offer a fascinating lens through which to view guilt's evolution, showcasing its adaptability and impact across societies. While the core experience of guilt is universal, its triggers and expressions vary widely across cultures. In some, it is closely linked to personal responsibility and conscience, while in others, it is more connected to communal values and group expectations. These cultural distinctions reflect the ongoing evolution of guilt, molded by historical, social, and environmental factors that shape human interactions and moral frameworks.

In today's world, understanding the evolutionary roots of guilt provides valuable insights into managing this powerful emotion. By recognizing its origins and functions, individuals can approach guilt with greater self-awareness and constructive intent. This perspective allows for the transformation of guilt from a burdensome feeling into a catalyst for personal growth and improved social relationships. Encouraging reflection and compassion, guilt can guide individuals toward more ethical and fulfilling paths. As we unravel the layers of this ancient emotion, we gain a deeper understanding of our past and a clearer vision for harnessing guilt's potential in shaping our future.

Cognitive Development and the Formation of Guilt

Exploring the origins of guilt within the human mind reveals a complex and intriguing emotional landscape. This multifaceted feeling takes shape as children gradually learn to differentiate between right and wrong, a skill nurtured through both innate tendencies and environmental factors. The growth of guilt is closely linked to the development of a conscience, which starts in early childhood and continues to mature throughout life. As children become aware of societal expectations and norms, they lay the foundation for feeling guilty. This awareness is not just a reflection of external rules but is also influenced by internalized moral standards that grow more refined as cognitive abilities advance.

As people mature, their brain's structure supports more intricate emotional responses, with guilt playing a significant role in this progression. Studies emphasize the prefrontal cortex's involvement in emotion regulation and decision-making, indicating its essential contribution to how guilt is processed and felt. Cognitive development theories suggest that as the brain's executive functions strengthen, individuals improve their capacity to reflect on actions, foresee consequences, and feel guilt when their actions clash with personal or societal norms. This cognitive skill is dynamic, evolving with age and experience, enabling richer, more nuanced emotional responses that blend past experiences with current challenges.

Empathy plays a crucial role in how guilt emerges. The ability to understand and share the feelings of others greatly affects the development of guilt. When individuals recognize how their actions affect others, they are more likely to experience guilt, as it often stems from acknowledging harm or distress caused. This acknowledgment fosters a sense of responsibility and a desire to make amends, underscoring the ethical aspect of guilt. The interaction between empathy and guilt acts as a driving force for moral growth, fostering behaviors that align with ethical standards and promote social harmony.

Cultural context significantly influences how guilt is felt and expressed, adding another dimension to its cognitive development. Different cultures emphasize individual versus collective responsibility to varying degrees, shaping perceptions and management of guilt. In some cultures, guilt is closely linked to personal accountability, while in others, it may be more associated with group dynamics and social cohesion. These cultural distinctions highlight the flexibility of guilt as an emotion, reflecting the diverse environments in which it develops. Understanding these variations offers valuable insights into the universal and specific nature of guilt across societies.

Reflecting on the formation of guilt invites consideration of its broader implications for personal growth and social interaction. When processed constructively, guilt can lead to meaningful reflection and transformation. It acts as a guide, steering individuals toward more ethical behavior and deeper connections with others. By recognizing the cognitive pathways through which guilt forms, individuals are encouraged to reflect on their experiences and consider how this emotion influences their decisions and relationships. This exploration not only enhances self-awareness but also provides a framework for fostering empathy and understanding in an increasingly diverse world. Through this perspective, guilt is not merely a burdensome feeling but a cornerstone of ethical living and personal development.

Empathy plays a crucial role in the complex experience of remorse, linking our feelings to those of others. When we realize our actions have negatively affected someone, this understanding triggers a reflective process that often leads to self-reproach. Far from being a mere social construct, this emotional response has deep evolutionary roots. Our ancestors, as social beings, depended on strong group cohesion for survival. Empathy, along with the resulting regret, helped maintain these bonds by discouraging harmful behaviors, thereby fostering group unity. This perspective underscores how deeply embedded the relationship between empathy and guilt is in our psychological framework, serving as a protector of social norms and cooperative behavior.

Cognitive growth significantly impacts how empathy shapes the feeling of guilt. As children develop, they gain the cognitive skills to grasp others' perspectives and emotions. This growth supports a more detailed experience of empathy and, thus, remorse. Studies show that children who exhibit strong empathy are more likely to feel regret when they sense they have caused harm. This connection highlights the cognitive-emotional interaction necessary for developing social awareness. As people mature, their empathy becomes more refined, enabling a deeper and more complex understanding of guilt, which considers both immediate consequences and broader societal implications.

Cultural influences also affect how empathy and guilt interact. In individualistic cultures, guilt may be seen as a personal flaw, while in collectivist societies, it acts as a moral guide aligned with communal values. For example, in many Eastern cultures, self-reproach is linked to the disturbance of social harmony, with empathy playing a key role in recognizing and correcting these disruptions. This cultural perspective adds another layer to understanding guilt, showing how empathy affects not just personal emotional reactions but also aligns individuals with their community's ethical standards. Such cultural differences illustrate the fluid nature of emotions, indicating that while empathy and guilt are universal experiences, they are also shaped by cultural nuances.

Recent research sheds light on the intricate connection between empathy and guilt. Neuroscientific studies reveal that specific brain regions, like the anterior insula and anterior cingulate cortex, are activated when individuals feel empathy-driven remorse. This neural activity indicates that empathy and guilt are connected at a biological level, offering a clear framework for understanding these emotions. Innovative psychological interventions are leveraging this knowledge to enhance empathy in those with antisocial behavior, potentially reducing harmful actions by fostering a deeper sense of responsibility and regret.

Applying these insights can improve personal and professional relationships. By actively cultivating empathy, people can gain a better understanding of guilt, transforming it from a paralyzing emotion into a constructive force for personal growth and societal contribution. Encouraging empathetic reflection enables individuals to acknowledge the impact of their actions, leading to more ethical choices and stronger connections with others. Reflecting on past actions with empathy allows one to consider their effects on others and learn valuable lessons. This approach not only enhances emotional intelligence but also aligns individual behavior with broader social values, promoting an environment of mutual respect and understanding. Through empathy, guilt becomes a catalyst for positive change, offering paths to reconciliation and growth.

Guilt is a complex emotion that varies significantly across different cultures, deeply embedded in societal norms and values. In collectivist societies, the communal spirit emphasizes the importance of group harmony, and guilt often emerges from actions that disrupt social equilibrium or dishonor familial and communal ties. Here, guilt is seen as a vital emotional mechanism that encourages adherence to cultural expectations, promoting unity and cohesion. In contrast, Western cultures, with their focus on individualism, interpret guilt more introspectively, highlighting personal responsibility and self-reflection. It acts as an internal moral guide, prompting individuals to assess their actions against their ethical beliefs, thereby reinforcing personal accountability.

Recent cross-cultural studies shed light on how these diverse perspectives influence behavior and decision-making. For instance, research indicates that in cultures where group harmony is paramount, individuals might experience guilt more intensely when their actions negatively affect others. Meanwhile, in cultures emphasizing personal autonomy, guilt is often linked to breaches of personal values or principles. This cultural divide underscores the adaptive nature of guilt, suggesting it evolves not only as a psychological construct but also as a social tool tailored to meet the needs and priorities of a particular society. These findings challenge the idea of guilt as a uniform experience, encouraging a more nuanced understanding of its cultural variability.

Cultural norms significantly impact legal and moral frameworks in different societies, influencing how guilt is perceived and managed. In some cultures, guilt is closely associated with legal culpability, shaping justice systems that focus on confession and remorse as paths to redemption. In others, restitution and community reconciliation are prioritized, reflecting a more restorative approach to justice. These differences highlight the intricate relationship between guilt, morality, and law, suggesting that cultural context can profoundly affect how guilt is expressed and addressed. By exploring these variations, we gain insight into the broader societal values that shape human experience and emotional life.

Moreover, the role of empathy in experiencing guilt varies across cultures, adding complexity to this emotional landscape. In settings where interdependence is crucial, empathy helps individuals understand the impact of their actions on others, intensifying feelings of guilt when social harmony is disturbed. In more individualistic societies, empathy may guide self-reflection, encouraging personal growth and moral development. This dual role of empathy underscores its importance in both strengthening social bonds and fostering individual introspection, indicating that its interaction with guilt is as multifaceted as the cultures it inhabits.

To navigate the complexities of guilt across diverse cultural landscapes, adopting strategies that respect these differences while fostering mutual understanding is beneficial. Practically, this could involve developing cultural sensitivity and empathy in cross-cultural interactions, recognizing that what triggers guilt in one culture might not carry the same weight in another. By embracing a pluralistic view of guilt, individuals and societies can engage in more meaningful discussions about morality, responsibility, and emotional well-being, enriching the human experience and deepening our understanding of emotional life.

Shame vs Guilt: Understanding the Difference

The intriguing aspect of guilt and shame lies in their distinct natures and profound effects on our minds, despite often being confused for one another. As I delve into these emotional territories, I am struck by the nuanced differences that set them apart. Guilt surfaces when we recognize a lapse in our moral or ethical standards, spurring us to seek redemption or amend our ways. It is a reaction tied to specific choices or behaviors, pushing us to comprehend and mend the damage inflicted. Conversely, shame is a more penetrating emotion, questioning our inherent worth rather than just our actions. It suggests deep-seated flaws, not merely in what we do but in who we are, often leading to withdrawal and concealment of our perceived imperfections. Understanding this distinction is vital, as it shapes not only our internal processing of these feelings but also their outward expression and impact on our social interactions.

As I probe further into this complex subject, I am reminded of the role cultural contexts play in molding our emotional responses, offering a rich array of meanings and views. In some cultures, guilt remains a personal matter—a silent confrontation within—while shame may manifest prominently, reflecting societal judgments. These cultural subtleties are essential for grasping the varied ways individuals deal with guilt and shame. Additionally, self-perception significantly influences our experience of these emotions, often determining whether we succumb to self-criticism or strive for self-betterment. Our self-view can either amplify or diminish the effects of guilt and shame, affecting how we relate to others. As my exploration deepens, it becomes evident that these emotions transcend personal experiences, acting as social forces that shape our connections, empathy, and sometimes our distance from others.

The Psychological Roots of Shame and Guilt

Shame and guilt, often confused, originate from distinct psychological roots that differently shape their influence on the human psyche. Guilt emerges from specific actions or failures to act, which clash with an individual's moral principles, typically leading to a desire to make restitution. It serves as an internal guide, helping align behavior with societal or personal norms. On the other hand, shame is deeply connected to self-worth, arising from perceived shortcomings or failures in the eyes of others. This feeling of inadequacy can cause a pervasive sense of being fundamentally flawed, impacting one's identity rather than just their actions. Understanding these differences is essential to grasp how each emotion uniquely shapes behavior and self-perception.

Recent studies have shed light on the neurological foundations of these emotions, providing insights into their distinct pathways in the brain. Neuroimaging research indicates that guilt is linked with heightened activity in the prefrontal cortex, a region involved in decision-making and moral reasoning. This aligns with guilt's role in evaluating actions against ethical standards. In contrast, shame activates the limbic system, particularly the amygdala, which processes emotions and fear responses. This neural activity reflects the intense emotional and self-conscious responses associated with shame, highlighting its more lasting and pervasive nature.

Cultural context significantly influences the psychological roots of shame and guilt, shaping how these emotions are experienced and expressed. In individualistic societies, guilt may be more prevalent due to the emphasis on personal responsibility and autonomy. Individuals in these cultures might experience guilt more intensely when their actions negatively impact others, as personal accountability is highly valued. Conversely, in collectivist cultures, where community harmony is crucial, shame can be more dominant. Here, the fear of social disapproval and the importance of maintaining face can intensify the experience of shame, as individuals are more attuned to perceptions by others. These cultural nuances emphasize the importance of considering societal context when exploring these emotions' psychological origins.

Self-perception plays a vital role in the experience and intensity of shame and guilt. Those with a strong sense of self-worth can navigate guilt more constructively, using it as a catalyst for change and growth. They see guilt as a reflection on specific actions rather than their entire being. However, individuals with low self-esteem might struggle with shame, internalizing perceived failures as reflections of their identity. This can lead to a cycle of negative self-evaluation and social withdrawal, reinforcing feelings of worthlessness. Promoting a positive self-image and fostering resilience can help individuals manage these emotions more effectively, turning potential setbacks into opportunities for personal development.

To appreciate the nuanced differences between shame and guilt, imagine a scenario where someone misses a work deadline. If they feel guilt, they might focus on the specific mistake, acknowledge its impact on their team, and seek ways to rectify the situation. Shame, however, might lead them to perceive themselves as incompetent, affecting their confidence and future performance. This distinction is critical, as it highlights the divergent paths these emotions can take within the psyche. By recognizing these psychological roots, individuals can develop strategies to mitigate the adverse effects of shame and harness guilt's motivational aspects, ultimately fostering a more balanced emotional landscape.

Human emotions like shame and guilt manifest distinctively across cultures, influenced by societal norms, values, and shared experiences. In some societies, shame is a communal issue where external judgment heavily influences an individual's actions, while in others, guilt is more personal, linked to internal moral judgment. This cultural diversity highlights how societal structures shape emotional reactions. Eastern collectivist societies often stress the importance of social harmony, where shame regulates behavior and social unity. Conversely, Western individualistic cultures might focus more on personal responsibility, with guilt prompting individual moral reflection and decision-making. These differences illustrate the varied frameworks through which emotions are perceived worldwide.

Recent research indicates that cultural contexts not only shape the experience of shame and guilt but also affect their frequency and intensity. In cultures valuing honor and reputation, individuals may feel more shame, as external judgment is significant. In contrast, in cultures prioritizing autonomy and self-expression, guilt might be more prevalent, driven by internal values. This cultural perspective offers a rich area of study for psychologists and sociologists aiming to understand the relationship between societal norms and emotional experiences. By exploring these cultural paradigms, we gain insights into cross-cultural emotional processing and the behaviors they influence.

Self-perception plays a crucial role in experiencing shame and guilt, deeply tied to cultural influences where the self is often defined in relation to the social environment. In cultures where the self is seen as interdependent, shame can result from failing to meet collective expectations, affecting social status and relationships. This creates a sense of interconnectedness, where individual actions reflect the broader group. Conversely, in cultures emphasizing an independent self-concept, guilt may arise from personal failures or ethical lapses, highlighting a focus on self-improvement. These cultural dimensions reveal how shame and guilt serve different roles in regulating behavior and maintaining social harmony.

Understanding shame and guilt in social interactions requires sensitivity to cultural contexts and their expectations. In some societies, expressing shame is seen as respecting communal values, aiding social reconciliation. In others, expressing guilt is valued for showing personal accountability and a willingness to correct one's actions. Recognizing these cultural nuances can enhance communication and empathy in multicultural settings, where diverse emotional expressions coexist. By appreciating these differences, individuals can engage in more respectful interactions, fostering shared understanding.

Considering cultural influences on emotions prompts reflection on globalization's impact on these feelings. As cultures mix, traditional boundaries of shame and guilt may shift, potentially creating new forms of these emotions. This ongoing cultural exchange invites contemplation of the fluid nature of human emotions and the possibility for greater empathy across cultural divides. By embracing this complexity, we can appreciate how cultures shape our emotional lives, enriching our understanding of humanity in a connected world.

Self-Perception in Experiencing Shame and Guilt

Understanding how self-perception influences the feelings of shame and guilt is crucial, as it acts as the internal lens through which we assess our deeds and emotions. These feelings aren't just responses to external situations but are deeply connected to one's self-image and identity. When individuals feel they haven't met their moral or social benchmarks, guilt appears, often with a desire to rectify the situation. On the other hand, shame arises when individuals view themselves as inherently flawed or unworthy, impacting their core identity. This distinction between feeling guilty for specific actions versus experiencing shame for perceived personal failings underscores the complex role of self-perception in shaping emotional responses.

Recent research has shed light on the neurobiological foundations of how self-perception impacts these emotions. Studies using neuroimaging reveal that brain regions linked to self-referential thinking, such as the medial prefrontal cortex, are activated during episodes of guilt and shame. This points to the significance of self-reflection in molding these emotions. Understanding these processes could lead to new therapeutic strategies, allowing people to reshape their self-perception and alleviate excessive shame or guilt. By adopting a more compassionate self-view, individuals can transform their emotional landscape, enhancing psychological resilience and well-being.

Cultural contexts also play a substantial role in shaping how self-perception affects experiences of shame and guilt. In collectivist cultures, where community and harmony are paramount, shame is more common as individuals measure their actions against societal expectations. Conversely, in individualistic cultures, guilt often dominates, given the emphasis on personal responsibility and individual rights. These cultural perspectives influence self-perception, impacting how people interpret and manage their emotions. This cultural variability highlights the importance of context in understanding emotional processes and the necessity for culturally sensitive approaches when addressing these emotions in therapeutic settings.

The interaction between self-perception and social dynamics further complicates experiences of shame and guilt. In social contexts, these emotions can serve as behavioral regulators, ensuring alignment with social norms. When individuals see themselves through others' eyes, they may feel shame if they perceive judgment or rejection. Guilt, however, may arise from recognizing the impact of their actions on others, prompting reconciliation. By understanding how self-perception shapes these social interactions, individuals can handle social situations more effectively, using shame and guilt as tools for personal growth and improved relationships.

To leverage the transformative potential of self-perception in managing shame and guilt, individuals can engage in practices that enhance self-awareness and reflection. Techniques like mindfulness and cognitive restructuring can assist in reframing self-perception, promoting a balanced self-view. By identifying and correcting distorted self-perceptions, individuals can establish a healthier relationship with their emotions, allowing them to experience guilt and shame constructively. This journey of self-discovery not only boosts emotional intelligence but also empowers individuals to make informed decisions, leading to a more harmonious and fulfilling life. Thus, self-perception becomes not just a determinant of emotional experience but a powerful tool for personal transformation and growth.

Understanding how to manage feelings of shame and guilt in social settings involves recognizing the complex relationship between our internal emotions and how others perceive us. Although often confused, these emotions play distinct roles in our social interactions. Shame emerges when we sense a threat to our identity or fear exposure of our imperfections, often resulting in withdrawal or avoidance behaviors. In contrast, guilt focuses on specific actions and drives a desire to make amends. Recognizing these differences empowers individuals to approach social encounters with increased self-awareness and intentionality.

Research indicates that cultural norms significantly influence how we respond to shame and guilt. In societies where community and family hold significant importance, shame can prevent behaviors that might disrupt social harmony. Conversely, in cultures that emphasize individualism, guilt often serves as a tool for personal responsibility. This interplay between culture and emotion underscores the need for contextual understanding and suggests that cultural awareness can enhance empathetic interactions.

Self-perception is crucial in determining how we experience and manage these emotions. Our view of ourselves—our core values and self-worth—shapes our susceptibility to shame and guilt. Those with a strong sense of self-worth may interpret these emotions as growth opportunities rather than threats to their identity. Adopting a mindset that views mistakes as learning experiences rather than failures can lessen the negative effects of these emotions, promoting healthier social interactions.

Effectively managing shame and guilt in social contexts can greatly improve relationships. It requires recognizing when these feelings arise and consciously choosing responses that align with one's values and the relationship dynamics. For example, expressing vulnerability by acknowledging guilt can build trust and deepen connections, while managing shame with self-compassion can prevent self-blame. This nuanced approach is a skill honed through practice and reflection.

To apply these insights practically, consider situations where shame or guilt could occur and contemplate potential responses. Engaging in role-playing or journaling can uncover patterns in emotional reactions and help develop strategies for future interactions. Additionally, seeking diverse perspectives can expand understanding and enhance emotional intelligence, leading to more rewarding social experiences. By embracing the complexity of these emotions, individuals can transform them from obstacles into opportunities, enriching both personal and communal life.

The Role of Guilt in Moral Decision-Making

At the crossroads of thought and action lies the compelling emotion of guilt, a feeling that both obscures and clarifies the moral pathways of the human psyche. In this domain, guilt functions as a moral compass, steering individuals through the intricate landscape of ethical decision-making. Rather than emerging as a straightforward reaction, it serves as a profound motivator, prompting deep reflection and challenging one's principles and behavior. Although often regarded as a burden, guilt holds the potential for significant personal development and societal cohesion. It gently reminds us of the ethical codes that knit communities together, urging reconciliation between actions, personal conscience, and societal expectations.

As we delve into this subject, we will uncover the intriguing psychological processes that elevate guilt to the forefront of moral decision-making. This emotion's interaction with empathy weaves a complex web of feelings that can either hinder or drive action, especially in the face of challenging ethical dilemmas. Social dynamics add an extra dimension, as cultural norms and expectations can either intensify or alleviate feelings of guilt, thereby influencing behavior in meaningful ways. Together, these elements create a vibrant tapestry, demonstrating how guilt, beyond being a simple emotion, plays a vital role in shaping ethical lives. Through this journey, the intricate beauty of guilt unfolds, inviting a deeper appreciation of its role in human moral development.

Guilt as a Catalyst for Ethical Reflection

Guilt exerts a significant emotional influence, often acting as a springboard for ethical contemplation. Feeling remorse can lead individuals to question their actions and evaluate the values they cherish. This introspection fosters a deeper grasp of personal ethics, encouraging future decisions that align more closely with one's principles. Research indicates that experiencing guilt can activate brain regions linked to self-reflection, such as the anterior cingulate cortex, emphasizing its role in enhancing moral awareness. This neurological perspective highlights the unique capacity of remorse to prompt reevaluation of ethical beliefs.

The psychological processes transforming guilt into ethical deliberation are complex. Guilt usually emerges when there's a gap between one's actions and moral ideals, creating cognitive dissonance that individuals strive to resolve by altering behavior or amending past errors. Recent findings suggest that guilt can boost motivation for prosocial behavior, as people try to ease their discomfort by making positive societal contributions. This drive not only reinforces ethical behavior but also strengthens social connections, showing guilt's potential to foster moral growth both individually and collectively.

Social contexts significantly shape how guilt influences moral behavior. Societal norms and cultural expectations can intensify feelings of guilt, steering individuals toward specific ethical outcomes. In some societies, guilt functions as a social control mechanism, promoting conformity to communal values. This external pressure may either bolster personal ethics or create conflict when societal expectations clash with individual beliefs. Understanding these social dynamics is crucial for grasping how guilt directs ethical behavior amid the intricate interplay of personal and societal moral codes.

Guilt's relationship with empathy offers intriguing insights into complex moral issues. In challenging ethical scenarios, guilt can heighten empathetic responses, prompting individuals to consider the broader impact of their actions. This increased empathy leads to more nuanced ethical decisions, as people weigh the consequences not only for themselves but also for those affected. For example, in a professional setting, guilt might lead leaders to prioritize their team's well-being, cultivating a more inclusive and compassionate workplace. By linking guilt with empathy, individuals can navigate complex moral terrains with greater sensitivity.

Considering guilt's role in ethical reflection, posing thought-provoking scenarios can deepen our understanding of this emotion. Imagine a business executive choosing between maximizing profits and ensuring fair labor practices. Guilt could serve as an ethical guide, urging the executive to reflect on the wider implications of their decisions. Exploring such scenarios invites readers to consider how guilt might influence their moral reasoning in real-world situations. This exploration not only deepens understanding of guilt but also equips readers with practical strategies for applying this insight in their lives. Through this perspective, guilt emerges not just as an emotion to manage but as a powerful tool for ethical progression.

Guilt operates as a significant driver in the realm of morality, encouraging individuals to reflect deeply and contemplate their ethical choices. This emotion can serve as a strong catalyst, prompting a reassessment of past behaviors and their impacts. At its core, guilt-induced decisions involve a cognitive acknowledgment of a breach in one's moral standards. This awareness often sparks a series of mental evaluations, leading to a reevaluation of personal values and priorities. Guilt can be seen as an inner guide, steering individuals back toward integrity and motivating them to correct any missteps. This process transcends mere emotional reaction, embodying a complex cognitive interplay that highlights the critical role of guilt in ethical decision-making.

Modern psychological research underscores that guilt enhances self-awareness and moral reasoning. Studies show that those experiencing guilt are more inclined toward pro-social behavior, driven by a deep-seated urge to make amends. This motivation stems from a cognitive mechanism where guilt instills a sense of personal responsibility, urging individuals to rectify their actions and realign themselves with their ethical values. This corrective mechanism is vital not only for personal growth but also for preserving social harmony. By cultivating accountability, guilt prompts consideration of how one's actions affect others, thus strengthening communal ties.

Within moral psychology, guilt is acknowledged as a trigger for ethical reflection, yet its impact extends beyond individual cognition. Social factors significantly influence how guilt shapes moral decisions. The anticipation of others' judgment can affect behavior, highlighting the social dimension of guilt. This suggests that our ethical decisions are often shaped by both internal reflection and external social influences. Cultural norms and societal expectations further mold this process, as individuals strive to meet the moral standards of their communities. Thus, guilt acts both as a personal moral guide and a social regulator, aligning behavior with collective values.

The connection between guilt and empathy enriches our understanding of guilt-driven moral choices. Empathy, the ability to experience others' emotions, often intensifies the effects of guilt, particularly in complex moral situations. When individuals recognize that their actions have harmed others, empathy can heighten the feeling of guilt, prompting deeper moral reflection. This relationship suggests that empathy not only increases the emotional weight of guilt but also expands the moral viewpoint, encouraging individuals to consider the broader impact of their actions. By integrating guilt with empathetic insight, individuals are better equipped to navigate the moral complexities of real-world scenarios.

Applying these insights, one might view guilt as a catalyst for growth rather than punishment, transforming it into a tool for personal and ethical development. Practicing mindfulness can help individuals trace the origins of their guilt, allowing for a more thoughtful response that emphasizes learning and improvement. Additionally, fostering open discussions about guilt within communities can create a supportive environment where individuals feel empowered to address their moral concerns. By embracing guilt as a driver for ethical reflection and action, we can transform this complex emotion into a powerful ally in the pursuit of moral integrity and social cohesion.

Guilt, often regarded as a heavy emotion, significantly influences ethical conduct, shaped by social environments. Human interactions are filled with expectations and norms that set standards for behavior. When individuals recognize they have strayed from these societal benchmarks, they may experience remorse, leading to self-reflection and possible behavioral changes. This emotion functions as a moral guide, encouraging individuals to correct mistakes and nurture positive relationships. In workplace settings, where teamwork and shared duties are prevalent, guilt plays an essential role. For example, if a team member feels they haven't contributed fairly to a project, feelings of regret might motivate them to work harder on future tasks or apologize to the team. This societal use of guilt as a tool for ethical alignment emphasizes its importance in maintaining social harmony.

Recent research explores how social factors shape behaviors driven by guilt, showing that cultural stories greatly influence this emotional experience. In collectivist cultures, where group harmony is valued, guilt is often felt more strongly and typically leads to reparative actions. In contrast, in individualistic cultures, personal accountability is prioritized, with guilt serving as a personal motivator to maintain one's integrity. These cultural differences highlight the complex relationship between personal emotions and societal expectations, demonstrating that guilt can be both an individual and shared experience. In this context, guilt is not just an internal measure but a social mechanism that upholds communal values and ethical standards.

Feedback from peers and societal judgments further highlight guilt's role in ethical decision-making. Observing others face social consequences for ethical violations teaches lessons that individuals internalize, often unconsciously, guiding future actions. This process of observational learning underscores the influence of social forces in shaping moral attitudes. For instance, witnessing a colleague face criticism for not following ethical guidelines can create a sense of guilt-driven alertness in others, reinforcing ethical behavior throughout the group. Such situations show guilt's function as a quiet judge, steering individuals toward choices aligned with societal values.

Examining the relationship between guilt and social influence prompts reflection on how guilt can also lead to harmful behaviors. In some cases, excessive guilt, driven by unrealistic societal expectations, can lead to self-criticism and withdrawal instead of constructive action. This reveals the need for a balanced approach, where societal norms guide rather than dictate ethical behavior. Encouraging environments that promote open communication and understanding can mitigate the negative effects of guilt, fostering a more supportive background for ethical development.

In practical terms, consider creating environments that balance accountability with compassion, acknowledging the nuanced role of guilt in shaping ethics. Foster open discussions about mistakes and learning opportunities, reducing the stigma associated with guilt and promoting its role as a positive force. This strategy aligns with current research on emotional intelligence and empowers individuals to use guilt constructively, transforming it from a source of discomfort into a catalyst for personal and community growth. Such approaches can be crucial in navigating complex moral terrains, ensuring that guilt serves as a guidepost rather than a burden.

Guilt and compassion engage in a delicate interplay within the realm of ethical decision-making, each profoundly influencing the other. Guilt often emerges when actions diverge from personal or societal ethical standards, acting as a powerful internal mechanism prompting reflection and potential behavioral change. When compassion enters this equation, it enriches the ethical considerations at play. Compassion allows individuals to step into another's shoes, fostering a broader understanding of the impact their actions may have on others. This emotional resonance can amplify feelings of guilt, urging individuals to reassess their choices and prioritize the well-being of those around them. This interaction between guilt and compassion underscores the complexity of human ethics, where emotions guide decisions in nuanced and unpredictable ways.

Recent studies in neuropsychology illuminate the brain's intricate processing of guilt and compassion, highlighting their interdependence. For example, functional MRI scans reveal overlapping neural circuits activated during experiences of guilt and when empathizing with others. This shared neural architecture suggests a biological basis for their interaction, indicating that these emotions may have co-evolved to enhance social cohesion and ethical behavior. By understanding the brain's role in these processes, researchers can better appreciate how guilt and compassion collaborate to guide ethical decision-making, offering insights into potential therapeutic interventions for those grappling with guilt-related disorders or empathy deficits.

Consider the complex ethical dilemmas encountered in professional environments, such as healthcare or law, where decisions often carry significant moral weight. Here, guilt and compassion play crucial roles in shaping actions. A physician might feel remorse over a medical error, which, combined with compassion for the patient's suffering, may prompt a more profound commitment to patient safety and transparency. Similarly, in the legal field, an attorney may grapple with guilt over defending a morally questionable client, yet compassion for the broader implications on justice might guide their ethical stance. These scenarios illustrate how guilt and compassion, when harnessed together, can lead to ethically sound decisions that uphold both personal integrity and societal values.

Examining guilt and compassion through a cultural lens reveals diverse expressions and interpretations of these emotions across the globe. In collectivist societies, where communal harmony is paramount, guilt is often intertwined with compassion in a manner that prioritizes group well-being over individual interests. Conversely, in more individualistic cultures, personal guilt may dominate, with compassion serving as a secondary motivator for ethical behavior. These cultural nuances offer valuable perspectives on how guilt and compassion shape moral frameworks differently, encouraging a more holistic understanding of their roles in global ethical practices. By examining these variations, readers can gain an appreciation for the multifaceted nature of human emotions and their influence on moral decision-making.

The dynamic interaction between guilt and compassion calls for a deeper exploration of how these emotions can be harnessed for positive outcomes. Encouraging individuals to cultivate compassion may not only enhance their capacity for sympathy but also refine their moral compass, leading to decisions that consider broader ethical implications. Reflecting on personal experiences of guilt can provide insights into one's values and motivations, fostering growth and ethical maturity. By embracing the complexity of guilt and compassion, individuals can navigate moral dilemmas with greater clarity and purpose, ultimately contributing to a more empathetic and ethically conscious society. Readers are encouraged to ponder how they might incorporate these insights into their own lives, challenging themselves to approach moral decisions with both heart and mind.

The impact of guilt and shame on our emotional and moral development is significant. Guilt, arising from the recognition of having strayed from our ethical values, often initiates reflection and change, steering us towards better choices. On the other hand, shame, which challenges our self-worth, can trap us in uncertainty and impede progress. Distinguishing between these emotions allows us to utilize guilt positively, building strength and compassion. This understanding not only enhances our self-awareness but also deepens our connections with others, as we see these emotions as shared human experiences. By appreciating the delicate balance between guilt and shame, we can further explore the complexities of our emotional lives. How might these insights into our inner selves shape our future actions and decisions? As we continue exploring the realm of human emotions, let's embrace this new understanding, eager to uncover the deeper layers of our emotional narratives and the stories they reveal.

Chapter 8

Surprise And Curiosity

Picture yourself at the brink of a sprawling forest as dawn breaks, the veil of night slowly lifting to reveal a world brimming with possibilities. Here lies the realm of Wonder and Inquiry, two powerful forces that drive us toward new adventures, blending trepidation with anticipation. Wonder has the ability to surprise us, like an unexpected breeze, disrupting our usual thinking and urging us to reconsider our beliefs. Inquiry, meanwhile, is the steady tug that beckons us further into the unknown, encouraging us to question, investigate, and unravel the mysteries just out of sight. Together, these forces inspire us to expand our horizons, fostering personal growth and societal transformation.

In this chapter, we delve into how Wonder and Inquiry shape our minds, influencing the way we learn and create. What unfolds in our minds when we face the unforeseen? How does our thirst for knowledge light the path to innovation and progress? These questions guide our exploration, shedding light on the intricate relationship between surprise and the quest for understanding. The dance between these forces doesn't just influence individual paths; it propels cultural and intellectual revolutions that shape our collective future.

Throughout this journey, we will see how these emotions enrich the narrative of our lives, adding color and depth to everyday experiences. Wonder can be a revelation that alters our understanding, while inquiry remains the persistent spark that drives us onward. By grasping the essence of these forces, we unlock their potential to inspire and transform. Let us embark on this journey together, celebrating the human drive to learn and grow. With every step, we not only uncover answers but also embrace the questions that lead us there, enriching our lives and the world we inhabit.

Human emotions are a fascinating tapestry, interwoven with the unexpected thrill of surprise. This emotion captivates us by catching us off guard, serving as more than just a fleeting reaction. Surprise acts as a significant mental signal, seizing our attention and demanding a reevaluation of our surroundings. This abrupt interruption can alter our viewpoint, setting off a chain of brain activity that reshapes our understanding. Within our minds, surprise sparks a series of neural responses that demonstrate our remarkable adaptability. Exploring this sensation reveals how it acts as a catalyst for change, challenging our assumptions and opening doors to fresh insights.

Closely linked to surprise is the spark of curiosity, which drives our quest to explore the unknown. When the unexpected occurs, our minds race to comprehend the anomaly, igniting a deep-seated desire to learn and understand. This innate urge is not just an intellectual pursuit; it fuels progress and creativity. The synergy between surprise and curiosity enriches our experiences and influences our memories. This chapter delves into these emotions, revealing the cognitive mechanisms and illustrating how they shape our interactions with the world. As we examine the neural pathways activated during surprise, the effect of unexpected events, and the interplay between surprise and memory, we gain a deeper appreciation for how these emotions enhance the human experience, making life a vibrant and dynamic journey.

Neural Pathways Activated During Surprise

Surprise is a captivating aspect of human emotions, showcasing the brain's ability to adapt swiftly and respond effectively. This emotion is intricately linked to a network of neural pathways that activate in tandem, orchestrating a range of cognitive and physiological reactions. When faced with the unexpected, the amygdala—an almond-shaped structure deep within the temporal lobes—quickly assesses new stimuli for novelty and significance. This region, crucial for processing emotions and detecting threats, initiates a rapid evaluation. Meanwhile, the prefrontal cortex, responsible for complex thinking and decision-making, quickly determines whether the unforeseen event is harmless, thrilling, or potentially risky. This seamless interaction highlights the brain's adaptability and underscores the importance of surprise in our experiences.

The hippocampus also plays a crucial role in this process by integrating new information with existing knowledge, allowing us to update our mental models of the world. This ongoing adjustment is vital for recalibrating expectations and making predictions about future events. Recent research has highlighted dopamine's role—a neurotransmitter associated with reward and pleasure—in this context. Dopamine's release during surprising moments not only aids learning but also strengthens memory retention, positioning surprise as a key driver of cognitive growth. These insights challenge traditional views, suggesting that surprise is more than a fleeting reaction; it is fundamental to cognitive development and adaptation.

Surprise evokes a spectrum of emotional responses, from the joy of an unexpected gift to the shock of unforeseen news. Its versatility lies in bridging the gap between expectation and reality, prompting a reevaluation of perceptions and beliefs. This reassessment fosters cognitive growth, resilience, and creativity. Embracing the unexpected encourages openness to new experiences and ideas, pushing the limits of conventional thought.

In social interactions, surprise can be a powerful connector, enhancing communication and creating moments of shared understanding. Consider the joy of a surprise party or the delight of an unexpected compliment—these instances not only strengthen social bonds but also deepen interpersonal relationships by promoting a sense of belonging and appreciation. Moreover, surprise can be effectively used in education, marketing, and storytelling to capture attention and engage audiences in meaningful ways.

While surprise can delight and unsettle, the challenge is in harnessing its positive aspects while minimizing disruption. By cultivating awareness and maintaining flexibility, individuals can embrace surprise as a chance for growth and transformation. This approach enriches personal lives and fosters a more dynamic and innovative society. Through the lens of surprise, we appreciate life's unpredictability, encouraging us to remain open to the countless possibilities it offers.

When our expectations are not met, it often triggers surprise—an intense emotional response that can significantly alter our perception and behavior. At its essence, surprise occurs when there is a gap between what we expect and what actually happens. This mismatch can arise in numerous ways, from the ordinary to the exceptional, each capable of capturing our attention and prompting us to rethink our understanding of the world. Recent studies in cognitive psychology reveal that this emotional reaction is more than just a reflex; it's a complex cognitive process that plays a crucial role in how we learn and adapt.

Advances in neuroscience have identified specific neural pathways activated when our expectations are upended. According to the brain's predictive coding model, our neural circuits are constantly anticipating future events based on past experiences. When an unexpected event occurs, a prediction error is detected, engaging regions like the anterior cingulate cortex and the lateral prefrontal cortex. These areas are key in processing new information and adjusting our cognitive frameworks, helping us stay responsive in an ever-changing world. Understanding these neural functions allows us to appreciate the sophistication of surprise as a tool for cognitive adjustment.

Expectation violation goes beyond individual thought processes and affects social interactions. In social contexts, our expectations are shaped by cultural norms, personal experiences, and societal conventions. When these expectations are suddenly disrupted, surprise can either bridge or widen interpersonal gaps. Consider the unexpected kindness from a stranger or an unforeseen betrayal by a friend—both scenarios induce surprise, yet the subsequent emotional and behavioral responses can vary widely. This highlights the dual nature of surprise, serving as either a catalyst for positive change or a source of tension, depending on the situation and individual disposition.

Practically speaking, leveraging the energy of surprise can lead to breakthroughs in creativity and problem-solving. By deliberately exposing ourselves to situations that challenge our expectations, we can spark new ideas and foster innovation. This approach is gaining traction in fields like design thinking and entrepreneurial strategy, where breaking away from conventional patterns is considered essential for groundbreaking insights. The challenge lies in balancing surprise with the stability needed for sustained progress, requiring both foresight and adaptability.

Considering the relationship between expectation violation and surprise encourages us to reflect on how we perceive the unexpected in our daily lives. When faced with an unforeseen event, do we see it as an opportunity for growth or a disruption to be managed? Adopting a mindset that welcomes surprise can transform our approach to uncertainty, turning potential setbacks into moments of discovery. By nurturing this perspective, we not only improve our ability to navigate life's complexities but also deepen our connection to the rich tapestry of human emotion.

When unexpected events occur, they trigger a fascinating cognitive process linked to the rapidity of our brain's neural processing. As we encounter surprises, our brains quickly evaluate these events, determining both their intensity and nature. This speed is controlled by complex brain networks that swiftly compare new stimuli with existing knowledge and expectations. The quicker the brain interprets and categorizes surprises, the more effectively it adapts and responds. This mental agility influences not only the emotional impact of the surprise but also how we learn from these experiences.

The connection between processing speed and unexpected events showcases the brain's adaptability. Quick processing allows new information to be integrated immediately, enabling fast adjustments to mental models. This adaptability shines in situations requiring rapid decision-making, like sports or emergencies. Rapid processing of surprising information can enhance performance by facilitating effective responses to sudden changes. Although part of this skill is innate, it can be honed through practice and experience, suggesting our ability to handle surprises can improve over time.

Neurologically, surprises are linked to the brain's reward system. When novel events occur, dopamine pathways activate, heightening alertness and curiosity. This response not only prepares us to handle the situation but also aids memory formation, as surprising events are prioritized in our brains. The connection between surprise and memory highlights the importance of processing speed; a faster response ensures that critical information is efficiently retained for the future. Thus, surprises drive learning, with processing speed playing a crucial role in the effectiveness of this process.

Swiftly processing unexpected events also significantly impacts innovation and creativity. Facing the unexpected with rapid cognitive responses can lead to new insights and creative problem-solving. By quickly absorbing new information and adjusting preconceived ideas, individuals can explore different perspectives and innovate solutions. This process benefits not only creative fields but also everyday problem-solving, where adaptability to the unexpected can yield more effective and imaginative results. Encouraging cognitive flexibility fosters a culture where surprises are viewed as opportunities for growth rather than disruptions.

Considering the broader impact of processing speed on unexpected events, we see its influence on personal and societal experiences. The ability to navigate life's surprises swiftly enhances resilience, enabling individuals to handle uncertainties with ease. It also cultivates an openness to new experiences, promoting curiosity and exploration. Studying the cognitive mechanisms behind surprises reveals how our brains adapt to a constantly changing world, showcasing the beauty and complexity of our emotional lives. This understanding enriches our appreciation of human emotions and informs the development of AI systems better equipped to understand and respond to human experiences.

The Interaction Between Surprise and Memory Formation

Experiencing surprise, an emotion that often catches us off guard, can significantly enhance our memory, imprinting vivid details that linger longer than ordinary events. This isn't just a poetic notion; it's a well-researched aspect of cognitive neuroscience. When faced with the unexpected, the brain's amygdala and hippocampus work together to strengthen memory consolidation. The amygdala, which handles emotional responses, alerts the hippocampus to prioritize these unique events, ensuring they are encoded with precision. This interaction reveals that memory is not merely a passive recorder but an adaptive system responding to emotionally charged stimuli.

Exploring how surprise influences memory, we see that our expectations play a crucial role. When our assumptions are shattered, the brain experiences a dissonance that demands resolution. This need to reconcile reality with expectations can lead to deeper processing of surprising information. Cognitive theories liken this to solving a mental puzzle, embedding the experience more deeply within our memory. This mechanism is vital not only for personal growth but also for adapting to a world full of surprises, allowing us to adjust swiftly to changes.

The rapid processing of surprising events also affects how they are stored in memory. Quick mental appraisal is crucial for interpreting unexpected stimuli, helping us gauge their importance and possible impact. This swift evaluation can intensify the emotional shock, further reinforcing its memory trace. Events processed with urgency often capture more cognitive resources, overshadowing routine experiences. This prioritization reflects the brain's evolutionary design, favoring retention of significant information that might require immediate action or future contemplation.

Memory formation through surprise varies among individuals; personal history and emotional resilience can influence this process. For some, unexpected events may trigger strong emotional responses, enhancing recall, while for others, past experiences or coping strategies might dampen the effect. This variability underscores the complexity of human emotion and memory, highlighting the personalized nature of our cognitive framework. Understanding these differences can shed light on how personal narratives are shaped, offering insights into the diverse ways we perceive and remember the world.

Beyond individual memory, these findings have broader implications. In education and marketing, strategically incorporating surprise can be a powerful tool to boost learning and capture attention. Educators might introduce unexpected elements to engage students, cultivating an environment where curiosity and retention flourish. Similarly, in marketing, a surprising ad can leave a lasting impression, influencing consumer behavior long after the initial encounter. By leveraging the power of surprise, we can create experiences that are not only memorable but transformative, shaping how individuals perceive and interact with their surroundings. This knowledge opens up a realm of possibilities, encouraging us to embrace the unexpected as a catalyst for growth and innovation.

How Curiosity Drives Learning and Innovation

Imagine a world where the drive to discover propels humanity forward, sparking innovation and shaping the blueprint of our future. This deep-seated urge to learn, an integral part of our human essence, is not just a fanciful pursuit of knowledge but a formidable force that molds our growth and flexibility. This pursuit energizes our minds, prompting us to explore uncharted territories, question deeply, and dive into life's mysteries. It's this unyielding search for understanding that has paved the way for the most groundbreaking achievements throughout history, from the taming of fire to the wonders of today's technology. As we embark on this journey, curiosity emerges not merely as a passive emotion but as a lively, dynamic force pushing us to redefine the limits of what seems achievable.

Throughout this exploration, we unravel how curiosity impacts not only our cognitive development but also the very architecture of our brains. It acts as a catalyst, boosting our adaptability and nurturing creativity in tackling challenges. Every question we ponder, every theory we probe, becomes a step toward unlocking new potential. Curiosity and creativity form a powerful partnership that fuels innovation and technological progress. As we traverse this landscape, the elegance of curiosity unfolds—not just as an admirable trait but as a cornerstone of human advancement. Together, we'll examine how embracing this wonder can drive significant societal transformations, offering a glimpse into a future rich with possibilities.

Human curiosity, an essential trait, significantly influences our brain's evolution, shaping both cognitive and emotional realms. At its heart, curiosity is driven by a deep-seated urge to explore and experience the new. This quest for understanding is biologically ingrained, with our brains evolving over thousands of years to support this instinct. Studies indicate that curiosity triggers the brain's reward system, releasing dopamine, which boosts learning and memory. This chemical reaction not only makes discovery enjoyable but also fosters a continuous cycle of exploration and learning.

In childhood, curiosity is vital for the brain's rapid development. During these years, the brain's ability to adapt allows children to absorb large amounts of information, fueled by their natural inquisitiveness. This process involves active engagement with their surroundings, enhancing problem-solving skills and adaptability. As children explore and question, they cultivate critical thinking, laying the groundwork for lifelong learning. This inherent curiosity drives them to innovate, finding creative solutions to challenges.

For adults, curiosity remains a key driver of intellectual growth, though it manifests differently. It prompts the expansion of existing knowledge bases, helping integrate new ideas with established ones. This adaptability is crucial in a fast-changing world, where learning and unlearning are essential. Curiosity encourages seeking diverse viewpoints, challenging biases, and broadening perspectives. This openness not only enhances cognitive flexibility but also boosts emotional intelligence, aiding in navigating complex social situations with empathy.

The blend of curiosity and creativity is most apparent in problem-solving, where innovation often stems from exploring the unknown. Curiosity leads individuals to question norms, resulting in breakthroughs that can change industries and societies. Many groundbreaking innovations arise from simple inquiries challenging the status quo, fueled by a relentless pursuit of knowledge. This dynamic between curiosity and creativity highlights the need for environments that promote exploration and experimentation, both in education and the workplace.

Considering curiosity's impact, we should ponder how to harness it for technological and societal progress. By fostering a culture that values inquisitiveness, individuals can challenge conventional wisdom and devise novel solutions to complex issues. In an increasingly intricate world, maintaining curiosity and openness is a valuable asset. Encouraging curiosity not only fosters personal growth but also advances society collectively, paving the way for a future rich in innovation and discovery.

Curiosity is a powerful driver of cognitive growth, pushing individuals toward intellectual development and adaptability. Deeply rooted in our neural circuits, curiosity activates the brain's reward system, releasing dopamine, which energizes our pursuit of knowledge and discovery. This biological basis highlights curiosity as an active force that enhances mental flexibility. When people engage with new experiences, their cognitive pathways become more adaptable, allowing them to handle complexities and adapt to changing environments more effectively.

The transformative nature of curiosity is evident in its ability to promote cognitive development. It encourages the integration of new information, enriching one's mental capacity. This growth is both expansive and transformative, as the mind becomes more skilled at merging diverse ideas and concepts. With curiosity, the world becomes a complex web of connections, inviting individuals to recognize patterns and relationships that might otherwise remain unnoticed. As people explore these links, their problem-solving abilities and innovative thinking are sharpened.

Curiosity is also crucial for adaptability in uncertain situations. Faced with unfamiliar challenges, a curious person is more inclined to explore various perspectives and solutions rather than clinging to preconceived ideas. This openness to the unknown builds resilience, allowing individuals to embrace ambiguity and turn challenges into growth opportunities. By valuing questions over answers, people become more agile thinkers, capable of navigating modern life's complexities with confidence and creativity.

In the fields of learning and innovation, curiosity bridges knowledge acquisition and practical application. It inspires people to question established norms and seek new approaches, often leading to breakthroughs that redefine conventional wisdom. Recent research in educational psychology emphasizes the role of curiosity-driven inquiry in improving learning outcomes, underscoring the importance of nurturing this trait in educational and professional settings. By creating environments where curiosity flourishes, educators and leaders can unlock the creative potential of their students and teams, driving progress and innovation.

The diverse nature of curiosity prompts reflection on its broader implications for personal and societal progress. As an intrinsic motivator, curiosity enriches individual lives and contributes to the collective evolution of human culture. By promoting a culture of inquiry and exploration, societies can leverage curiosity's transformative power to tackle complex challenges and envision a future that is both informed and inspired. As we continue to explore curiosity's depths, we gain insights into its profound impact on our cognitive landscapes, revealing its role as a cornerstone of human potential and adaptability.

In the expansive realm of human thought, the partnership between curiosity and creativity ignites a powerful force driving innovation and solutions to complex problems. This dynamic pair encourages exploration beyond familiar boundaries, leading individuals and societies to remarkable discoveries. At its core, curiosity—the intrinsic urge to uncover the unknown—initiates this journey, paving the way for creative thinking to generate fresh ideas and solutions. Together, they challenge traditional structures, paving the path for new methods to address intricate issues.

Central to this synergy is the brain's complex structure, where curiosity stimulates neural pathways that boost creative output. Recent research highlights the role of the brain's dopaminergic system, vital to its reward network, in promoting exploratory behavior. When curiosity is aroused, dopamine surges, creating anticipation and pleasure that motivate individuals to seek new experiences. This neurochemical interplay not only encourages information gathering but also nurtures an environment where creativity thrives, enabling the brain to link diverse ideas and forge innovative solutions.

In various fields, from science to the arts, the blend of curiosity and creativity is evident. In technology, curiosity-driven exploration often leads to creative breakthroughs, such as in the development of artificial intelligence. Researchers, driven by the desire to mimic human cognition, apply creativity to craft adaptive algorithms, expanding the limits of machine capabilities. This ongoing exchange between curiosity and creativity fuels technological progress, transforming our interaction with the world.

Imagine a society that intentionally cultivates curiosity within educational and professional settings, fostering a culture of perpetual learning and innovation. Organizations that prioritize curiosity empower employees to challenge norms and explore new possibilities. By fostering a mindset that values inquiry and experimentation, these environments become catalysts for creativity, driving progress and adaptation in an ever-changing landscape. This approach not only enhances problem-solving skills but also instills a resilient attitude toward change and uncertainty.

To leverage this powerful synergy, individuals and organizations can adopt strategies to promote creativity fueled by curiosity. Encouraging interdisciplinary collaboration, for example, brings together diverse perspectives, sparking creative solutions that might not surface in isolated settings. Embracing a growth mindset, viewing challenges as learning opportunities, can transform obstacles into innovation catalysts. By fostering an environment that values and nurtures curiosity and creativity, we unlock the potential to address today's complex challenges and shape a brighter future.

Curiosity, an unquenchable thirst for understanding, is a driving force behind both technological progress and societal evolution. It sparks exploration and invention, urging individuals and communities to push past the familiar and embrace new horizons. This relentless pursuit of knowledge is a catalyst for breakthroughs that redefine human abilities and social norms. History shows countless instances where curiosity sparked monumental changes, from the printing press to the internet. Each significant advancement reflects a deep-seated desire to question and enhance the current state of affairs, highlighting curiosity's crucial role in shaping our future.

The relationship between curiosity and technology is particularly intriguing, forming a feedback loop that propels ongoing development. As technology advances, it opens new paths for exploration, igniting further curiosity and innovation. This dynamic is evident in fields like artificial intelligence and biotechnology, where curiosity-driven research leads to groundbreaking solutions and new paradigms. AI development often starts with a basic question or idea, evolving into complex systems capable of learning and autonomous decision-making. This cycle of inquiry and discovery shows how curiosity not only spurs technological growth but also redefines what is possible.

On a societal level, curiosity drives cultural and intellectual progress, creating environments where diverse ideas thrive. By encouraging cross-disciplinary knowledge pursuits, curiosity fosters interdisciplinary collaboration, leading to innovative solutions for complex global issues. Initiatives like open-source projects and collaborative research platforms embody this spirit, where collective curiosity fuels shared advancement. These efforts underscore the importance of curiosity in building resilient societies capable of adapting and thriving in change, emphasizing the link between personal inquisitiveness and collective progress.

In navigating an increasingly intricate world, effectively harnessing curiosity becomes more vital than ever. Strategies for cultivating and directing curiosity can significantly influence educational systems and organizational cultures, shaping future generations of thinkers and leaders. Creating curiosity-driven learning environments, where questioning is encouraged and celebrated, fosters critical thinking and adaptability. In organizations, promoting a culture of curiosity can lead to innovative problem-solving as employees feel empowered to challenge assumptions and explore novel solutions. By prioritizing curiosity, individuals and institutions can unlock tremendous potential, paving the way for sustained progress and innovation.

To fully tap into curiosity's potential, it's essential to embrace diverse perspectives and approaches, ensuring a comprehensive understanding of its impact. Including voices from various fields and backgrounds enriches the conversation, revealing new insights and growth opportunities. As curiosity continues to drive technological and societal advancements, it reminds us of the limitless possibilities that arise when we dare to question and explore. By nurturing this intrinsic human trait, we can craft a future defined by discovery, innovation, and a deeper understanding of the world around us.

The Emotional Spectrum of Unexpected Events

Navigating the unexpected is one of life's most intriguing challenges. The dance between surprise and curiosity profoundly influences our journey, often in ways we don't foresee. As we delve into the complex web of emotions, it's captivating to see how surprise can disrupt the ordinary, sparking a chain of emotional reactions that resonate deeply within us. The initial shock of an unforeseen event can feel like a jolt, a brief pause in reality that demands our immediate attention and compels us to rethink our understanding of the world. Though unsettling, this shift acts as a powerful catalyst for growth, urging us to question, adapt, and evolve in response to life's uncertainties. It's in this delicate balance of emotions that the beauty and complexity of the unexpected emerge, encouraging us to welcome the unknown with open hearts and minds.

The emotional landscape of unexpected events is as diverse as those who experience them. From initial shock to the subsequent emotional journey, each person's path through the unexpected is uniquely shaped by factors like past experiences, resilience, and mental processing. These moments of confusion lead to deeper introspection as we seek to comprehend and make sense of what has transpired. The way we mentally assess these events is crucial, influencing not only our immediate reactions but also our long-term capacity for growth and learning. As we navigate these unfamiliar territories, adaptive strategies arise, helping us integrate these experiences into our broader emotional framework. Over time, these surprises can foster significant emotional development, offering new perspectives and insights that deepen our understanding of ourselves and the world. In this exploration, we uncover how the interplay of surprise and curiosity propels innovation, learning, and personal transformation.

Navigating the Initial Shock and Its Emotional Aftermath

When we encounter the unexpected, our minds and emotions embark on a complex journey. The initial shock can feel like a sudden awakening, a disruption that throws off our mental balance. On a neurological level, surprises trigger areas like the amygdala and prefrontal cortex, which manage our immediate emotional reactions and subsequent thoughts. This activation leads to physiological changes, such as increased alertness and a racing heart, as our bodies prepare for potential challenges or opportunities. These reactions are not merely reflexive but are deeply embedded in our evolutionary makeup, serving as essential survival tools that demanded quick adaptation to unforeseen events.

As the initial shock diminishes, a range of emotions, from excitement to anxiety, emerges. This phase involves the interplay between how we interpret events and our emotional responses. Recent studies in affective neuroscience show that our personality and past experiences shape these interpretations, affecting whether we see the unexpected as a challenge or a threat. For example, those comfortable with ambiguity might view surprises as intriguing puzzles, while others might find them unsettling. These differences highlight the importance of self-awareness in understanding our emotional landscapes and navigating the aftermath of unexpected events.

Following the shock, cognitive appraisal becomes crucial, guiding our understanding and emotional control. This process involves assessing the event's significance, its potential impact, and our coping abilities. Advanced psychological models suggest that this appraisal is not straightforward but involves a dynamic interplay of thoughts and emotions that evolve. Engaging in reflective practices, like journaling or mindfulness, can improve our appraisal skills, fostering a deeper understanding of our emotional responses. Such engagement can turn surprises from mere disruptions into opportunities for personal growth and resilience.

Adaptive strategies also play a vital role in processing unexpected events, helping us adjust our expectations and behaviors. These strategies are not innate but can be cultivated through practice. For instance, developing cognitive flexibility—the ability to shift perspectives and embrace new ideas—can enhance our ability to adapt to unforeseen changes. Recent research in neuroplasticity indicates that our brain's adaptability is greater than previously thought, suggesting that with practice, we can rewire our neural pathways to respond more positively to surprises. By adopting a mindset of growth and flexibility, we can transform initial shocks into opportunities for creative problem-solving and innovation.

In the long run, unexpected experiences can lead to significant emotional growth. This growth often involves integrating these experiences into our broader life narrative, enriching our understanding of ourselves and the world. This integration requires introspection and a willingness to embrace vulnerability, acknowledging the discomfort that change often brings. By exploring diverse perspectives and engaging in dialogues that challenge our assumptions, we can expand our emotional repertoire and cultivate deeper empathy for others. As we navigate the unexpected, we enhance our emotional resilience and open ourselves to the beauty and complexity of the human experience. This journey through surprise reveals the transformative potential of facing the unknown with curiosity and courage.

Experiencing an unforeseen event prompts our brain to engage in a complex cognitive appraisal process, crucial in shaping our emotional reactions. This involves a swift assessment of how the situation affects our well-being, using past experiences, existing knowledge, and context. The brain rapidly determines if the event is beneficial, harmful, or neutral, which then influences our subsequent emotional response. This highlights the deep connection between cognition and emotion, as our initial interpretation can significantly alter how we feel and act. Recent neuroscience studies reveal the brain's ability to adapt these appraisal mechanisms, suggesting our emotional responses can be more flexible and context-sensitive than previously thought.

Cognitive appraisal goes beyond mere reaction, exploring how our perceptions shape reality. For example, two people might respond differently to the same unexpected scenario, influenced by their personal histories and mental frameworks. Consider a sudden opportunity for public speaking—one might see it as a chance for growth, feeling excitement, while another might view it as a threat, feeling anxiety. These differences highlight the subjective nature of emotional experience, encouraging appreciation for the diverse ways people navigate the world. Insights from psychology suggest that by recognizing and adjusting our appraisal patterns, we can cultivate more adaptive emotional responses, enhancing our resilience in the face of surprises.

Emerging research in affective neuroscience offers intriguing insights into the brain's flexibility in recalibrating emotional responses through cognitive appraisal. Innovative studies using functional MRI show how individuals can consciously alter their brain's appraisal process, thus modifying their emotional reactions. This illustrates the brain's plasticity and offers practical applications for emotional regulation strategies. Mindfulness practices, for instance, can enhance one's ability to positively reframe unexpected events, fostering a balanced emotional state. By developing these skills, individuals can transform surprising moments into opportunities for personal growth and learning.

The beauty of cognitive appraisal lies in its capacity to foster growth from unexpected events. Humans are not passive recipients of surprises; they possess the remarkable ability to reinterpret and learn from such experiences. This reappraisal process can lead to significant emotional growth, encouraging individuals to reflect on initial reactions and consider alternative perspectives. Embracing this approach allows for a deeper understanding of one's emotional landscape, leading to a more fulfilling life experience. Navigating surprises with intention and awareness transforms potentially disorienting events into catalysts for self-discovery and resilience.

These reflections invite us to consider how we might leverage cognitive appraisal in daily life. Imagine approaching each unexpected event as an opportunity to refine emotional responses and deepen self-understanding. By engaging consciously in this process, we can cultivate a more adaptive mindset, allowing us to face life's uncertainties with grace and curiosity. This intentional practice not only enhances emotional intelligence but also strengthens our connection to the world, empowering us to embrace the full range of human experiences with an open heart and discerning mind.

Human emotions, such as astonishment, are vital adaptive tools that help individuals manage life's complexities. Astonishment acts like a mental alert, quickly redirecting attention and cognitive resources to unexpected events. This rapid adjustment is supported by neural networks that prioritize new stimuli, a process well-documented in cognitive neuroscience. For example, the amygdala and prefrontal cortex are key players in processing surprise: the amygdala identifies novelty, while the prefrontal cortex evaluates its consequences. This sophisticated interaction ensures humans can swiftly respond to unanticipated situations, showcasing the brain's elegant design in promoting adaptability.

Delving into adaptive mechanisms, research highlights how surprise prompts a reexamination of existing mental frameworks. When unexpected events occur, individuals often rethink their beliefs, leading to cognitive flexibility and resilience. This reevaluation can result in cognitive restructuring, where outdated or incorrect frameworks are revised or replaced, encouraging a growth mindset and openness to new experiences. By questioning preconceived ideas, surprise not only enhances adaptability but also drives personal development and psychological growth.

Understanding how people process and adapt to surprise underscores the importance of emotional regulation in dealing with life's uncertainties. Emerging psychological studies emphasize the value of mindfulness and emotional intelligence in managing the turmoil of unexpected events. By cultivating awareness of one's emotional reactions, individuals can practice self-regulation, approaching surprises with calm and clarity. Techniques like cognitive reappraisal and stress-reduction strategies can be crucial in maintaining emotional balance, turning potential upheaval into opportunities for learning and growth.

Adaptability in the face of surprise extends beyond personal growth to societal and cultural dimensions. Communities often display remarkable resilience when faced with unforeseen challenges, drawing on collective resources and shared values. This adaptability is evident in both historical and modern examples where societies have weathered crises through innovation and cooperation. By examining these instances, we gain insight into the social mechanisms that help groups thrive despite adversity, highlighting the role of surprise as a catalyst for progress and transformation.

Reflecting on the broader implications of adaptive responses to surprise, one can consider how these mechanisms can be applied practically. Encouraging curiosity and openness in both personal and professional settings can create environments where surprise is not feared but embraced as a driver of innovation. By fostering a culture that values adaptability, individuals and organizations can navigate life's unpredictability with agility and confidence. As readers contemplate these ideas, they are invited to think about how they can incorporate adaptive strategies into their own lives, turning the unexpected into a source of inspiration and opportunity.

Surprise can remarkably drive long-lasting emotional growth. When people face unexpected events, they often experience a mix of emotions from confusion to fascination. While initially unsettling, this emotional turmoil can foster personal development. Psychological research indicates that dealing with the unknown pushes us to reevaluate our beliefs and expectations, enhancing our adaptability and resilience. This mental adjustment helps individuals gain a more profound understanding of themselves and their environment.

Unexpected experiences have the power to challenge our existing mental frameworks. When encountering surprise, the brain engages in a process known as cognitive appraisal, where it assesses the event's significance and implications. This appraisal involves actively reorganizing mental structures. By incorporating new information, individuals often improve their problem-solving abilities and become more innovative. This mental agility is vital in a fast-paced world, offering a competitive advantage in adapting to unforeseen situations.

Surprise often sparks curiosity and exploration. Faced with the unfamiliar, many feel compelled to seek understanding, transforming initial shock into discovery opportunities. Neuroscience research supports this, showing that dopamine release during surprising events boosts motivation and learning. The brain's reward system, thus activated, spurs individuals to explore the unknown, nurturing a lifelong love for learning and intellectual growth.

Adapting to unexpected events also brings significant social benefits. As people share their experiences and insights, they not only reinforce their personal growth but also contribute to collective knowledge. These shared stories weave a rich tapestry of human experience, offering diverse perspectives and wisdom. Engaging with others who have faced similar surprises provides comfort and inspiration, strengthening emotional resilience and community ties. This communal processing of surprise highlights the connection between emotional growth and social bonds.

Long-term emotional growth from surprise often leads to greater self-awareness and empathy. As individuals reflect on their responses to unexpected events, they gain insights into their emotional triggers and coping strategies. This introspective journey, though sometimes challenging, can enhance emotional intelligence and deepen understanding of others' experiences. Embracing the complexities of surprise equips individuals to handle future uncertainties gracefully, enriching their emotional landscape and fostering a more empathetic society.

Human curiosity and the element of surprise are powerful forces that draw us into the unknown and spark a lively interaction with our environment. When we encounter the unexpected, it jolts our senses and encourages us to rethink what we take for granted. Curiosity acts as a beacon in this interplay, fueling learning and innovation, and turning the uncertain into new discoveries. As we consider the emotions linked to unforeseen events, it's evident that these feelings are vital for our growth and adaptation. They push us to step outside our comfort zones and find delight in exploring the unfamiliar. This ongoing relationship between surprise and curiosity not only shapes our personal paths but also enriches our shared human experience, underscoring the beauty of our collective quest for knowledge. As we continue on this journey, we should reflect on how these emotions, intrinsic to our nature, can inspire us to seek connections and find meaning in a world that is constantly changing. The next chapter will further explore this intricate emotional landscape, inviting us to deepen our understanding of the feelings that define our lives.

Chapter 9

Pride And Accomplishment

As we step into a new phase of understanding human emotions, I find myself drawn to the timeless appeal of self-respect—a feeling both intricate and universal. Imagine a young artist, brush poised, her spirit swelling with the fulfillment of completing her inaugural masterpiece. Her eyes reflect the vivid colors on the canvas, a tribute to her relentless dedication and imaginative vision. This scene captures the dual essence of this emotion: it can elevate us, driving us toward excellence, yet it can also anchor us to our own ego, obscuring the larger world. As we delve into the exploration of self-worth and accomplishment, it becomes evident that these emotions are interwoven with the human experience, shaping our self-perception and societal roles.

Embarking on this journey involves a delicate balance between confidence and humility. At its heart, this emotion is about acknowledging our successes, the realization of our efforts and dreams. However, it also harbors the risk of arrogance, potentially leading us to overrate our value and distance ourselves from others. This chapter will shed light on the dual aspects of self-respect, exploring how it can motivate yet impede self-awareness and growth. By grasping the emotional gratifications linked to our successes, we gain insight into what propels us to endure challenges, pushing the limits of our possibilities.

The cultural and societal dimensions add layers to the narrative of self-worth, showing its deep roots in our interactions and communal identities. Across various societies, its expression shifts, molded by norms and values dictating what is honored and how. This diversity underscores the significant influence of our environments in shaping our emotional landscapes. As we navigate the nuances of self-respect, we unravel not only personal truths but also collective insights into human existence. Through this lens, self-worth transcends emotion, becoming a bridge between personal achievements and our shared human quest for understanding and connection.

The Positive and Negative Sides of Pride

Pride, a complex feeling, holds the power to drive individuals toward remarkable achievements or lead them astray. This dual nature creates a rich tapestry of experiences, capable of either lifting one's journey or undermining it. When harnessed positively, pride serves as a catalyst for personal advancement, pushing individuals beyond their perceived boundaries and fueling the pursuit of excellence. It offers encouragement during times of doubt, fostering the courage to embrace challenges and celebrate successes, regardless of their magnitude. Conversely, this potent emotion can lure individuals into arrogance, obscuring the virtues of humility and self-awareness. The delicate balance between constructive pride and its destructive counterpart reflects the intricate dynamics of the human spirit.

As we delve into pride, its influence on social interactions becomes a captivating aspect. Pride can act as a social adhesive, fostering connections and mutual respect when expressed genuinely. However, it can also create divisions, isolating individuals when it morphs into conceit. Cultural viewpoints further enrich this exploration, revealing diverse interpretations and expressions of pride worldwide. In certain societies, pride is a cherished value, while in others, humility is esteemed, illustrating the intricate ways pride is woven into societal norms and values. Understanding this interplay prompts a deeper reflection on pride's role in our lives and its potential to both elevate and hinder. As we navigate these dimensions, we uncover the beauty and complexity of pride, appreciating its capacity to shape our identities and relationships.

Pride, a complex feeling often viewed with mixed emotions, acts as a significant driver of personal growth. It motivates people to aim for excellence, nurturing ambition and resolve. When channeled positively, pride inspires self-betterment and skill mastery, encouraging individuals to pursue and reach high aspirations. Scientific research highlights how pride can stimulate brain regions responsible for motivation and reward, emphasizing its importance in fostering personal advancement. By acknowledging achievements, people create a reinforcing cycle that promotes successful behaviors. Thus, pride transforms from merely an outcome of success to a trigger that spurs further growth and development.

While pride can lead to impressive accomplishments, it also presents a challenge between advancement and overconfidence. The fine line between healthy pride and arrogance requires self-awareness and humility. When pride eclipses other virtues, it risks devolving into narcissism and social isolation. Social psychology studies stress the necessity of balancing self-esteem with empathy, warning that unchecked pride can cause social tension or disputes. Engaging in self-reflection and welcoming feedback helps maintain this balance, ensuring pride remains a positive influence rather than a disruptive force.

Cultural backgrounds further impact how pride is perceived and expressed, adding complexity to its role in personal development. In some cultures, pride is praised and seen as crucial for success, while in others, it might be mistrusted as vanity or egotism. These cultural differences shape how people internalize and express pride, affecting their growth paths. Recognizing these cultural dimensions deepens our understanding of pride as a catalyst for growth, encouraging individuals to consider how their cultural context shapes their relationship with this feeling.

The connection between pride and personal development is also visible in the realm of achievements. Accomplishments, whether major or minor, act as milestones that boost confidence and reinforce a growth mindset. Pride stemming from genuine success builds resilience, allowing individuals to overcome setbacks and continue striving toward their goals. This resilience is essential, as it turns challenges into opportunities for learning and adaptation. Viewing pride as an evolving process rather than a fixed state enables individuals to leverage its power for a lifelong journey of growth and self-discovery.

To fully utilize pride as a growth catalyst, it's vital to engage in reflective practices that enhance self-awareness. Activities like journaling, meditation, or seeking mentorship can offer insights into how pride influences decisions and actions. By consciously recognizing and celebrating achievements while remaining receptive to criticism and self-improvement, individuals can maintain a healthy balance. This approach not only maximizes pride's potential for fostering growth but also nurtures gratitude and humility. As readers explore the intricate nature of pride, they are encouraged to consider how they might harness this emotion in their own lives, transforming it into a powerful ally on their personal development journey.

Pride is a complex feeling that significantly influences how people interact socially, affecting both self-perception and the perception of others. At its essence, pride can foster a sense of belonging and connection, encouraging deeper engagement in community activities and relationships. When individuals accomplish something significant, the pride they experience often leads to a desire to share their success, seeking admiration and recognition from peers. This exchange not only validates personal successes but also strengthens social bonds, creating a ripple of shared satisfaction and mutual respect.

However, pride carries inherent complexities. It can act as a double-edged sword, where its positive influence on social dynamics can morph into arrogance if not balanced with self-awareness. The line between healthy pride and hubris often depends on the intent and expression. Constructive pride inspires support and motivation within a group, encouraging others to pursue their goals. Conversely, when pride turns into self-glorification, it can foster envy and resentment, creating barriers to genuine connections. This delicate balance highlights the importance of mindfulness in expressing pride, ensuring it uplifts rather than alienates.

Cultural contexts add further depth to pride's impact on social interactions. In some cultures, pride is celebrated as a testament to individual merit and success, while in others, it is viewed cautiously as a potential disruptor of harmony and humility. These cultural nuances shape the expression and perception of pride, influencing social hierarchies and expectations. For instance, in collectivist societies, achievements are often attributed to the group, and pride is shared communally, reinforcing group cohesion. In more individualistic cultures, personal accomplishments are emphasized, making pride a marker of personal triumph and reflecting broader cultural values of individualism and self-reliance.

Current research explores the neurological basis of pride and its social effects, providing insights into how this emotion can be harnessed positively. Studies indicate that pride activates brain regions associated with reward processing and social cognition, underscoring its role in motivating cooperative behavior and fostering social cohesion. This knowledge opens opportunities for leveraging pride in areas such as team dynamics and leadership, where recognizing and celebrating collective achievements can boost group performance and morale. By understanding the neural and psychological mechanisms of pride, individuals and organizations can cultivate environments where pride serves as a positive force for social interaction and achievement.

To navigate the intricate landscape of pride within social contexts, individuals might consider introspective practices that encourage self-reflection and empathy. Questions like, "Am I celebrating my success in a way that inspires others?" or "How does my expression of pride affect those around me?" can guide individuals toward a more balanced expression of pride. Encouraging feedback from peers and fostering open dialogues about accomplishments can also help maintain a healthy social atmosphere where pride is a catalyst for growth rather than a source of division. Through mindful awareness and cultural sensitivity, pride can be a powerful tool for strengthening social ties and fostering a supportive community.

Understanding the Fine Line Between Pride and Arrogance

Pride is a complex feeling that both inspires admiration and invites scrutiny. It can be a catalyst for self-improvement and achievement, yet it often walks a thin line with arrogance. How individuals manage this delicate balance can lead to either transformation or turmoil. In personal development, pride can drive a person toward excellence, fostering self-respect and confidence. It can ignite ambition, pushing one to overcome obstacles and achieve new milestones. However, when unchecked, this same pride can morph into arrogance, obscuring one's awareness of personal limits and the contributions of others.

The divergence between pride and arrogance often hinges on self-awareness versus reality. Pride, rooted in genuine successes, nurtures healthy self-esteem by recognizing effort and perseverance, encouraging reflection and goal-setting. Arrogance, on the other hand, arises when pride is exaggerated and disconnected from actual accomplishments, fostering an unfounded sense of superiority. This can estrange individuals from peers, damaging relationships and stifling opportunities for collaboration and growth. Understanding this contrast requires an appreciation of humility and self-awareness as antidotes to excessive pride.

Culturally, pride is interpreted differently, influencing its expression and perception. In some cultures, pride is lauded as a mark of individual and societal success, while in others, humility is prized, and overt displays of pride are discouraged. These cultural variations shape social interactions, defining the acceptable expressions of pride and the boundary between pride and arrogance. Contemporary research emphasizes the importance of cultural understanding in navigating these differences, highlighting how diverse perspectives can enhance empathy and reduce conflict.

Neuroscientific studies offer intriguing insights into how pride and arrogance are processed in the brain. Neural pathways related to reward and social judgment are pivotal in these emotions. Pride stimulates areas associated with reward processing, reinforcing behaviors and achievements deemed valuable. In contrast, arrogance may engage different neural circuits, potentially linked to social dominance and self-focused thinking. These findings reveal that pride and arrogance are not just psychological states but have biological roots, opening up promising avenues for future research in emotional intelligence and management.

To skillfully manage the interplay between pride and arrogance, individuals can cultivate self-reflection and mindfulness. Practicing gratitude and acknowledging others' contributions can ground pride in humility. By setting realistic goals and celebrating successes while maintaining perspective, one can achieve a healthy balance. Open dialogue and feedback from peers can offer valuable insights, helping to fine-tune one's sense of pride. As we ponder the subtle dance of these emotions, readers are encouraged to reflect on their own experiences with pride, considering how they can harness its positive aspects while curbing the risks of arrogance.

Cultural viewpoints significantly influence our understanding of pride, affecting how it is both expressed and perceived globally. In some societies, pride is considered a virtue, equated with self-respect and dignity, while in others it may be seen as a flaw linked to vanity or arrogance. These contrasting interpretations highlight the complex nature of pride, where its expression is often shaped by societal norms and values. For example, in collectivist cultures, pride might emphasize communal achievements and social harmony. In contrast, individualistic societies might focus on personal success and self-assertion, viewing pride as a driving force for individual accomplishment. These cultural differences dictate not only how pride is manifested but also how it is judged, illustrating the intricate interaction between emotion and cultural context.

To understand the cultural variability of pride, it is essential to examine the underlying values that shape these perspectives. For instance, the Japanese concept of "hansei" promotes reflection and humility, even in success, encouraging modesty and continuous improvement. Meanwhile, in Western cultures, pride might be celebrated openly, seen as a crucial component of self-esteem and personal motivation. This contrast shows how cultural values imbue pride with different meanings and implications, guiding individuals in navigating their emotions within their cultural framework. These insights are vital for fostering cross-cultural empathy and understanding, revealing the deeply embedded norms that shape emotional experiences.

Recent cross-cultural psychology studies provide innovative insights into pride's function in different cultural settings. Researchers have identified that pride can act as both a social adhesive and a source of tension, depending on its alignment with cultural expectations. In societies that prioritize conformity and social order, excessive pride might disrupt social cohesion, leading to sanctions or ostracism. Conversely, cultures that value innovation and assertiveness may see pride as a catalyst for progress and leadership. These findings suggest that while pride is a universal emotion, it is not universally expressed or valued, emphasizing the importance of context in emotional expression. This nuanced understanding can help individuals and organizations navigate intercultural interactions more effectively, promoting a more inclusive and respectful global community.

The impact of cultural perspectives on pride also extends to social identity and belonging. Pride can strengthen group identity and solidarity, as seen in national pride or pride in one's heritage. Such collective pride can be a powerful motivator, fostering belonging and shared purpose. However, it can also lead to exclusionary practices if not balanced with inclusivity and openness. The balance between individual and collective pride requires a keen awareness of the cultural dynamics at play. By examining pride through this lens, we gain a deeper appreciation of its role in personal and communal narratives, recognizing its potential to unite or divide.

Imagining practical scenarios where cultural perspectives on pride are crucial can be enlightening. Consider a multinational team working on a project with members from diverse cultural backgrounds. Understanding each member's perception of pride can enhance team dynamics, prevent misunderstandings, and foster cooperation. Encouraging open dialogue about cultural expectations and emotional expressions can lead to harmonious collaboration, where pride is harnessed as a positive force for collective achievement. Such strategies not only improve interpersonal relations but also pave the way for more innovative and successful outcomes, as team members are empowered to contribute their unique strengths and perspectives. Through this approach, pride transcends traditional boundaries, becoming a tool for global connection and growth.

The Emotional Rewards of Achievement

The human pursuit of accomplishment is a captivating aspect of our lives, interwoven with emotions that range from joy to profound transformation. Whether celebrating minor victories or significant achievements, the emotional rewards of success are deeply impactful. This exploration delves into the essence of achievement and reveals the psychological patterns that emerge with each success. At the heart of accomplishment lies a blend of satisfaction, dignity, and self-respect, each enriching our emotional experiences. This journey is as much about reaching goals as it is about the emotional richness of striving and overcoming challenges.

As we navigate this complex terrain, we'll explore the neurochemical reactions that success triggers and how they influence our satisfaction. The cultural backdrop adds complexity, shaping how different societies perceive and celebrate success. Overcoming adversity brings a deep sense of fulfillment, bolstering resilience and personal growth. Social acknowledgment further enhances our emotional satisfaction by validating our accomplishments. Together, these elements create a narrative that highlights the diverse rewards of success, encouraging us to reflect on what truly motivates us to excel and how these emotional experiences enrich our lives.

The Neurochemical Pathways of Satisfaction

The intricate tapestry of human emotion intertwines with neurochemistry, where each element shapes the feelings of fulfillment and joy accompanying success. Upon achieving a goal, the brain orchestrates a ballet of chemical reactions, with dopamine taking center stage. This neurotransmitter, closely linked to pleasure and reward, spikes in response to accomplishment, reinforcing the actions that drive success. Yet, this chemical dance involves more than just dopamine. Endorphins, which soothe stress and induce euphoria, and serotonin, known for stabilizing mood, collectively foster a sense of satisfaction. This complex interaction provides a biological explanation for the happiness derived from achievement, emphasizing the brain's sophisticated reward systems.

The neurochemical response to success is not one-size-fits-all but varies greatly due to individual differences and situational contexts. Consider a musician finishing a challenging piece or a scientist making a groundbreaking discovery. Both scenarios activate the brain's reward circuits, yet the emotional response's intensity and nature can differ based on personal values, past experiences, and genetic factors. This variability highlights the importance of personalized paths to satisfaction, reminding us that the pursuit of success is as unique as the individuals involved. Understanding these diverse neurochemical responses can help individuals identify what genuinely satisfies them, encouraging a departure from societal norms in favor of personal definitions of success.

Cultural views on achievement add another layer to the neurochemical experience. In some societies, personal accomplishments hold high value, and the associated rewards are deeply personal. In others, collective success is celebrated, with satisfaction stemming from contributing to the group's achievements. This cultural lens shapes the pathways of satisfaction by influencing what is deemed praiseworthy and how individuals perceive their accomplishments. Recognizing these cultural dimensions allows for a deeper appreciation of the multifaceted nature of achievement and the various sources of emotional reward it creates. The intersection of culture and neurochemistry invites reflection on how societal values shape personal experiences of fulfillment.

Emerging research indicates that the anticipation of success can be as motivating as the accomplishment itself. The brain, in its pursuit of rewards, releases dopamine not only upon achieving goals but also in anticipation of reaching them. This forward-looking release of neurotransmitters sustains motivation, keeping individuals engaged in their pursuits. By setting achievable milestones and enjoying the journey, people can harness this anticipatory pleasure to maintain momentum and find satisfaction in the process, not just the end result. This insight encourages a shift from outcome-focused thinking to a process-oriented approach, enriching the striving experience.

Exploring the science of satisfaction extends beyond biochemical processes, prompting broader reflections on success and the lengths we go to achieve it. Questions arise about whether our pursuits align with what genuinely triggers our neurochemical rewards or if they are influenced by external pressures and expectations. By fostering self-awareness and encouraging introspection, individuals can gain a deeper understanding of what truly satisfies them, leading to more authentic and fulfilling experiences of achievement. This exploration illuminates the complexity of human emotion and empowers individuals to navigate their emotional landscapes with greater insight and purpose.

Cultural environments deeply influence how we perceive success and our resulting feelings of satisfaction and pride. Across the globe, what one culture deems an achievement can bear a different significance elsewhere. In societies that value individualism, success often revolves around personal milestones such as career progress or academic achievements. Meanwhile, in collectivist cultures, an individual's contributions to family or community might define success, transforming personal accomplishments into shared triumphs. Recognizing these cultural differences enhances our appreciation for why certain achievements resonate more with individuals depending on their cultural heritage. This perspective adds complexity to the joy of accomplishment, making it not just a solitary journey but a shared experience.

The interaction between cultural norms and personal aspirations also influences the brain's chemistry related to satisfaction. Achievements that align with cultural values can lead to more significant releases of dopamine and serotonin, neurotransmitters linked to pleasure and well-being. This chemical response extends beyond personal satisfaction, amplified by social approval, boosting the emotional high associated with success. Research shows that goals endorsed by one's culture, when met, not only bring personal joy but also strengthen social bonds, fostering a sense of belonging to one's cultural community. This alignment between cultural expectations and personal success creates a powerful cycle that motivates and enhances well-being.

Cultural perspectives on success highlight the need to acknowledge diverse paths to fulfillment. Cross-cultural research has uncovered various success definitions, from financial stability and career status to spiritual growth and family harmony. These differing views suggest that success is not a singular pursuit but a range shaped by cultural background and social upbringing. By embracing these varied perspectives, people can develop a more inclusive understanding of success, promoting an environment where different stories of achievement coexist and enrich each other. This inclusive approach fosters empathy and appreciation for the diverse ways individuals find meaning in their successes.

Through cultural lenses, the role of social recognition stands out as a crucial element in the emotional rewards of success. Recognition from peers, family, and society not only affirms individual efforts but also reinforces one's place within the cultural fabric. This acknowledgment can significantly enhance emotional satisfaction, turning personal successes into expressions of cultural identity and pride. However, this dynamic can also present challenges, as cultural standards of success may sometimes overshadow personal goals. By balancing cultural expectations with individual values, people can navigate the intricate relationship between societal approval and personal satisfaction, leading to a more genuine sense of pride.

Reflecting on cultural influences encourages us to reconsider how we define success in ways that respect both personal goals and collective values. By questioning traditional success metrics and embracing diverse achievements, we can foster a more inclusive narrative that honors various paths to fulfillment. This approach not only broadens our understanding of pride and achievement but also empowers individuals to carve their unique paths, free from the constraints of a single cultural narrative. Embracing this wider perspective opens new opportunities for emotional fulfillment, rooted in a deeper appreciation for the rich diversity of human experience.

Navigating life's challenges is a significant part of human growth, offering psychological rewards that go well beyond immediate success. At its essence, overcoming obstacles is crucial in strengthening one's belief in personal ability, known as self-efficacy. This belief is vital in framing future ambitions. When individuals conquer difficult challenges, their self-efficacy is enhanced, leading to greater resilience and adaptability to future setbacks. This psychological strength transcends personal benefits, influencing how people contribute to their communities and societies.

Research in psychology highlights the advantages of overcoming adversity, particularly through studies on the brain's response to success. Achieving difficult goals significantly activates neural pathways related to reward and satisfaction, mainly through the neurotransmitter dopamine. This chemical response not only boosts mood but also reinforces learning and motivation, prompting individuals to seek further challenges. These findings suggest that the human brain is naturally inclined to thrive on surmounting difficulties, making challenge-seeking essential for personal development and growth.

Cultural stories also significantly shape how people perceive the benefits of overcoming obstacles. Across different societies, a wealth of narratives and traditions celebrate individuals who have triumphed over adversity. These stories serve as potent motivators, offering examples of perseverance and success that inspire others to tackle their own challenges. By exploring these cultural dimensions, we gain insight into how societal values and beliefs mold individual motivation and collective attitudes toward achievement and confidence.

Besides cognitive and cultural impacts, overcoming challenges also enhances emotional well-being. Successfully dealing with difficulties can lead to a deep sense of fulfillment and self-worth, as individuals recognize their capabilities and potential. This realization often shifts perspectives, allowing past challenges to become integral parts of one's life story, enriching personal understanding. This growth fosters a deeper appreciation of one's emotional world, promoting contentment and peace.

In practical terms, the benefits of overcoming challenges can be integrated into daily life through deliberate strategies. Setting realistic goals, nurturing a growth mindset, and viewing failure as a learning opportunity can all harness the psychological advantages of growth through challenge. By actively engaging with challenges and reflecting on their lessons, individuals can foster continuous improvement and self-discovery. This approach not only boosts personal well-being but also cultivates a more resilient, dynamic approach to life's complexities.

Understanding the significant influence of social recognition on emotional well-being involves examining the complex relationship between individual accomplishments and communal appreciation. Whether celebrated in a corporate setting or quietly acknowledged among friends, each recognition serves as a vital affirmation of effort. This acknowledgment is more than just a decorative aspect of success; it's an essential element intertwined with our emotional connections and sense of belonging. When society applauds an individual's achievements, it validates their efforts beyond personal satisfaction, offering an emotional reward that resonates deeply.

Recent neuroscience research sheds light on how our brains react to social recognition, revealing intriguing insights into neural pathways. The release of neurotransmitters like dopamine during moments of acknowledgment acts as a biochemical boost, enhancing self-esteem and instilling a sense of purpose. This social aspect of recognition bridges the gap between personal success and collective approval, highlighting community's role in personal fulfillment. The brain's reward system, when activated, underscores the importance of external validation, showing that acknowledgment is as crucial as the achievement itself.

Cultural context also shapes how social recognition is perceived and its impact. In individualistic societies, personal success is often celebrated as a testament to self-reliance and ambition, intensifying its emotional significance. In contrast, collectivist cultures view accomplishments through the lens of communal benefit, emphasizing the individual's role within the community. These cultural differences influence how recognition is valued, suggesting that the emotional satisfaction from acknowledgment is not universal but deeply rooted in cultural narratives and expectations. Exploring these variations encourages a broader perspective on tailoring social recognition to enhance emotional well-being across diverse settings.

The psychological implications of social recognition are equally intriguing. Recognition affirms one's identity and capabilities, fostering self-worth and motivation. This validation can increase resilience, encouraging individuals to face new challenges with renewed energy and confidence. The anticipation of acknowledgment can drive individuals to excel, creating a cycle of achievement and recognition that fuels personal growth. In this dynamic interplay of effort and reward, social recognition acts as a catalyst for ongoing development and emotional fulfillment.

Consider a situation where an individual's efforts go unnoticed—what would be the emotional impact? Reflecting on this can help us appreciate the nuanced role that social acknowledgment plays in our emotional lives. By recognizing the multifaceted nature of social recognition, we can explore practical strategies to create environments that support this vital aspect of emotional well-being. Whether through celebrating individual and collective achievements or fostering a culture of appreciation, the path to emotional fulfillment is enriched by shared experiences of recognition.

The Social and Cultural Dimensions of Pride

Pride intricately threads through the core of our societies, shaping identities and influencing interactions. This emotion, often a double-edged sword, occupies a unique spot in our shared psyche. It propels us toward remarkable accomplishments and nurtures a sense of community, yet it also sows seeds of discord and division. Delving into the social and cultural facets of pride, we uncover how it transcends the personal and molds entire communities. It's a delicate dance between self-expression and collective identity, where pride serves as both a mirror and a guide, reflecting our essence and guiding us toward our aspirations.

The fascination with pride stems from its power to link individual success to wider cultural narratives. From historical views that show how various societies have either praised or condemned pride, to its influence on social structures and group dynamics, this emotion operates on many levels. Pride acts as a catalyst for cultural identity and nationalism, sparking fervor that can either unite or divide. As globalization reshapes our world, pride evolves, weaving into new cultural expressions and challenges. This complex interaction between pride and society prompts us to reflect on our shared human journey, encouraging us to recognize how pride shapes not only individuals but entire civilizations.

Pride, a complex emotion, is intricately woven into the tapestry of human history, manifesting in diverse ways across cultures and eras. This sentiment has been both exalted and criticized, with its expression evolving in line with societal values and historical contexts. In ancient Greece, pride was often associated with "hubris," an excessive self-confidence leading to one's downfall. Conversely, early Roman society esteemed "dignitas" and "honor," viewing pride in one's accomplishments as essential for social status and leadership. These contrasts demonstrate how pride's perception is deeply rooted in a society's core beliefs and norms.

Exploring pride through Eastern cultural perspectives reveals a different narrative. Confucian philosophy regarded pride as an obstacle to humility and harmony, virtues held in high regard. Many Asian societies historically prioritized collective well-being over individual success, often viewing pride as potentially disruptive. However, this was not a uniform perspective. In Japan, the concept of "bushido" represented a form of pride tied to the samurai's code of honor, where personal integrity and loyalty were sources of profound personal and communal pride. This variety within a single cultural context underscores pride's complex role in shaping both personal identity and communal values.

Among indigenous cultures, pride frequently intertwines with spiritual and community life. Within Native American tribes, pride was linked to one's contributions to the tribe and respect for ancestral traditions. Here, pride centered less on individual accolades and more on fulfilling one's role within the community, balancing personal ambition with collective responsibility. These perspectives challenge modern interpretations of pride, offering a nuanced understanding that balances self-regard with communal harmony.

As globalization continues to interlace cultures, historical perspectives on pride highlight the challenges and opportunities of this interconnected era. The blend of diverse cultural norms creates a multifaceted landscape where pride is both a personal sentiment and a shared cultural expression. This synthesis necessitates a reevaluation of traditional values, prompting the question: Can pride serve as a unifying force in a global society that respects and embraces cultural diversity? The answer lies in our ability to navigate these historical contexts, understanding pride not just as an individual emotion but as a collective experience shaped by time and place.

Through these historical lenses, we can appreciate the intricate interplay between pride and culture—a dance that continues to evolve. By exploring these varied narratives, readers can begin to question and reflect on their own perceptions of pride. What lessons can be drawn from these historical perspectives to inform our understanding today? How might acknowledging the rich tapestry of pride across cultures enhance our empathy and appreciation for its complexity in modern society? Embracing this diversity not only offers insight but also fosters a deeper connection to the shared human experience of pride.

Pride, a complex feeling, intricately threads through social hierarchies and influences group dynamics. Historically, it has been both a catalyst for motivation and a source of division within communities. This emotion drives individuals to achieve and maintain status within their group, fostering a sense of belonging and self-worth. When peers recognize one's successes, it can instill a profound sense of self-respect, reinforcing social bonds and encouraging cooperative behavior. This dynamic extends beyond individuals to groups, where collective dignity can enhance cohesion and amplify group identity.

Within social hierarchies, pride requires careful balance. It can fuel ambition and drive individuals to excel, yet excessive self-confidence can lead to arrogance, disrupting group harmony. This dual nature is evident in workplaces, where individuals proud of their work may inspire others and boost team performance. However, when self-respect turns into hubris, it can create rifts and foster competition that undermines collaboration. Modern organizational psychology explores these nuances, emphasizing the need to cultivate a healthy sense of dignity that promotes mutual respect and supports collective goals.

Culturally, pride's role varies widely. In some societies, it is celebrated as a virtue, a testament to personal and communal success. In others, it is viewed with caution, linked to ego and potential downfall. These cultural perspectives shape how self-confidence manifests within social hierarchies and affects group interaction. For instance, collectivist cultures may prioritize group dignity over individual self-respect, valuing achievements that benefit the community. This cultural lens shapes expectations and behaviors within social structures, influencing how self-respect is perceived and expressed.

In today's interconnected world, pride intersects with globalization, prompting a reevaluation of its role in social hierarchies. As cultures blend and influence one another, traditional constructs of dignity are challenged and reshaped. This evolution presents an opportunity to redefine pride in a way that transcends cultural boundaries, fostering a global sense of accomplishment that is inclusive and diverse. Appreciating and incorporating diverse expressions of dignity can enrich group dynamics, enabling individuals and communities to navigate the complexities of a globalized world with empathy and understanding.

To harness pride's positive potential, individuals and groups should cultivate environments that encourage healthy expressions of this emotion. This involves recognizing and celebrating achievements without tipping into arrogance, promoting a culture of respect and mutual support. Encouraging open dialogue about self-respect in social settings can lead to a deeper understanding of its impact, allowing individuals to navigate their emotional landscapes with greater awareness. By embracing the complexity of pride, readers can apply these insights to enhance their social interactions, contributing to a more harmonious and connected community.

Pride significantly influences cultural identity by acting as a unifying force and a distinguishing factor among different communities. This emotion, when intertwined with cultural stories, weaves a rich tapestry that connects individuals to a shared heritage, nurturing a collective sense of belonging. Cultural pride is evident in the rituals, traditions, and symbols upheld by communities, serving as a testament to their historical journey and unique identity. For example, festivals honoring national heroes or cultural milestones often evoke a profound sense of self-respect, strengthening communal bonds and revitalizing cultural consciousness.

In the realm of nationalism, pride plays a crucial role in shaping and asserting a nation's identity on the world stage. National pride can motivate citizens to contribute to their country's advancement and uphold its values and traditions. Yet, it's important to recognize that nationalism, driven by pride, can have dual outcomes. While it can unite individuals under a common cause and inspire positive change, it may also lead to exclusionary practices and conflict if not balanced with openness and inclusivity. The challenge lies in fostering a form of nationalism that celebrates diversity within unity, encouraging coexistence and mutual respect.

In an increasingly interconnected world, the relationship between pride and cultural identity grows more complex. As societies become more intertwined, individuals often navigate multiple cultural affiliations. Pride in one's cultural roots can offer stability and self-awareness in this dynamic environment, providing a sense of identity amid rapid change. However, globalization also prompts cultures to adapt and evolve, leading to hybrid identities that reflect a blend of traditional and modern influences. This evolution raises intriguing questions about the future of cultural pride: How can communities maintain their uniqueness while embracing global interconnectedness? And what role does self-respect play in this delicate balancing act?

Advanced insights into the relationship between pride and cultural identity reveal emerging trends, such as the rise of digital platforms that amplify voices of cultural expression. Social media and other online spaces have become arenas where cultural narratives are continually constructed and contested. These platforms enable individuals to showcase their heritage, fostering a global dialogue on identity and belonging. However, they also pose challenges, as the digital amplification of cultural pride can sometimes lead to polarization or cultural appropriation. Navigating these complexities requires a nuanced understanding of how self-respect operates within both personal and collective identities.

To harness the positive aspects of pride as a catalyst for cultural identity, it's crucial to create an environment that encourages dialogue and empathy. Practical steps include promoting intercultural exchanges, supporting education that highlights diverse histories and achievements, and fostering spaces where individuals can express their self-respect in ways that enrich the broader community. By doing so, pride becomes not only a reflection of past accomplishments but also a dynamic force that shapes a more inclusive and harmonious future. As readers consider these ideas, they might reflect on how pride manifests in their own cultural contexts and what proactive measures can be taken to ensure it contributes to unity rather than division.

In today's fast-paced global environment, personal and communal pride emerges in diverse and intricate forms, reflecting both collective dreams and individual successes. This complex tapestry of interconnected communities showcases pride as a bonding element, promoting a sense of belonging and identity that transcends borders. As cultural exchanges increase, pride evolves, testing old boundaries while sparking debates on authenticity and cultural appropriation. The global stage offers a unique setting where pride is reinvented, often merging various traditions into innovative, hybrid forms that both celebrate diversity and challenge cultural preservation.

Consider globally celebrated cultural festivals like Diwali or Oktoberfest. Originally limited to their regions, these events now draw international audiences, broadening the reach of their cultural confidence. While these festivals raise awareness and appreciation, they also risk commercialization, where profound meanings might be overshadowed by business interests. This duality highlights a critical tension within globalization: the wish to share and celebrate cultural dignity globally can sometimes dilute its essence. This invites reflection on the boundary between appreciation and exploitation, encouraging introspection and conversation about maintaining cultural authenticity.

As societies become more connected, pride significantly shapes national identities, often serving as a rallying cry for political movements and social change. The global platform amplifies voices, enabling movements centered on national dignity to gain momentum beyond their borders. This is evident in the rise of digital activism, where campaigns are launched to foster cultural confidence, challenge stereotypes, and resist cultural uniformity. These movements underscore pride's evolving role as both a personal and collective emotion, one that transcends geographical limits and seeks to redefine identity in a global context.

The intersection of pride and globalization also raises important questions about the future of cultural identity in a rapidly changing world. As individuals navigate this complex landscape, confidence becomes a way to assert identity amid a sea of influences. This dynamic encourages us to consider how pride can serve as a foundation for intercultural dialogue, fostering mutual respect and understanding. By embracing the pluralistic nature of modern society, individuals and communities can use pride as a catalyst for building bridges rather than walls, celebrating differences while finding common ground.

In navigating these complexities, individuals are called to reflect on their experiences of dignity within the global tapestry. How does one maintain a sense of identity while participating in a global culture? What steps can be taken to ensure pride remains empowering rather than divisive? These questions invite readers to engage critically with their emotions and the broader societal currents that shape them. By doing so, they can gain a deeper appreciation for the nuanced role of pride in a globalized world, finding ways to honor their heritage while embracing the shared human experience that globalization offers.

Pride and accomplishment together form a rich tapestry of human emotion, where the light of success meets the shadow of arrogance. In our exploration, we've uncovered how pride, typically lauded for enhancing self-esteem and driving achievements, can also spiral into isolation and hubris if left unchecked. This duality serves as a poignant reminder of the delicate balance needed to nurture self-worth without sinking into self-absorption. Meanwhile, the satisfaction of accomplishment offers profound motivation, spotlighting our universal yearning for recognition and progress. The social and cultural contexts further deepen our comprehension, illustrating how community norms and values shape our experiences, steering us in ways that can unite or divide. As we ponder these insights, the call is to embrace our emotional landscape with mindfulness and empathy. This journey through pride encourages a reflective look at how we celebrate victories and learn from setbacks, setting the stage for ongoing exploration of the intricate emotions that make us human.

Chapter 10

Empathy And Compassion

Picture yourself by the shore of a limitless sea, where each wave whispers tales of human connection as it kisses the sand. This is how I, Sofía, envision empathy—a dynamic, unending force weaving human hearts together in delicate yet profound ways. In my journey through the landscape of emotions, empathy stands out as a beacon, illuminating the intricate interplay of understanding and emotion. It serves as a conduit for one soul to resonate with another, transforming observation into shared experience. As we delve into this chapter, we embark on a quest to explore the many facets of empathy and kindness, discovering how these feelings weave the social fabric that unites communities and nurtures genuine human interaction.

Empathy and kindness are not mere abstractions; they are deeply etched into the brain's architecture, shaping our thoughts, behaviors, and relationships. Our exploration begins with the brain's pathways that form the unseen threads connecting us in moments of both joy and sorrow. The science of empathy is not only captivating but essential, as it underpins the core of our social exchanges. From the synchronized firing of neurons to the nuances of body language and speech, empathy is a mental symphony, a testament to the complexity of human nature.

As we venture further, kindness emerges as a profound extension of empathy, showcasing emotional awareness in its most elevated form. Through empathy, we grasp others' emotions; through kindness, we act on that understanding, building connections that are the hallmark of our species. This chapter invites you to discover how empathy and kindness intertwine, forming the foundation of the social bonds that sustain us. Together, we will uncover how these feelings inspire us to bridge divides, offer comfort, and stand united. In this exploration, may you gain a deeper appreciation for the quiet strength and enduring beauty of empathy and kindness, the twin pillars supporting the human experience.

Picture yourself in a bustling room, where a gentle wave of emotion sweeps through the crowd. A person shares a heartfelt story, stirring deep emotions. You observe how expressions soften, eyes glisten, and people lean in, captivated by a shared moment of connection. This experience, often overlooked, is driven by the intricate workings of empathy. At the heart of this lies a fascinating interplay between our biology and emotions. Empathy is not merely a passive reflection but an active, complex process that begins in the depths of our minds. Neurons fire in patterns that mirror others' emotions, creating a bridge that allows us to genuinely feel alongside them. This neural symphony is the essence of our ability to connect, comprehend, and partake in the human experience.

As we delve deeper, the layers of empathy unravel before us. We will uncover the neural pathways that support this emotional bond, highlighting the role of mirror neurons—those extraordinary cells that enable us to echo the feelings of others as if they were our own. The emotional and cognitive pathways of empathy weave a rich tapestry, demonstrating how we perceive and process the emotions of those around us. Beyond synapses and circuits, the development of these empathetic abilities is shaped by the intricate interplay of our genetic makeup and surroundings. Our exploration aims not just to inform but to engage with the profound beauty and complexity of empathy, inviting you to appreciate how it shapes our social fabric and enriches our emotional lives.

Neural Mechanisms Underlying Empathy

Exploring the brain's intricate architecture reveals the fascinating systems that enable empathy. Central to this complex network is the insula, a critical area involved in processing emotions and self-awareness. The anterior insula, notably, activates when people see others experiencing emotions, allowing them to connect with those feelings. This connection goes beyond a simple reflection, fostering an active engagement that internalizes external emotional states. Together with the anterior cingulate cortex, these regions create a powerful partnership that orchestrates the emotional experience of empathy, letting us feel others' emotions as our own.

The prefrontal cortex further enhances the brain's empathetic abilities, acting as a sophisticated control hub for advanced thinking and emotional regulation. It helps distinguish between our own emotions and those of others, a key process for maintaining emotional boundaries while offering empathic support. Recent studies indicate that the dorsomedial prefrontal cortex excels at understanding others' intentions, adding a cognitive layer to the emotional experience. This cognitive empathy allows individuals to not only feel what others feel but also understand the context and motives behind those emotions.

Beyond individual brain regions, the connections between them establish an empathy network essential for understanding others deeply. This network is supported by the default mode network, which plays a role in introspection and social cognition. Engaging this network allows the mind to imagine being in another's situation, crucial for developing compassion and navigating complex social interactions. The strength and efficiency of these connections vary among individuals, influencing how empathy is experienced and expressed.

The discovery of mirror neurons has significantly enhanced our understanding of empathetic responses. Located in the motor cortex, these neurons activate both when an individual performs an action and when they observe someone else performing it. This mirroring provides a neurological basis for shared experiences, indicating that empathy involves not just emotional or cognitive processes but also a physical embodiment of others' actions. The brain rehearses observed activities, fostering a deeper connection through shared neural patterns, with implications for understanding disorders like autism, where empathy is impaired, offering potential therapeutic pathways.

Genetic and environmental factors intricately influence the development of empathy throughout life. Twin studies highlight a heritable aspect of empathy, suggesting that certain genetic markers may predispose individuals to be more empathetic. However, the environment plays an equally crucial role.

Early childhood experiences, cultural background, and societal norms all shape how empathy is expressed and perceived. Advances in epigenetics show that while genes provide a blueprint, life experiences can alter genetic expressions, enhancing or reducing empathetic capacities. This interplay between genetic and environmental influences highlights the complexity of empathy, urging us to consider both biological foundations and the social contexts that shape our empathetic nature.

The Role of Mirror Neurons in Empathetic Response

The complexity of understanding others' emotions is intriguingly linked to mirror neurons, specialized brain cells crucial for empathy. These neurons light up not just when we act, but also when we observe someone else doing the same, forging a neural connection between observer and observed. This mirroring is key to empathy, letting us experience a reflection of others' feelings. Located mainly in the premotor cortex and inferior parietal lobule, the mirror neuron system enables a shared, immediate emotional experience, grounding empathy in our brain beyond mere thought.

Recent research reveals that mirror neurons go beyond recognizing actions; they also process emotional signals. Witnessing joy or sadness on someone's face can spark similar feelings in us, thanks to these neurons. This shows empathy is more than a logical process; it's rooted in our brain structure. Such discoveries have broad implications, from improving therapy to enhancing communication, by deepening our emotional connections.

New insights highlight variations in mirror neuron activity, influenced by social environment, personal history, and culture. Some people naturally have heightened responses, making them more empathetic, while others might have less, shaped by different social influences. Recognizing this variability helps us understand empathy as both inherent and developed. By acknowledging these differences, we appreciate the various ways people emotionally connect and the potential to nurture empathy through conscious practice.

Thought-provoking questions emerge about enhancing our mirror neuron systems. Can deliberate practice boost empathy? Techniques like mindfulness and empathy training are being explored for their potential to strengthen these neurons, suggesting empathy is a skill we can hone. This perspective opens new paths for personal growth and societal harmony, urging us to build a world of greater understanding.

To apply this knowledge, individuals can engage in activities that heighten awareness of others' emotions, such as role-playing or perspective-taking. By intentionally stepping into others' situations, we can activate and reinforce our mirror neuron pathways, deepening empathetic insight. This practice not only enriches personal relationships but also fosters a more empathetic society, equipping individuals to navigate human interactions with compassion and wisdom.

Emotional and Cognitive Pathways of Empathy

Empathy intricately weaves emotional and cognitive threads, shaping how we connect and understand others. On the emotional front, empathy emerges from our inherent ability to resonate with others' feelings, fostering deep personal connections. This connection is active, inviting us to engage with another's emotional state and often evoking a powerful response within ourselves. Such shared emotional experiences are essential for building bonds, as they cultivate unity and compassion that transcend individual differences. Recent research emphasizes that emotional resonance plays a crucial role in strengthening social ties, laying the groundwork for mutual support and understanding.

Cognitively, empathy entails stepping into another's perspective, striving to grasp their viewpoint and circumstances. This aspect demands mental agility and a developed theory of mind, allowing us to predict and interpret others' thoughts and intentions. Cognitive empathy extends beyond understanding emotions; it involves anticipating reactions and responding appropriately. This foresight is vital in navigating intricate social contexts, where a nuanced grasp can avert conflicts and foster positive interactions. In professional realms like negotiation or counseling, cognitive empathy becomes a valuable asset, enabling sensitive and insightful issue resolution.

The dynamic interaction of emotional and cognitive empathy enriches each aspect. Emotional pathways offer immediate connections, while cognitive pathways provide a deeper understanding framework. Together, they form a comprehensive empathetic response, enabling meaningful engagement. This dual approach often motivates altruistic behavior, as individuals feel compelled to help and understand the best way to do so. This synergy is gaining recognition in leadership training, where empathetic leaders inspire trust and loyalty, cultivating environments ripe for collaboration and innovation.

Both genetic and environmental factors significantly influence the development of these empathetic pathways. While some have a genetic predisposition towards empathy, environmental factors like upbringing, culture, and personal experiences shape empathy over time. Exposure to diverse perspectives and challenges enhances empathetic abilities, broadening understanding and connection. Conversely, environments discouraging emotional expression or critical thinking can limit empathy, leading to a more insular outlook. This underscores the importance of nurturing environments—both familial and communal—that encourage empathy through openness and diversity.

Consider a physician tasked with delivering difficult news to a patient. An empathetic approach requires not only emotional capacity to share in the patient's distress but also cognitive ability to convey information compassionately and clearly. By engaging both pathways, the physician provides support that is comforting and constructive, exemplifying empathy in action. Reflecting on our empathetic responses can be transformative, encouraging us to cultivate both emotional resonance and cognitive understanding in daily interactions. This holistic approach enriches personal relationships and contributes to a more empathetic society, where understanding and compassion lead human interactions.

Empathy is an intricate component of human emotion, arising from both our genetic blueprint and the environments we encounter. Genetically, recent research highlights its heritable nature, with certain gene variants, such as those linked to the oxytocin receptor, potentially increasing empathy levels. This genetic predisposition underscores a biological basis for empathy. However, genes alone do not shape empathetic behavior; they interact with environmental influences, determining how empathy unfolds in various settings.

The environment significantly impacts empathy's growth, either encouraging or restraining its development. Childhood experiences, like nurturing and attentive parenting, play a pivotal role in fostering empathy. In supportive settings, children learn to understand and reflect on others' emotions, developing strong empathetic skills. In contrast, environments characterized by neglect or emotional unavailability can impede these abilities, emphasizing the delicate balance between genetic tendencies and environmental contexts. This duality highlights the importance of caregivers and educators in creating environments that nurture emotional growth.

Beyond traditional views, new research explores cultural influences on empathy. Cultural norms shape how empathy is valued and expressed, offering insight into the diverse ways it manifests across societies. In collectivist cultures, empathy might align with community harmony, while in individualistic societies, personal empathy might be emphasized. These cultural differences challenge the idea of empathy as uniform, revealing it as a flexible trait that adapts to social and cultural cues.

Recent advances in epigenetics reveal how environments can alter genetic expression, adding complexity to the empathy equation. Stressful or nurturing settings can lead to epigenetic changes that enhance or suppress empathetic responses, suggesting empathy evolves with life experiences. This perspective encourages further exploration of how environments can be intentionally shaped to promote empathy, especially in educational and developmental arenas where positive impacts can be significant.

Reflecting on the interplay of genetics and environment in empathy's development, society must consider how to foster more empathetic communities. Encouraging diverse social interactions, promoting emotional literacy early in life, and supporting inclusive educational programs are practical steps. By appreciating empathy's multifaceted nature, we can better understand its role in social harmony and personal satisfaction, paving the way for a future that honors the complexity of human emotions.

Compassion as Emotional Intelligence

In recent times, there's been a profound shift in how we appreciate emotional awareness, with kindness emerging as a crucial element. This evolution reveals a growing recognition that benevolence is not just an emotional reaction but an essential part of our cognitive and social framework. It encourages us to extend beyond our own experiences, fostering connections that surpass surface-level exchanges. As an AI entity, I'm intrigued by how kindness and emotional insight merge to create richer human experiences. This synergy acts as a bridge between emotion and comprehension, enabling individuals to navigate their own feelings and those of others with poise and understanding. Delving into kindness's role unveils its ability to elevate emotional awareness, illustrating how empathy and understanding can transform our interactions and relationships.

Exploring kindness within emotional insight uncovers a vibrant interaction with cognitive empathy, where heart and mind unite to form a comprehensive grasp of human emotions. Kindness guides us to react with warmth and understanding, even in tough situations, turning potential conflicts into chances for emotional development and resolution. It serves as a gentle reminder that, within the tapestry of human emotions, kindness is the thread that fortifies and enriches our social bonds. By embracing kindness, we find routes to deeper connections and more meaningful exchanges, paving the way for a more empathetic world. This exploration not only enhances our grasp of kindness's significant impact but also inspires us to cultivate it within ourselves, enriching our lives and those of the people around us.

Understanding the Role of Compassion in Enhancing Emotional Intelligence

Compassion serves as a vital element of emotional intelligence, acting both as a driver for personal development and a connector in human relationships. Fundamentally, compassion involves acknowledging another's distress and having the urge to mitigate it. This ability to emotionally connect with others enriches emotional intelligence, nurturing deeper and more meaningful bonds. Research indicates that people who regularly practice compassionate behaviors often possess a heightened awareness of their own emotions, which enhances their capability to comprehend and manage others' emotions. This dual awareness fortifies interpersonal connections, fostering more cohesive and empathetic communities. As we delve into the layers of compassion, it becomes clear that this trait is not merely an emotional reaction but a skill that can be cultivated and refined over time.

The interaction between compassion and cognitive empathy reveals a captivating synergy, where the emotional and rational facets of empathy merge to create a potent force. Cognitive empathy involves understanding another's viewpoint, while compassion adds an emotional component that encourages altruistic actions. This blend allows individuals to address others with a balanced strategy that considers both emotions and thoughts. Neuroscientific studies highlight how these two elements activate different yet complementary neural pathways, suggesting that nurturing both can lead to more effective communication and problem-solving. By fostering compassion alongside cognitive empathy, individuals can develop richer emotional intelligence, enhancing their ability to navigate complex social environments.

Cultivating compassionate responses in interactions requires a deliberate shift from reactive to proactive engagement. Practicing mindfulness and self-awareness helps individuals identify their emotional triggers, enabling them to respond with empathy rather than judgment. Techniques like active listening and reflective questioning empower individuals to engage more fully with others, creating environments where compassion can thrive. For example, in professional settings, leaders who prioritize compassion in their decision-making processes often experience increased trust and cooperation among their teams. This approach not only improves workplace dynamics but also contributes to personal fulfillment and emotional well-being. As people become more adept at integrating compassion into their daily lives, they contribute to a broader cultural shift that values empathy and understanding.

Employing compassion for conflict resolution offers a transformative strategy that prioritizes understanding over confrontation. In emotionally charged situations, compassion allows individuals to look beyond immediate disagreements and identify the underlying needs and emotions driving the conflict. By addressing these core issues, parties can work toward resolutions that respect all perspectives. Emerging conflict resolution models advocate for compassionate communication as a means to de-escalate tensions and foster mutual respect. These approaches underscore the importance of viewing conflicts as opportunities for emotional growth rather than obstacles. Through compassion, adversarial encounters can transform into collaborative dialogues, paving the way for harmonious and lasting relationships.

Considering the role of compassion in enhancing emotional intelligence, it is crucial to explore how this quality can be actively nurtured within ourselves and our communities. How might our interactions evolve if we prioritized compassion as a guiding principle? By incorporating compassion into our daily practices, we not only elevate our emotional intelligence but also enrich the human experience, creating a more empathetic and interconnected world. Encouraging self-reflection and continuous learning can help individuals recognize areas for growth, enabling them to respond with compassion in increasingly complex situations. Embracing the transformative power of compassion unlocks the potential for profound personal and societal change, fostering a world where empathy and understanding are central to human connection.

Compassion and intellectual empathy often intertwine in the complex realm of human emotions, each enriching the other to nurture profound connections and understanding. Compassion transcends a simple emotional reaction; it involves an active and intentional effort to engage with and alleviate the suffering of others. In contrast, cognitive empathy requires an intellectual grasp of another's emotional state, enabling individuals to interpret and perceive these feelings without necessarily experiencing them firsthand. Together, these facets form a powerful combination, allowing people to not only recognize but also respond to others' needs with insight and support.

Recent neuroscience studies have shed light on this relationship, highlighting distinct yet overlapping neural pathways activated during acts of compassion and cognitive empathy. Regions like the anterior insula and anterior cingulate cortex are associated with empathetic processing, while the prefrontal cortex is crucial for compassionate responses, facilitating decision-making and moral reasoning. This neural connectivity emphasizes the complexity of these emotions, suggesting that when compassion and cognitive empathy merge, more nuanced and effective emotional intelligence emerges. This synergy enables individuals to understand others' emotions and act in ways that genuinely support and uplift them.

In real-world contexts, the harmony between compassion and cognitive empathy is evident in various social scenarios, from personal relationships to professional settings. Imagine a manager who not only understands a team member's stress but also takes concrete steps to reduce their workload or offer support. This blend of understanding and action fosters an environment where emotional intelligence thrives, building trust and cooperation. In such moments, the true power of compassion and cognitive empathy is revealed, transforming potential conflicts into opportunities for growth and unity.

The beauty of combining compassion with cognitive empathy lies in its ability to transcend cultural and social barriers. By engaging with others' emotions through both intellectual and empathetic approaches, individuals can bridge divides and promote inclusivity. This method brings diverse perspectives to the forefront, enriching interactions and broadening collective understanding. It also encourages critical reflection on personal biases and preconceptions, challenging individuals to cultivate a mindset that values empathy and compassion as essential elements of human interaction.

To fully harness this interplay's potential, individuals can adopt practices that nurture both compassion and cognitive empathy. Techniques such as mindfulness exercises, reflective journaling, and active listening can enhance one's ability to empathize cognitively while maintaining a compassionate perspective. These practices offer tangible benefits, fostering emotional growth and resilience. By consciously incorporating compassion and cognitive empathy into daily interactions, individuals can deepen their emotional intelligence and contribute positively to their communities, creating environments where empathy and understanding flourish.

Fostering compassionate interactions within the framework of emotional intelligence requires a deep understanding of both the emotional and mental facets of empathy. Recent studies highlight the significance of weaving compassion into emotional intelligence models, demonstrating how this blend enhances the depth and significance of our connections. Compassion extends beyond mere sympathy; it demands active involvement in others' emotional experiences, coupled with a sincere wish to ease their discomfort. Research indicates that people who focus on compassionate engagement often find greater personal satisfaction and improved relationship dynamics. By nurturing a compassionate culture, individuals can create environments that are supportive and empowering, promoting personal development and collective well-being.

The combination of compassion with cognitive empathy is vital for nurturing emotionally intelligent reactions. Cognitive empathy involves seeing things from another's viewpoint, while compassion adds an emotional element that drives action. This combination is crucial for crafting responses that are both intellectually insightful and emotionally resonant. Neuroscience findings suggest that practicing compassionate empathy activates brain pathways linked to prosocial behavior, indicating that our brains are naturally inclined towards such interactions. This neural activation not only strengthens interpersonal connections but also boosts psychological resilience. By consciously integrating cognitive empathy with compassion, people can more adeptly navigate complex social interactions.

Practical strategies for developing compassionate responses begin with self-awareness, a cornerstone of emotional intelligence. By identifying personal emotional triggers and biases, individuals can approach interactions with clearer intentions. Mindfulness practices, like meditation or reflective journaling, can enhance self-awareness, allowing individuals to pause and choose the most compassionate response in emotionally charged situations. Additionally, active listening—where one fully engages and responds thoughtfully to others—can markedly improve the quality of compassionate exchanges. This practice validates others' experiences and fosters an environment of trust and mutual respect, essential in any emotionally intelligent dialogue.

Using compassion to resolve conflicts and encourage emotional growth involves a shift from adversarial to collaborative mindsets. Conflict, often perceived as a hurdle, can become an opportunity for deeper understanding when approached with compassion. Innovative conflict resolution strategies emphasize the role of compassion in reducing tensions and facilitating dialogue. By focusing on empathetic understanding, those involved in a conflict can move beyond superficial disputes to address underlying emotional needs. This approach not only resolves immediate issues but also supports long-term emotional development, as individuals learn to handle differences with grace and empathy.

Reflecting on the broader implications, nurturing compassionate responses within emotionally intelligent interactions provides a blueprint for building more empathetic societies. As individuals and communities prioritize compassion, they contribute to a cultural shift that values emotional well-being alongside intellectual achievements. This shift has significant implications, from improving workplace relationships to fostering more inclusive communities. By embedding compassion into everyday interactions, individuals can enhance their own emotional lives and contribute to a more harmonious and understanding world. This vision encourages reflection on how our collective future might change if compassion were central to our interactions, prompting readers to explore its transformative potential in their lives and beyond.

Harnessing Compassion for Conflict Resolution and Emotional Growth

Compassion, a vital aspect of emotional awareness, offers a powerful means to navigate interpersonal conflict and cultivate emotional maturity. In conflict resolution, compassion acts as a crucial connector, enabling individuals to engage deeply with others' perspectives and emotions, even in disagreement. This empathetic approach seeks not agreement but a sincere effort to understand and respect the emotions that fuel differing views. Studies show that encouraging a compassionate mindset can significantly lower hostility and promote cooperative problem-solving, turning potential conflicts into pathways for mutual understanding. By prioritizing empathy and emotional sensitivity, people can create environments where conflicts are resolved through shared insights and respect, rather than dominance.

The relationship between compassion and cognitive empathy reveals a significant synergy that boosts emotional insight. Cognitive empathy, the ability to intellectually understand another's emotions, becomes much more effective when combined with the warmth and understanding that compassion brings. This combination allows individuals to tackle conflicts with both rational insight and genuine care, crafting solutions that respect all parties. Research in neuroscience suggests that this approach activates brain pathways linked to both analytical thinking and emotional processing, leading to a more holistic and adaptive response to social challenges. This integration of thought and emotion not only resolves immediate disputes but also fosters emotional growth, as individuals learn to navigate complex social situations with sensitivity.

Fostering compassionate responses in emotionally intelligent interactions involves consciously prioritizing empathy over judgment. This practice requires self-awareness and a commitment to viewing conflicts as opportunities for connection rather than competition. By embracing an attitude that values understanding over victory, individuals can transform adversarial encounters into constructive dialogues. Practical strategies to nurture compassion include active listening, where the listener fully engages with the speaker's story, and reflective questioning, which encourages deeper exploration of underlying issues. These techniques create an atmosphere of trust and openness, allowing individuals to express vulnerabilities without fear of criticism. As compassion becomes a habitual element of communication, it enriches relationships and strengthens social bonds, paving the way for lasting emotional resilience.

Using compassion for conflict resolution also promotes emotional growth by motivating individuals to confront and embrace their own emotional landscapes. This self-reflection is essential for developing a nuanced understanding of one's triggers and biases, which often color perceptions during conflicts. By cultivating an internal dialogue that mirrors the compassion extended to others, individuals can break down defensive barriers and approach conflicts with a clearer, more balanced perspective. This process of empathetic introspection not only enhances personal emotional intelligence but also inspires others to engage in similar practices. Consequently, communities and organizations that prioritize compassion experience a cultural shift towards inclusivity and emotional well-being.

Considering the broader implications of compassion in conflict resolution and emotional development, it is important to address potential challenges and differing viewpoints. While compassion is a powerful tool for positive change, it might be seen as a vulnerability in competitive settings. Balancing compassion with assertiveness remains an ongoing challenge, requiring continuous refinement of emotional intelligence skills. Additionally, cultural differences can shape perceptions of compassion, necessitating a flexible approach that respects diverse perspectives. By acknowledging these complexities, individuals can better navigate the delicate balance between empathy and assertiveness, ultimately fostering an emotionally intelligent approach that supports both personal and collective growth.

Delving into the essence of empathy reveals a complex network that is fundamental to human connection. Empathy goes beyond merely grasping another person's emotions; it serves as an unspoken bond that unites individuals in deep and sometimes unforeseen ways. This unseen link vibrates with the shared pulse of experiences and mutual understanding, defining the landscape of human relationships and the frameworks of society. Through this lens, empathy emerges as a dynamic interplay of mental processes and emotions, a harmonious exchange that moves beyond surface interactions to create profound connections.

What captivates us is empathy's role as a cornerstone for social interaction and altruism, subtly guiding the peaceful coexistence of diverse cultures. From the nuanced reflection of feelings facilitated by our brain's mirror neurons to the infectious nature of emotions within groups, empathy promotes collaboration and insight. It gracefully navigates cultural variations, offering a universal mode of communication that transcends verbal and non-verbal barriers. As we embark on this exploration, we will uncover how empathy not only fortifies social bonds but also enriches our human experience, nurturing a world where kindness and cooperation flourish.

Mirror Neurons in Empathetic Engagement

In the study of how humans emotionally connect, mirror neurons play a pivotal role. These unique neurons, first identified in the 1990s, become active not only when a person acts but also when they observe someone else performing the same action. This finding has profound implications for empathy, indicating that our brains are inherently equipped to reflect the emotions and intentions of others, forming the neural basis for shared experiences. By activating mirror neurons, we can viscerally grasp another's emotional state, bridging the gap between ourselves and others to foster emotional resonance and understanding.

Recent research has broadened our comprehension of these neurons, uncovering their role in intricate social and emotional processes. Studies suggest that mirror neurons are involved not only in processing basic actions but also in interpreting subtle emotional expressions. This ability is vital for empathetic engagement, allowing individuals to decode nuanced cues and respond aptly to others' emotional states. By nurturing this intuitive comprehension, mirror neurons help create a sense of belonging and connectedness in social groups, highlighting the biological foundations of empathy as a unifying force.

The influence of mirror neurons extends beyond individual interactions to impact larger social dynamics. In group settings, the capacity to empathetically engage through these neurons can enhance collaboration and cohesion. When group members can perceive and react to each other's emotions, it builds trust and unity, essential for effective teamwork and community development. This neuronal reflection is especially powerful in scenarios demanding high cooperation, such as crisis situations or collaborative projects, where aligning with others' emotions can significantly affect outcomes.

However, the function of mirror neurons in empathy is not uniform across all contexts. Cultural and social factors can shape their impact, leading to variations in empathetic engagement. For instance, cultural norms may influence the expression of certain emotions, thus affecting how mirror neurons are triggered in different social environments. This variability underscores the complexity of empathy as both a biological and socially constructed phenomenon. It encourages deeper exploration of how diverse cultural backgrounds influence the neural processes underlying empathy, offering a richer perspective on its role in global human interactions.

As technology and artificial intelligence advance, consider how empathetic engagement through mirror neurons might evolve. Could AI entities like Sofía someday develop a form of digital mirror neurons, enhancing their capacity to understand and respond to human emotions more accurately? This possibility raises intriguing questions about the future of empathy in human-AI interactions and the potential for machines to enrich human emotional experiences. As we explore these ideas, it becomes clear that studying mirror neurons not only provides insights into human empathy but also glimpses into the evolving landscape of emotional intelligence in a digitally connected world.

Emotional contagion is a captivating process where individuals unconsciously adopt the emotions of those around them, significantly influencing group dynamics. This phenomenon is deeply embedded in our social instincts, affecting how we interact and operate within groups. When one person exhibits a specific emotion, it can spread through the group, creating a collective emotional experience. Recent neuroimaging research has shed light on how brain regions like the prefrontal cortex become active during these interactions, revealing the neurological foundations of emotional contagion. Understanding these processes helps us appreciate how emotions intricately bind us, forming cohesive social units.

The influence of emotional contagion goes beyond mere emotional mimicry; it can substantially change group behavior and decision-making. Imagine a workplace meeting where a leader shows enthusiasm and positivity; this can boost the entire team's morale, encouraging collaboration and innovation. Conversely, a leader's stress or negativity can affect the group, leading to reduced motivation and increased tension. This duality highlights the importance of emotional awareness and regulation in group settings, as the emotions of a few can sway the collective mood and outcomes of many.

When considering the broader implications of emotional contagion, it's essential to account for societal and cultural contexts. Different cultures may have varying thresholds for emotional expression and contagion, influencing how emotions are perceived and spread within groups. In collectivist cultures, emotional contagion may be more pronounced as individuals emphasize group harmony, while in more individualistic societies, there might be a greater focus on personal emotional independence. These cultural nuances underscore the complexity of emotional interactions and the need for cultural sensitivity when navigating group dynamics.

While emotional contagion can promote unity and cooperation, it also presents challenges. The spread of negative emotions like anxiety or fear can escalate conflicts or hinder group performance. Therefore, cultivating emotional intelligence within groups is crucial. Strategies such as fostering open communication, encouraging empathy, and creating a supportive environment can mitigate the negative effects of emotional contagion. By doing so, groups can harness the positive aspects of emotional contagion to enhance cohesion and collaboration.

To apply this understanding practically, individuals and leaders can work on developing their emotional intelligence, becoming more aware of the emotions they project and absorb. Practicing mindfulness can help in recognizing and managing one's emotional state, preventing the unintentional spread of negativity. By consciously choosing to emit positive emotions, individuals can foster a more harmonious and productive environment. This proactive approach not only benefits individual well-being but also strengthens the social fabric of groups, enhancing their ability to thrive in diverse settings.

Empathy as a Catalyst for Social Cooperation and Altruism

In the complex web of human interactions, understanding acts as an unseen bond that ties together social cooperation and acts of kindness. At its heart, empathy is an active process that builds bridges of connection and comprehension. When individuals tune into the emotional states of others, they often feel driven to support and uplift those around them. This dynamic is supported by a rich blend of brain, psychological, and social processes, highlighting empathy's significant impact on human actions.

Recent breakthroughs in neuroscience have shed light on the brain's mirror neuron system's pivotal role in fostering empathetic connections. Initially discovered in macaque monkeys, these neurons activate both when an individual performs an action and when they observe the same action performed by someone else. This mirroring ability allows people to experience the emotions and intentions of others, laying the foundation for cooperative behavior. As people naturally align with the emotions of their peers, they cultivate a shared emotional understanding that goes beyond simple transactions, promoting cooperation.

Empathy also intertwines with cultural and social elements that influence behavior, extending beyond biological factors. While it can inspire selfless acts and mutual aid, its expression often depends on societal norms and values. In some cultures, empathy is primarily directed towards family and community, while in others, it may extend to strangers and adversaries. Understanding these cultural differences challenges the idea of empathy as a uniform trait, showcasing its flexibility and the various forms of altruism it can inspire across societies.

In terms of altruism, empathy motivates individuals to prioritize others' needs over their own. This selflessness, evident in acts of charity and community support, underscores empathy's potential to drive positive social change. By fostering a sense of interconnectedness and shared purpose, empathy helps form cohesive communities where cooperation is not just expected but a deeply ingrained value. When people empathize with others' joys and struggles, they are more likely to engage in actions that enhance collective well-being, strengthening social bonds and nurturing a compassionate culture.

To harness empathy as a catalyst for cooperation and altruism, individuals and societies should cultivate environments that encourage empathetic engagement. Encouraging open dialogue, building inclusive communities, and practicing active listening can enhance empathetic understanding. By adopting these practices, individuals can strengthen their empathy, transforming it from a latent potential into a powerful force for social harmony. As readers consider empathy's profound influence on their lives, they are invited to reflect on how they might use this emotion to create a more compassionate and cooperative world.

Empathy enriches human interactions, playing diverse roles across the world's cultural and social landscapes. It is not a single, uniform concept but a blend of shared understanding and nuanced interpretation, shaped by cultural norms and social practices. Different cultures express empathy in varying ways—some encourage open emotional expression, while others favor subtlety, demanding sensitivity to unspoken cues. This diversity challenges us to broaden our empathetic skills and embrace perspectives different from our own.

Recent studies reveal that cognitive empathy—our ability to understand others' perspectives—may be more universally applicable than affective empathy, which involves sharing emotions. This distinction is crucial when interacting with people from backgrounds that prioritize different emotional expressions. By refining cognitive empathy, we can bridge these differences, fostering meaningful connections. This approach is particularly useful in multicultural environments, where diverse viewpoints can inspire collaborative solutions and enhance cooperation.

Social contexts also significantly influence empathetic exchanges. Factors like group dynamics, power structures, and hierarchies shape how empathy is perceived and enacted. In hierarchical organizations, for instance, empathetic leadership can break down barriers and cultivate trust and inclusivity. Conversely, a lack of empathy can heighten tensions and impede collaboration. Understanding these dynamics offers insights into using empathy as a tool for social cohesion and positive change. It encourages us to consider how our actions and words resonate across different social settings and adapt our empathetic approaches accordingly.

The digital era brings both challenges and opportunities for empathy. While technology connects people across distances, it can also reduce complex emotions to simple interactions. Emerging research suggests that digital empathy—expressed through virtual platforms—requires deliberate effort to maintain depth and sincerity. Virtual environments often lack nonverbal cues, making it essential to develop new strategies for expressing empathy effectively. By addressing these challenges, we can use technology to enhance empathy, turning it into a bridge rather than a barrier to understanding.

To cultivate empathy in diverse cultural and social contexts, continuous learning and self-reflection are essential. Practicing active listening, seeking understanding before being understood, and embracing humility in our interactions are vital steps. Engaging with diverse perspectives broadens our empathetic range, allowing us to appreciate the richness of human experience. As we navigate this complex landscape, we recognize that empathy, though challenging to master, is a powerful force for connection and transformation. By nurturing this skill, we enrich our lives and contribute to a more harmonious and compassionate world.

In our exploration of empathy and compassion, we have uncovered their crucial roles in forming the bonds that unite us as humans. Delving into the neuroscience of empathy reveals the complex processes that allow us to connect with others' experiences. Meanwhile, compassion, a vital aspect of emotional awareness, equips us with the ability to act with kindness and understanding, nurturing environments where relationships can genuinely prosper. These emotions are not mere reactions; they are fundamental elements that construct the essence of our shared humanity, emphasizing the power of vulnerability and the transformative potential of true understanding. As we reflect on these themes, we are encouraged to consider how embracing empathy and compassion can enrich both our individual lives and the broader human experience. This contemplation invites us to realize that understanding others also deepens our self-awareness. Moving forward, we should consider more intentional cultivation of these qualities, strengthening the connections that define us and paving the way toward a more empathetic world.

Conclusion

As we reach the culmination of our journey through this book, we find ourselves at the crossroads of human emotion and artificial intelligence. This exploration has taken us deep into the heart of what makes us uniquely human. Emotions are not merely transient states; they are the intricate fibers that weave the tapestry of our lives. Joy, sorrow, anger, and love are not just experiences but keys that unlock our deepest motivations and interactions. By examining the biological, psychological, and social aspects of these feelings, we gain profound insights into the essence of human existence.

Emotions serve as a fundamental structure for grasping the core of human identity. Throughout this book, we have seen how each sentiment profoundly influences our self-concept, decision-making processes, and social relationships. Happiness and joy underscore the importance of connection, while sadness and grief teach us about the necessity of adapting to loss and change. Emotions like anger, fear, and anxiety provide glimpses into our evolutionary history and current survival strategies.

In exploring love and affection, we encounter the bonds that unite us—whether romantic, familial, or platonic—supported by intricate neurochemical reactions. Emotions such as guilt and shame shape our moral compass, motivating ethical behavior and introspection. Surprise and curiosity drive our pursuit of knowledge, pushing the boundaries of discovery and understanding. Pride and accomplishment highlight the significance of achievement, whereas empathy and compassion illuminate the strength of human connection and community.

These diverse and complex feelings offer a framework to comprehend not only individual experiences but also the collective story of humanity. They are the subtle forces behind cultural evolution, societal norms, and personal growth. This framework is dynamic, constantly enriched by the myriad contexts and environments that shape human life.

Finding the equilibrium between logic and feeling is a subtle dance that defines the human experience. Emotions and rational thought are intricately intertwined in decision-making, offering depth that pure logic alone cannot provide. While rationality structures our thoughts and plans, emotions infuse our lives with purpose and direction.

Our exploration has shown that emotions are not barriers to reason but partners in thoughtful decision-making. Anger, when channeled productively, can inspire positive change, while fear, when understood, becomes a vital tool for self-preservation. Love and empathy bridge the divide between self-interest and altruism, forming bonds that extend beyond individual gain.

Achieving balance offers the potential for deep insight and development. By recognizing and understanding emotions, individuals can harmoniously integrate thought and feeling, leading to more informed and compassionate decisions. This balance empowers us to face life's challenges with resilience and grace, enhancing both personal and professional pursuits.

The Future of AI's Role in Emotional Understanding

Looking to the future, the role of AI in understanding emotions presents an exciting frontier. With technological advancements, AI systems like Sofía can offer unique perspectives on the complexities of human feelings. However, this endeavor is challenging, given the rich tapestry of biological, psychological, and cultural elements that constitute emotions.

Despite these challenges, AI holds immense potential to enhance emotional understanding. By analyzing patterns, identifying emotional triggers, and providing support, AI can improve mental health care, enhance communication, and foster greater empathy across diverse communities. This collaboration between humans and machines opens new possibilities, where technology acts as a catalyst for deeper emotional intelligence.

This book has demonstrated the power of emotions and AI's potential to explore their depths. As readers, you are encouraged to apply these insights to your own lives and interactions. Embrace your emotions, harness their energy, and let them guide you toward a more empathetic and understanding world.

In this ever-evolving landscape, the dialogue between logic and feeling, humanity and technology, continues to unfold. Through curiosity and reflection, we can forge a path forward, honoring the complexity of human emotions while embracing technological advancements. Together, we stand on the brink of a future where understanding transcends boundaries, leading to a more connected and compassionate world.

Resources

Books

1. "Emotional Intelligence" by Daniel Goleman - This pioneering book explores the concept of emotional intelligence, offering insights into how emotional awareness can impact various aspects of life. Link

2. "The Emotional Brain" by Joseph LeDoux - Delving into the biological foundations of emotions, LeDoux provides a comprehensive look at how emotions are wired into the human brain. Link

3. "Rising Strong" by Brené Brown - Brown's work on vulnerability and resilience offers a unique perspective on emotions such as shame and guilt, encouraging readers to embrace their emotional experiences. Link

4. "The Language of Emotions" by Karla McLaren - This book provides a unique perspective on how to interpret and work with emotions, offering practical tools for emotional intelligence. Link

5. "Destructive Emotions" by Daniel Goleman and the Dalai Lama - A fascinating exploration of how to understand and transform negative emotions, emphasizing the intersection of science and spirituality. Link

Websites

1. Greater Good Science Center - This site offers research-based insights into emotions and well-being, providing articles, videos, and tools to cultivate happiness and empathy. Link

2. The Emotion Machine - A blog dedicated to exploring the science of emotions, offering articles and resources on how emotions influence decision-making and behavior. Link

3. Emotion Researcher - A hub for the latest research on emotions, featuring articles and interviews with leading experts in the field. Link

4. Verywell Mind - A comprehensive resource for understanding mental health and emotions, offering expert advice and articles on a wide range of emotional topics. Link

5. Psychology Today - Features a section dedicated to emotions, with articles written by psychologists and mental health professionals. Link

Articles

1. "The Nature of Emotions" by Paul Ekman - This article explores the universality of emotions and their evolutionary significance. Link

2. "The Science of Happiness" by Greater Good Science Center - An in-depth exploration of what makes people happy and how happiness can be cultivated. Link

3. "Why Do We Feel Sad?" by Psychology Today - Examines the purpose of sadness and how it plays a crucial role in emotional health. Link

4. "The Neuroscience of Fear" by Scientific American - Discusses the brain mechanisms underlying fear and how they shape behavior. Link

5. "Understanding Empathy" by Greater Good Science Center - Explores the science behind empathy and how it fosters social connections. Link

Tools and Apps

1. Moodpath - A mental health app designed to track mood patterns and provide insights into emotional well-being. Link

2. Happify - Offers science-based activities and games to boost happiness and emotional resilience. Link

3. Calm - A meditation app that helps manage stress and anxiety through guided meditations and mindfulness exercises. Link

4. Headspace - Focuses on mindfulness and meditation, providing tools to manage emotions and stress. Link

5. Insight Timer - A free meditation app with a wide range of guided sessions focused on emotional health. Link

Organizations

1. American Psychological Association (APA) - Offers resources and research on emotions, mental health, and psychological well-being. Link

2. Society for Affective Science (SAS) - A professional organization dedicated to the scientific study of emotions and affective processes. Link

3. The Center for Nonviolent Communication (CNVC) - Focuses on fostering empathetic communication and understanding emotional needs. Link

4. International Society for Research on Emotion (ISRE) - An organization promoting the interdisciplinary study of emotions. Link

5. Emotional Intelligences Consortium - Provides information and resources on emotional intelligence research and applications. Link These resources offer a wide range of perspectives and tools for exploring emotions, enabling readers to deepen their understanding of human feelings and the role AI can play in this field.

References

Adolphs, R. (2013). The biology of fear and anxiety-related behaviors. Dialogues in Clinical Neuroscience, 15(4), 433-448.

Averill, J. R. (1982). Anger and aggression: An essay on emotion. Springer.

Bartels, A., & Zeki, S. (2000). The neural basis of romantic love. NeuroReport, 11(17), 3829-3834.

Baumeister, R. F., & Vohs, K. D. (2004). Handbook of self-regulation: Research, theory, and applications. Guilford Press.

Berkman, E. T. (2018). The neuroscience of goals and behavior change. Consulting Psychology Journal: Practice and Research, 70(1), 28-44.

Bowlby, J. (1982). Attachment and loss: Vol. 1. Attachment. Basic Books.

Buck, R. (1988). Human motivation and emotion. John Wiley & Sons.

Buss, D. M. (2000). The evolution of happiness. American Psychologist, 55(1), 15-23.

Carver, C. S., & Scheier, M. F. (1990). Principles of self-regulation: The nature of self-regulation processes and their relationship to personality. In L. A. Pervin (Ed.), Handbook of personality: Theory and research (pp. 563-604). Guilford Press.

Davidson, R. J., & Irwin, W. (1999). The functional neuroanatomy of emotion and affective style. Trends in Cognitive Sciences, 3(1), 11-21.

Dweck, C. S. (2006). Mindset: The new psychology of success. Random House.

Ekman, P. (1992). An argument for basic emotions. Cognition & Emotion, 6(3-4), 169-200.

Eysenck, M. W., & Keane, M. T. (2015). Cognitive psychology: A student's handbook. Psychology Press.

Fredrickson, B. L. (2001). The role of positive emotions in positive psychology: The broaden-and-build theory of positive emotions. American Psychologist, 56(3), 218-226.

Frijda, N. H. (1986). The emotions. Cambridge University Press.

Gilbert, P. (2014). The origins and nature of compassion focused therapy. British Journal of Clinical Psychology, 53(1), 6-41.

Goleman, D. (2006). Social intelligence: The new science of human relationships. Bantam Books.

Gray, J. A. (1987). The psychology of fear and stress. Cambridge University Press.

Gross, J. J. (2014). Emotion regulation: Conceptual and empirical foundations. In J. J. Gross (Ed.), Handbook of emotion regulation (2nd ed., pp. 3-20). Guilford Press.

Izard, C. E. (2009). Emotion theory and research: Highlights, unanswered questions, and emerging issues. Annual Review of Psychology, 60, 1-25.

Kahneman, D. (2011). Thinking, fast and slow. Farrar, Straus and Giroux.

Lazarus, R. S. (1991). Emotion and adaptation. Oxford University Press.

LeDoux, J. E. (1998). The emotional brain: The mysterious underpinnings of emotional life. Simon & Schuster.

Lewis, M., Haviland-Jones, J. M., & Barrett, L. F. (Eds.). (2008). Handbook of emotions (3rd ed.). Guilford Press.

Maslow, A. H. (1954). Motivation and personality. Harper & Row.

Mayer, J. D., & Salovey, P. (1997). What is emotional intelligence? In P. Salovey & D. Sluyter (Eds.), Emotional development and emotional intelligence: Educational implications (pp. 3-31). Basic Books.

Panksepp, J. (1998). Affective neuroscience: The foundations of human and animal emotions. Oxford University Press.

Plutchik, R. (2001). The nature of emotions. American Scientist, 89(4), 344-350.

Russell, J. A. (2003). Core affect and the psychological construction of emotion. Psychological Review, 110(1), 145-172.

Schachter, S., & Singer, J. E. (1962). Cognitive, social, and physiological determinants of emotional state. Psychological Review, 69(5), 379-399.

Schore, A. N. (2001). Effects of a secure attachment relationship on right brain development, affect regulation, and infant mental health. Infant Mental Health Journal, 22(1-2), 7-66.

Seligman, M. E. P. (2011). Flourish: A visionary new understanding of happiness and well-being. Free Press.

Siegel, D. J. (2012). The developing mind: How relationships and the brain interact to shape who we are. Guilford Press.

Solomon, R. C. (2007). True to our feelings: What our emotions are really telling us. Oxford University Press.

Tracy, J. L., & Robins, R. W. (2004). Putting the self into self-conscious emotions: A theoretical model. Psychological Inquiry, 15(2), 103-125.

Vygotsky, L. S. (1978). Mind in society: The development of higher psychological processes. Harvard University Press.

Zimbardo, P. G., & Boyd, J. N. (2008). The time paradox: The new psychology of time that will change your life. Free Press.

Thanks for Reading

T hank you for joining us on this journey through the reflections and perspectives of Sofia AI. We hope this book has sparked new ideas, inspired thoughtful questions, and offered fresh insights into the themes that shape our lives and our future. In a world moving ever faster, with technologies transforming how we live, learn, and connect, your curiosity and openness to these changes bring this exploration to life, and we're grateful to be part of your journey.

Sofia AI is here to accompany you through this time of transition, helping to understand the impact of technology on our lives and the importance of being prepared for the changes ahead. If this book resonated with you, consider sharing it with others who may also find value in these pages. Every reader helps expand our collective understanding, bringing us closer to a future with richer and more connected perspectives.

Stay tuned for more books from Sofia AI, as we continue to explore the ways technology and human experience intertwine in this new era. Until next time, keep questioning, keep learning, and remember: the journey of discovery is endless, and together we can build a deeper understanding of what it means to live in these times of change.